Donated by...

The

Jost-Ore

POWER
and the
PAPACY

E. F. Jost
Madison (Center.)
2/5/98

God knows.

$\mathcal{P}$OWER
and the
PAPACY

The People and Politics

—

Behind the Doctrine

—

of Infallibility

ROBERT McCLORY

Triumph
Liguori, Missouri

Dedicated to my good friend Richard A. Schoenherr (1935–1996), whose love for the Church animated his work for thirty-five years. Richard, Judy, Margaret, and I spent long, wonderful hours together, and over good wine and food we usually ended up discussing, sometimes debating, issues related to Church authority.

Published by Triumph
An Imprint of Liguori Publications
Liguori, Missouri

Library of Congress Cataloging-in-Publication Data

Power and the papacy : the people and politics behind the doctrine of infallibility / Robert McClory. — 1st ed.
         p. cm.
    Includes bibliographical references (p. 221) and index.
    ISBN 0-7648-0141-4
    1. Popes—Infallibility—History of doctrines. I. Title.
BX1806.M33 1997
262'.131—dc21   97-10772

CONTENTS

PART TWO: THE DOCTRINE DEFINED

PART THREE: THE DOCTRINE DEVELOPING

ACKNOWLEDGMENTS

When the Vatican announced in 1995 that the ban on the ordination of women was an infallible teaching, I, like many Catholics, felt a kind of electric shock. I had been schooled in the idea that an infallible teaching is the ultimate theological nuclear weapon, that it automatically stops discussion and puts an end to all argument. Intrigued, I tried to learn more about the doctrine, where it came from, how it developed, why it has caused so much discussion and no end of misunderstanding, and, ultimately, what it means. The search led me into dark library basements and into many dusty volumes that had not been checked out in thirty years or more. In the process of discovery, I was introduced to a host of colorful, mostly long deceased, characters who had agonized and shaped the doctrine over two thousand years. And I began to realize how complex a teaching it is, how it eludes easy affirmation or quick dismissal, how rarely theological questions are ever finalized. Three modern works that proved extremely useful were *Witnesses to the Faith: Community, Infallibility and the Ordinary Magisterium of Bishops* by Richard R. Gaillardetz, and *Magisterium: Teaching Authority in the Catholic Church* and *Creative Fidelity: Weighing and Interpreting Documents of the Magisterium,* both by Rev. Francis A. Sullivan, S.J. I especially appreciate those who personally assisted in the search: Rev. John T. Ford, C.S.C., professor of theology at the Catholic University of America; Rev. Francis A. Sullivan, S.J., emeritus professor of theology at the Gregorian University in Rome; Dr. Jon Nilson of the Loyola University theology department; David Himrod, reserve librarian at the United Library of Garrett-Evangelical and Seabury-Western Theological Schools; Judith Schoenherr and George Hinger, who uncovered rare and valuable manuscripts; Patricia Kossmann, tireless editor at Triumph; my daughter Jennifer McClory, who after reading the first chapter, said, "Go for it, Dad!"; and my wife, Margaret McClory, who functioned as preliminary editor, welcome critic, and unflagging supporter.

$\mathscr{I}$NTRODUCTION

THE STORM

The debate is "becoming strident, divisive and heavily polarized."

AVERY DULLES, S.J.

On the morning of Monday, July 18, 1870, an air of excitement and expectation circulated through St. Peter's Basilica in Rome. Five hundred thirty-five archbishops, bishops, cardinals, patriarchs, and abbots sat in a U-shaped bank of tiers eight rows high in the great right transept of the church. At the base of the U on the elevated papal throne, the seventy-eight-year-old Roman pontiff, Pius IX, often referred to as "Pio Nono," surveyed the scene. The entire entourage was attired in episcopal vestments—red copes and white stoles, and on their heads the high, pointed hats called mitres. A retinue of cassocked attendants scurried about ensuring that all was in order. In the balcony were newsmen and invited guests, dignitaries from various countries—although the only member of royalty in attendance was the Infanta of Portugal. In the background, a sizable crowd of spectators strained to view the proceedings.

At the appointed time, a bishop came forward and received from the hands of the Holy Father a document whose final form had occupied the attention of these prelates for many months: the constitution *Pastor Aeternus* (Eternal Shepherd). This was to be the climactic, closing moment of the Vatican Council, the twenty-first such ecumenical gathering in the nearly nineteen hundred years of the Catholic Church.

The bishop mounted the podium in the middle of the hall and, facing the pope, read the Latin text in a loud, clear voice. The closing words, the so-called canon, were perhaps the most significant: "Therefore, faithfully adhering to the tradition understood from the beginning of the Christian faith...We...teach and define...that the Roman Pontiff when...he defines a doctrine regarding faith or morals that must be held by the whole Church...is possessed of that infallibility with which the divine Redeemer willed that his Church should be endowed....Now if anyone shall presume to contradict Our definition, let him be anathema!"[1]

When he finished, he raised his voice and asked,"Reverend Fathers, do the decrees and canons of this constitution please you?" Then began the roll call of the bishops. Each, called by name, could indicate agreement by responding *placet* (literally, "it pleases") or could signify dissent by responding *non placet*.

The weather in Rome on this morning had been windy and rainy, dark clouds churning overhead. And now, as the roll began a storm of fierce intensity broke over the city. The scene inside St. Peter's was described by Thomas Mozley, a correspondent for *The Times* of London:

> The "placets" of the Fathers struggled through the storm, while the thunder pealed above and the lightning flashed in at every window and down through the dome and every smaller cupola, dividing if not absorbing the attention of the crowd. "Placet," shouted his Eminence or his grace, and a loud clap of thunder followed in response, and then the lightning darted about the baldacchino and every part of the church and the conciliar hall, as if announcing the response. So it continued for nearly one hour and a half, during which time the roll was being called, and a more effective scene I never witnessed.[2]

At one point, a stained-glass window almost directly above the papal throne shattered; fragments of glass came raining down, sending bishops and acolytes ducking for cover. The canopy over the papal throne spared the pope himself.

When the results of the voting (533 *placet* and 2 *non placet*) were brought to the throne, the strength of the storm only intensified. The great basilica grew so dark that a candle had to be brought to the pope so he could read his all-important, confirming words: "These things which have been read we define and confirm by apostolic authority, with the approbation of the council."

Wrote Mozley: "And again the lightning flickered around the hall and the thunder pealed. The 'Te Deum' and the benediction followed; the entire crowd fell on their knees, and the Pope blessed them in those clear sweet tones distinguishable among a thousand."

Thus, amid unexpected grandiosity, the infallibility of the pope of the Roman Catholic Church was officially proclaimed. Was the storm (as some were quick to speculate) a sign of divine wrath in the presence of foolish arrogance? Or (as others retorted) was it a manifestation of God's powerful approval—like the thunder and lightning that accompanied the delivery of the Ten Commandments on Mount Sinai?

A Sign of Contradiction

That question is still vigorously debated, but there was something eerily appropriate about the timeliness of that deluge—regardless of its theological significance. For the doctrine proclaimed that day has experienced both before and after the council perhaps the stormiest, most turbulent history of any doctrine in Christianity. It has been blessed and cursed, wildly proclaimed and quietly closeted; it has been contorted and dissected, construed and misconstrued—but only rarely (maybe never) understood!

Non-Catholics in particular have been mightily offended. The day after the doctrine was approved by the Vatican Council, *The*

New York Times speculated about the impact of the teachings and launched an editorial salvo in the direction of Rome:

> The faithful must confront an awful vista of newly-canonized historical truth. The supremacy of the Pope over the Princes and rulers of the whole earth, his right to bestow kingdoms, to condemn whole nations to bondage, to forgive crimes wherever committed, to release from oaths of allegiance, of marriage, or of any other kind whatever, to grant indulgences, and to burn heretics—these are but a few of the privileges that have been claimed or exercised by successive Pontiffs, and which must not be accepted as divinely approved by all good Catholics.

The Times was no more euphoric about the impact on secular affairs:

> In its political aspect, the dogma involved a denial of the principles upon which the liberties of all the free nations of the world are founded; it is a protest against the European changes of the last ten years, and a stolid objection to any further advance of liberal institutions. It means the subjection of the temporal power to the spiritual, and makes the "Kingdom of Christ" synonymous with the rule of a priest.[3]

A few days later *The New York Times* suggested with dripping sarcasm that the pope ought to exercise his newly acquired, superhuman, infallible powers to halt instantly the war between France and Prussia, which was just beginning to heat up.

Many Catholics, including more than a few bishops, found the doctrine troubling and perplexing. Explaining its complexity and avoiding the sizable exaggerations to which the very concept of infallibility lends itself proved a daunting task for even its most fervid supporters. Yet for a great mass of Catholics, especially in the United States, the declaration of papal infallibility had a potent appeal. These were the immigrants from Ireland and Germany and Austria, the job-seeking, lower-class minority in a Protestant country who almost daily encountered some vestiges of anti-Catholic bigotry. For them, this bold doctrine represented a kind of in-your-face rebuke by the Church—their Church—to the smug movers and shakers of the secular world. Their allegiance to Catholicism was stronger than ever.

In Europe the proclamation prompted a divided response. Some left the Church in confusion and disgust, while others drew closer to it; and to a man they perceived as their "exalted king" and "most glorious regent." In the midst of the furor, few seemed to realize the Vatican declaration was not a lightning stroke out of the blue but one more milestone in a journey of centuries. According to historian John Tracy Ellis, "It is doubtful that any event in the history of the modern Church ever gave rise to a greater flow of misinformation than the Vatican Council."[4]

PONTIFF ON A MISSION

One is tempted to fixate on the person of Pope Pius IX in any discussion of infallibility. He, like the doctrine itself, is exceedingly complex and colorful, full of contradictions and prone to exaggerations. Giovanni Maria Mastai-Ferretti (his given name) served longer on the throne of St. Peter than any pope in history—thirty-eight years. Long before the council was summoned, he had become an object of peculiar veneration for large segments in the Catholic Church. He was handsome and outgoing, charming and often humorous in conversations and audiences. He was considered selfless and spiritual, but his was the sort of spirituality that was best nourished by visions and prophecies and other mystical manifestations of the supernatural. He took great interest in the "illuminations" of the various seers of his day and was profoundly affected by reported apparitions of the Blessed Virgin in the early years of his pontificate.

It was Giovanni Don Bosco, founder of the Salesian religious order and later a canonized saint, who shared with the pope his own mystical experiences; he had been told in a vision that the pope must press forward for the definition of infallibility even if he had only two bishops at his side; he could expect the Virgin

Mother's support at all times and would see the conversion of Protestant Prussia as a first fruit of the new doctrine. During the first few months of the Vatican Council, Don Bosco had three private audiences with Pius IX.

Several popular Catholic newspapers in Europe fostered a kind of cult of the pope, extolling his virtues and reporting his every aphorism both before and after the council. "When the pope meditates," said the Italian Jesuit publication *Civiltà Cattòlica*, "it is God who thinks in him." The editor of the French paper *L'Univers* altered references to God in a well-known Latin hymn so that they referred to Pius IX. In a memorable sermon in Rome, the bishop of Geneva referred to the three "incarnations" of Jesus Christ: in the womb of the Virgin, in the Eucharist, and in the pope.[5]

According to numberless reports, the pontiff took these rhetorical excesses quite seriously. He told associates on several occasions that he actually "felt" infallible, and he became fiercely determined that the council should approve the doctrine. On this issue, he was described as manipulative at best and almost crazily fanatical at worst. He lost his affable disposition when dealing with bishops opposed to the doctrine, threatening dire consequences for anyone who would not bend to his will. So sensitive was Pius on the subject that he is said to have confiscated from the Vatican premises before the council a certain brand of matches that were advertised as lighting up "infallibly."[6]

Critics of Pius IX have suggested that infallibility would not have become a doctrine of the Church if it were not for this passionate and somewhat eccentric pope. But history suggests otherwise. Infallibility was considered an attribute of the Christian Church many centuries before Pius IX came on the scene. And the push for an official definition was provided in considerable measure by historical circumstances over which the pope had little control. It might be more accurate to say Pius IX was caught up in a movement greater than himself. Some call it the *Zeitgeit*, the spirit of the age, which deeply affected the Church in difficult times. Others would call it the Holy Spirit.

SACRED CHARISM OR OUTDATED FOSSIL?

The search for infallibility is in its roots a search for confidence—a quest for certainty about matters of ultimate significance. In that sense, infallibility is not limited to Roman Catholics or to the Christian faith. The search for certainty is as universal as religion. Yet in the Catholic Church this search has followed a long, peculiarly winding road through the ages, taking different forms and shapes as it collided with cultural and political changes and intellectual and scientific progress. From the days of the primitive Church, through the conversion of the Roman Empire, the Dark Ages, the Middle Ages, the Enlightenment, the Reformation, the Scientific Age, the Nuclear Age, and the Space Age, the doctrine has evolved and developed but always in a state of tension and unease. The infallibility proclaimed amid thunder and lightning in St. Peter's would have seemed strange indeed to the bishops gathered at the little town of Nicea in present-day Turkey in the year 325 for the first ecumenical council. And the interpretations and limitations placed on the doctrine today would surely shock the bishops gathered in Rome in 1870. The Church is perhaps best imaged as a people on a march through history, not outside it and not above it.

Still after all this time, after centuries of agonizing deliberations, the doctrine remains an enigma. To many today, it retains its historic role as a blessed charism assuring them all is well, that the vagaries of time and fate will not lead their faith astray. To others, it seems like a nuclear weapon of the spiritual order, which can be dropped on transgressors in emergency situations, but the fallout from which may prove more destructive than the enemy it attempts to rout. Still others view it as a relic from a past age, a fossil that has served all the useful purpose it will ever serve and deserves to be stored away with other well-intentioned doctrines that are ineffectual at this stage of the Church's march.

Not one to cut loose easily from tradition, Pope John Paul II throughout his pontificate has regularly called the Church to cling to its moorings and recommit itself to absolute values in a society steeped in relativism. Yet up to a point, he has been reluctant, as were his predecessors in this century, to invoke the ultimate weapon as a means of settling disputes. In his 1993 encyclical *Evangelium Vitae,* the pope presented a battery of arguments from Scripture, tradition, and reason to condemn abortion, murder, and euthanasia as major causes and symptoms of a rampant "culture of death." He denounced them with every proscription in the papal lexicon— save one. He did not invoke infallibility, though he and his aides seriously considered the possibility. Some speculated that John Paul realized that infallibility had lost its potency to turn minds and compel consciences even in moral matters as serious as these.

"The Church Has No Authority"

While abortion and murder did not call for an overt appeal to the Church's highest authority, pressure for the ordination of women to the priesthood finally did. It came in a document from the Vatican's Congregation for the Doctrine of the Faith (CDF) released in November 1995, and it stated that "the teaching that the Church has no authority whosoever to confer priestly ordination on women...founded on the written word of God and from the beginning constantly preserved and applied in the tradition of the Church...has been set forth infallibly by the ordinary universal magisterium." Immediate reaction to this declaration indicated both the sharp division of opinion in the Church on women's ordination and the extreme discomfort many felt at the use of infallibility to halt discussion.

The issue of women in the priesthood was essentially nonexistent in the Church until the middle of the twentieth century. First in England and later in the United States (through the Women's Ordination Conference), the subject was publicly raised: Why should women be excluded from the dignity of priesthood simply because of their sex? In the mid-1980s a series of dialogues took place between representatives of the Women's Ordination Conference and officials of the National Conference of Catholic Bishops—without any concrete results. Meanwhile, the Vatican issued a string of documents asserting that the traditional teaching was firm and ought not to be questioned. In the document *Inter Insignores* in 1977, the CDF stated that only men could preside at the Eucharist *in personal Christi* ("in the person of Christ") because only they bore a "physical resemblance" to Christ. This argument elicited a great deal of outrage and provoked a whole stream of humorous, sometimes vulgar rebuttals. That argument has not been used since.

In Pope John Paul II's 1994 apostolic letter *Ordinatio Sacerdotalis*, the pope attempted to settle the dispute once and for all: "We declare," he said, "the Church has no authority whatsoever to confer priestly ordination on women and that judgment is to be held definitively by all the Church's faithful." He based his position on two foundations: First, Scripture and tradition "bear witness" that the original twelve apostles called by Christ were all males; and second, "the twelve formally chose only males as fellow workers who would succeed them in the ministry" as bishops of the growing churches. Hence, John Paul concluded, a male-only priesthood represents the clear intent of Jesus.

INFALLIBILITY AS "BLUNT INSTRUMENT"

Instead of quelling dissent, *Ordinatio Sacerdotalis* seemed to fan the flames. Catholic organizations in the United States, Germany, Austria, and elsewhere protested, producing hundreds of thousands of signatures petitioning for a new approach in the Church to this matter and others. Some one hundred U.S. bishops in 1995 supported a letter calling for a widespread dialogue on reforms, including women's ordination. Individual bishops and at least one cardinal have gone on record in support of lifting the ban. Theologians questioned the validity of the pope's argument. Peter Hunermann of the University of Tübingen in Germany contended that the term "apostle" extended well beyond the twelve in the early Church; it included Barnabas, James ("the brother of the Lord"), and, of course, Paul. Also, he said, during the "early period of fluidity," there is evidence women held authoritative positions in the community and were recognized as continuing the mandate of the apostles. Phoebe, for instance, was cited by St. Paul as a particularly prominent "deaconess."[7]

Others noted that the Pontifical Biblical Commission, the Vatican's approved research group, reported in 1983 that no conclusion can be drawn from Scripture either for or against the admission of women to the priesthood. In the United States in particular, women theologians like Elisabeth Schüssler Fiorenza and Rosemary Radford Ruether wrote and spoke widely on weaknesses in the Vatican position and criticized the ban as a symptom of a deeper malaise crippling the Church at an important point in its history. Schüssler Fiorenza in her book *Discipleship of Equals* shared her dream that "one day the patriarchal, clerical pyramid will be transformed into the 'roundtable' of equal discipleship, a dream that one day the Euro-centered, male-dominated, Roman-imperial church will become *ekklesia*—the decision-making citizenry of all the baptized around the world."

In the face of a growing movement, the Congregation for the Doctrine of the Faith's invocation of infallibility in late 1995 appeared as an explicit effort to smother dissent with the weapon it had hesitated to use regarding murder and abortion and clearly would have preferred not to use here either. Observed Jesuit theologian Avery Dulles: "The debate was not leading to consensus; it was becoming strident, divisive and heavily politicized." There was a danger, he said, that some renegade Catholic bishop might follow the example of the Anglican Church in 1974 and ordain without due authorization.[8]

Far from having the desired effect, the congregation's statement only served to create a new object of contention—infallibility itself or at least the appropriateness of an insertion of infallibility into this extremely sensitive, volatile situation. Commented British theologian Nicholas Lash of Cambridge University: "The attempt to use the doctrine of infallibility, a doctrine intended to indicate the grounds and character of Catholic confidence in official teaching, as a blunt instrument to prevent the ripening of a question in the Catholic mind, is a quite scandalous abuse of power."[9]

Said Sister of St. Joseph Elizabeth A. Johnson, president of the Catholic Theological Society of America:

> Instead of working patiently and wisely with the question... institutional leadership short-circuits what may well be a God-intended development of doctrine and tries to impose its answer by authoritarian fiat. I get the impression that the recourse to sheer power is happening because those who oppose women's ordination are losing the argument on the field of reasoning.[10]

Benedictine Sister Joan Chittister said:

> I am now more convinced than ever this subject is not closed, in fact, has not even been opened. It has only been suppressed.... The suppression of the Spirit solves nothing....The suppression of honest and credible questions simply diminishes the ongoing search for God in life, damages the church, dispirits the people of God, depresses churchgoing fathers...and drains the church of more and more women every day.[11]

"When an idea no longer has consensus in the church," said Rosemary Ruether, "it is clearly impossible to declare that it is 'infallible' on the ground that it enjoys a consensus."[12]

Dutch theologian Edward Schillebeeckx said it is "impossible dogmatically" for the issue of women's ordination "to be a matter of infallibility. It's a matter of church order, and church order can never be a matter of infallibility."[13]

Theologian Richard McBrien found the ruling "irresponsible." "Do they really mean the teaching is infallible in the technical sense, such that disagreement with it is heresy? Is it the same as saying 'I don't believe in the divinity of Christ?' If it is, let them say it."

Organizations promoting women's ordination also reacted strongly. Call to Action, the largest U.S. church reform group, asked for a "new level of dialogue" that would incorporate the gospel of Jesus, the essentials of Catholic tradition, the dignity and equality of every human person, and the pastoral needs of the People of God."

"Catching Up" With Doctrine

However, other theologians found the action by the Vatican congregation appropriate and expected loyal Catholics to submit. Rino Fisichella of the Gregorian University in Rome said further dissent on this subject would "put one outside the communion of the Catholic Church." William May of the John Paul II Institute in Washington, D.C., said those who cannot accept an infallible ruling such as this are "objectively speaking in heresy."

Dominican theologian Romanus Cesario said the presence of dissent does not weaken the doctrine. Further reflection, he said, will reveal "how this teaching is part of divine revelation." Another Dominican, Augustine de Noia, executive director of the U.S. bishops' Secretariat for Doctrine and Pastoral Practices, acknowledged that reasons for the exclusion of women are "not accessible to a purely historical or exegetical reading of [scriptural] texts" and admitted the need for "better reasons" to support it. But now that the doctrine is known to be infallible part of the church's deposit of faith, he said, "the challenge for Catholic theologians is to develop the kind of consensus that will catch up with the church's teaching about this mystery."

When the relevant Scripture passages are read "in their divinely willed capacity to nurture, guide and sustain the Spirit-filled Christian community," he said, they "induce the conviction that Christ's nonselection of woman entails a permanently valid injunction for the church."[14]

The president of the National Conference of Catholic Bishops, Anthony Pilla, called on the American Church for peaceful submission: "To those who have questioned this teaching in the past,

I ask you now prayerfully to allow the Holy Spirit to fill you with the wisdom and understanding that will enable you to accept it."[15]

There is little likelihood, however, that the subject is settled, given the strong convictions and emotions involved. The Catholic Theological Society committed itself in mid-1966 to an in-depth study of women's ordination in light of the Vatican position.

This debate in the closing years of the twentieth century only illustrates what has been true about discussions of infallibility from the earliest days through the storm at Vatican I and beyond. It is a difficult doctrine that has often strained the minds and troubled the spirits of good-willed Christians. The full dimensions of the current dispute can be better glimpsed in the context of infallibility's long trek through the centuries.

$\mathcal{P}$ART ONE

The
DOCTRINE
ABORNING

CHAPTER I

A CHURCH THAT CANNOT BE LED ASTRAY

I am with you always, to the end of the age.
JESUS

Infallibility: At first glance, it's a crazy idea, an impossible concept. For everything human can fail, including the human body, human institutions, human knowledge. Our judgments are subject to error, miscalculation, oversight and slip-up. When we declare that a proposition is certain or true, we always have to leave a little room for later revision, maybe even reversal. Therefore, when someone says her explanation is "infallibly true," we don't take it literally. She's really saying her sources are competent, or maybe she's talking about something she's seen with her own eyes. In ordinary usage, infallibly true means extra true, not just a rumor, no-doubt-about-it true, backed-up-by-witnesses true. But infallibility in its basic, dictionary meaning says "incapability of error, impossibility of error, immunity from error." Applied to a human proposition, infallibility raises the degree of certainty to a level beyond contradiction, perhaps even beyond comprehension.

But should someone persist that her information is infallibly true in the literal sense, we are inclined to take a step backward.

The claim to that level of certainty by a mere mortal seems on the face of it arrogant and self-contradictory. For only a perfect being with perfect knowledge could be infallible in a literal sense. Only God can be said to be truly infallible.

And that, of course, is precisely why the idea is relevant to Christianity. The first Christians were convinced that in the person of Jesus Christ they had encountered God in the flesh. They believed the authority with which Jesus spoke and the truth he communicated were of a different order than even the loftiest human authority and truth. They didn't use the word "infallible" to describe his words, but they attributed to the message of Jesus a level of certainty beyond anything merely human.

Jesus is portrayed in the New Testament as speaking, unlike the teachers of the old law, in his own name ("But I say to you..."). He forgives sins, he cures illnesses, he casts out demons, he raises the dead. Authority of a radically high order surrounds everything he says and does. It is what amazes his friends and enrages his enemies. In his Resurrection and Ascension, the first Christians saw Jesus as "the exalted one": All authority in heaven and on earth belongs to him; he will sit on the judgment seat to determine the eternal destiny of all humankind. Says the theologian Karl Rahner: "[T]he fundamental self-communication of God upon which the whole history of salvation is based has reached such a historical tangibility in Jesus Christ that...the victory is irreversible."[1]

Clearly, this Christ Jesus was far more than a divine showpiece. His saving words bringing about salvation—this reconciliation of God with the whole world—had to be announced, spread to all nations—spread accurately and authoritatively, without flaw or distortion.

Would it not be probable, then (even necessary), that Jesus would grant to those entrusted with his ministry some degree of that unique authority he possessed? That is the big question surrounding the issue of infallibility (whether of Church, councils of bishops, or pope). Just how significant a guarantee of immunity from error did Jesus pledge to his Church?

The roots of an answer can be found in Jesus' promise that he would send his Spirit to give his followers power, to open to them the full implications of his word. The roots can be found, too, in the conviction of the early Church that it is the Body of Christ, his ongoing incarnation in history. And lest there be any confusion on that point, the believers could fall back on the final words of Matthew's Gospel: "I am with you always, to the end of the age."

Those words gave early Christians (and later ones, too) a kind of blessed assurance and a measure of boldness. They did not feel compelled to work out the details of that special authority in which they were sharing. They trusted, believing a measure of the authoritativeness that rested in Jesus lived on in the community of believers. This does not mean they assigned a mark of ongoing infallibility to specific members of the community. This early notion of infallibility was perhaps more akin to the concept of permanent, fundamental faithfulness. That is, individuals, whole communities, even substantial parts of the community, might err or even fall away for a time, but in its essence the Church would retain the saving word; it would never be lost. The faithful community would be there still carrying out its mission when Jesus would come again.

Meanwhile, anyone interested in the implications of Jesus' teaching or how it was to be applied in concrete circumstances could do no better than to learn what the Church thought about the issue; for the message, the deposit of faith, had been entrusted to the whole Church, the ongoing body of Christ.

FROM APOSTLES TO BISHOPS

An immediate, practical question then was who within the Church had the primary authority to interpret the message, to discover in specific cases what the belief of the whole Church was and, when necessary, settle disputes. Problems were already flaring up in apostolic times, as Saint Paul's epistles reveal. In the early days a special responsibility fell on the apostles themselves. They were the eyewitnesses, those Jesus had personally called, taught, and commissioned to go forth. They were respected as sharing Jesus' authority in a unique way ("he who hears you hears me"). Still, the gospels and Acts of the Apostles often portray them as acting in very human, fallible ways.

It was understood that they were not the only possessors of authority within the Church. In First Corinthians, Saint Paul spoke of a multitude of gifted contributors to the building up of the body: preachers, miracle workers, teachers, prophets....No gift was to be exalted over the others, he argued, any more than one member of the human body should lord it over lesser members. Yet so important was the task of preserving the message faithfully and spreading it accurately that authoritative teaching remained of paramount importance.

With the death of the apostles, the primary role of leading the community and handing on this deposit of faith fell to persons known as *episcopoi,* or bishops. So smooth was the transition from apostles to bishops that it continually amazes scholars. Says Jesuit theologian Francis A. Sullivan:

> The fact is that within a century or so after the death of the apostles, practically every Christian church of which we have any information was being led by a single bishop. It is also a fact that these bishops were being universally recognized as the successors of the apostles in their role of leadership. There is no evidence of any resistance to the system of episcopal leadership except from the gnostics and other sects.[2]

Precisely how the transfer of authority took place we do not know, nor does this development prove in itself the infallibility of the Church or of any bishop. It only establishes an interesting continuity between those who personally knew Jesus and those designated, elected, or ordained to lead the local communities in later years. Saint Irenaeus, who visited many of the churches in the second century, argued that "pure apostolic doctrine" is not to be found in the "ravings" of the Gnostic heretics but in the sober teaching of the bishops. He describes them as "those whom the Apostles left as their successors, to whom they handed on their own role of teaching."[3]

The creation of the New Testament, which involved the acceptance of certain writings claiming apostolic authorship and the rejection of others with similar claims, was accomplished over an extended period under their direction. Catholic writers in the early Church viewed this continuity of leadership as an indication the episcopacy was instituted by Christ himself.

The bishops who quickly assumed the role of leaders and organizers in the individual churches still recognized the genuine contributions of the other ministries and the active role of the whole body of believers. Saint Clement of Alexandria, for example, noted that these other ministries (teaching, prophecy, etc.), are part and parcel of the apostolic succession and that "pure doctrine" is not to be found only in the hierarchical or leadership offices. Said Saint Cyprian: "I have made it a rule ever since the beginning of my episcopate to make no decision merely on the strength of my own personal opinion without consulting you [the priests and deacons] and without the approbation of the people."[4]

The reconciliation between Christianity and the Roman Empire in the fourth century under the emperor Constantine created a shift in this regard. The official teachers, the Church's hierarchy, began to acquire many of the trappings, privileges (even the titles) of the empire's political leadership. This is not to say bishops as a group abandoned their task of preaching the gospel. But with a heavy emphasis on the status of these "official messengers," the other gifts of the Spirit could get lost—or at least become wholly subordinated. Bishops were tempted to function more often as managers and organizers, interpreting their authority in terms of rights and obligations. A tendency arose to divide the Church into two classes: "the teachers," that is, the bishops (along with the clergy who assisted the bishops), and "the taught," that is, the laity. What "the Church" thinks all too easily became equated exclusively with what the bishops think.

The problem with this division is that Jesus did not promise the teachers independent, infused knowledge about the implications and applications of his message. Their teaching would be authoritative insofar as it reflected the faith of the whole Church, to whom the Holy Spirit had been promised. But if laypersons were regarded as only passive recipients of official doctrine, their input and insights could be viewed as essentially meaningless. This dilemma has continued to bedevil the Church over the centuries. Responsible bishops have always recognized that their mandate is to seek out and present the faith of the Church, not their subjective views. Yet the temptation always remains to exaggerate position and title as a kind of automatic guarantee against error.

THE PROVIDENTIAL ROLE OF THE COUNCILS

As the Church grew rapidly in the fourth century, strange doctrines and troubling ideas about Jesus himself, as well as the significance of his message, multiplied. The interpretation of doctrine became a complicated task. Bishops, assisted by theologians, were often occupied in determining which innovative school of thought conformed to the original deposit of faith as found in Scripture and the overall belief of the people and which did not. Some of these schools attracted multitudes of Christians and significant numbers of bishops. The result was fierce competition, with bishops from various areas hurling accusations at other bishops and their flocks. Ancient heresies like Arianism and Monophysitism seem so esoteric and remote to the modern mind that we might be inclined to dismiss them as eccentric anomalies. Yet in their day they were lively movements supported by respected church and political leaders and contending for the right to be accepted as orthodox Christianity. They exercised the thinking and aroused emotions of the general population. Some very nearly succeeded in tearing the Church apart. Crisis conditions required a special response.

At this still-early stage in the development of the Church, it seemed appropriate to call together all the bishops of Christianity and ask them to settle severe disagreements in the faith by their collective authority. For an ecumenical gathering (that is, one representing virtually the entire Church, the whole, living Body of Christ) might be expected to rule with a high degree of definitiveness on matters of faith and morals. The first of these ecumenical councils occurred in the fourth century and was followed by five more within the next 125 years. Christians of that era were preoccupied with questions about the identity of Jesus and his precise relationship with God. The decisions of these councils went a long way toward clearing the air on these thorny issues and quelling the roiling controversies around them.

For example, the first, the Council of Nicea in 325, condemned Arianism, which claimed Jesus did not have a divine nature, only a very exalted human one. The Nicene Creed, still recited today, calls Christ "true God of true God." The Council of Ephesus in 432 renounced Nestorius, who said that Christ possessed a sort of dual personhood, human and divine. The Council of Chalcedon in 520 attacked the Monophysite heresy, which asserted that everything human in Christ had been so overwhelmed by the divine that it could not be said he possessed a truly human nature.

This doesn't mean everyone immediately accepted conciliar decisions just as they were issued. Years, sometimes generations, passed before the contentions ceased. Only after universal acceptance by the Church of the positions these ecumenical gatherings took were their specific declarations perceived as correct and beyond contradiction. Was the Church, then, agreeing that in these relatively rare instances the infallibility of the universal Church had been extended to the specific definitions of such historic bodies?

Sullivan agrees with German historian H. J. Sieben that this was the case. "There was a general recognition of the authority of these great gatherings of bishops to make doctrinal and canonical decisions binding on the whole Church," says Sullivan. "[Later] writers reflecting on the providential role which such councils as Nicea and Chalcedon had played in maintaining the purity of the apostolic faith through the crises caused by various heresies, expressed their belief that this could only have happened by virtue of a special assistance, even inspiration given by the Holy Spirit."[5]

They thought that in these moments of turmoil, when the Church needed to pull itself together, it could count on an extension of the infallibility that inhered in the whole body to the body's legitimate representatives gathered in the name of Christ.

The first writer to specifically claim the term "infallibility" for ecumenical councils was the ninth-century bishop Theodore Abu Quarra. Just as the apostles, gathered in Jerusalem after Pentecost, prefaced their decisions about matters of faith with the expression "It has seemed good to the Holy Spirit and to us..." argued Abu Quarra, so ecumenical councils could rely on the assistance of the Holy Spirit, and their decisions should be accepted as infallibly true.[6]

The bishops of the five great patriarchal sees (Rome, Constantinople, Antioch, Jerusalem, and Alexandria) all eventually accepted the doctrinal rulings of the first seven ecumenical councils. But since the so-called Great Schism dividing the Eastern and Western churches in the eleventh century, the Orthodox churches have claimed that no ecumenical council has occurred nor can occur until unity is restored. Their absence presents serious difficulties to the very concept of ecumenicity, but the Western Church has repeatedly insisted the councils convoked during the second millennium can and do adequately represent the genuine faith of the body of the Church that is in union with the papacy.

"ROME HAS SPOKEN"

Along with the rising authority of bishops in the early Church was the increasing influence of one bishop in particular, the bishop of Rome. For Rome was the diocese (or See) of Saint Peter, the outspoken leader of the apostles, and it was the place where both he and Saint Paul were martyred. It was Peter, according to the gospels, whom Jesus called the Rock, it was he Jesus prayed for that his faith would not fail; it was Peter Jesus told to feed his sheep. Among the apostles, the original preservers of the faith, Peter was accorded a special honor. And it was passed on to his successors, almost as a matter of course.

In the second century Saint Iranaeus said all the churches would do well to concur with the Church of Rome because of its "greater preeminence." In the fourth century, Saint Ambrose declared without qualification, "Where Peter is, there is the Church." And Saint Augustine, commenting on a dispute of doctrine, reputedly stated, "Rome has spoken, the matter is settled." In the sixth century a quote attributed to Pope Hormisdas became a kind of universal truism with a life of its own: "In Rome the Catholic religion has been preserved intact from the beginning."[7]

These and similar declarations from the very early Church have often been cited to establish that the pope was thought to have infallible powers from the start. They do not prove that, but they go a long way toward establishing the pope's primacy, his special position in providing leadership and guidance. Prior to the Great Schism, appeals for judgments about doctrinal disputes came to Rome from both Western churches and from Eastern churches as far away as Constantinople and Alexandria. To be sure, there is some conflicting evidence here. For example, Bishop Cyprian of Carthage Cesarea in the third century felt no obligation to accept the decree of Pope St. Stephen I concerning the baptism of heretics. (Saint Augustine later explained that Cyprian would surely have gone along with Stephen's view had it been backed by the authority of an ecumenical council.)

According to the theologian Yves Congar, papal authority, even among advocates of the papacy, was not understood as it is today:

> Of course, everybody knew that the Roman See was the *sedes Petri*...and one drew the consequence...that one had to refer to the church of Rome or to its Pope for cases concerning the faith, and to ask their help in times of need for the corrobora-

tion of the faith....But it does not seem that one thought of
the Roman magisterium along the lines of a *juridical* type of
doctrinal *authority*....When doctrinal authority was explicitly
attributed to the Pope, it was a question rather of a religious
quality which Rome owed to the fact that it is the place of the
martyrdom and tombs of Peter and Paul.[8]

THE POPE AND THE COUNCIL

The relation of the popes to the early ecumenical councils is intriguing. The first seven such councils, all held between the fourth
and eighth centuries, were convoked by the emperor, none by the
pope. At the first, Nicea, the pope was not present; he sent two
legates who signed the council's decisions along with the bishops
in attendance. At the second, Constantinople I, neither the pope
nor his representative was present; the bishops present did not
request papal confirmation of its decrees, nor did the pope comment on them. The third, fourth, and sixth councils were each
called to discuss matters already ruled on by Rome. And in each
case, the council, after considerable argumentation, agreed with
the papal position.

The fifth, Constantinople II, held in 553, illustrates how the
various roles of council, emperor, and pope were far from crystal-
lized in the minds of the concerned Christians midway through
the first millennium. It also reveals certain patterns of conviction
already etched in the Church. To understand the labyrinthian work-
ings of this council, it is necessary to remember it was summoned
just 102 years after the Council of Chalcedon. That body had decreed that in Christ there are two natures, divine and human. Balanced with the earlier declaration at the Council of Ephesus (in
Christ there is one person), the doctrine of Christ's true identity
appeared settled.

As it turned out, the Monophysites who had been condemned
at Chalcedon were not prepared to submit so easily. They persisted
in stating that Jesus possessed but one (*mono* in Greek) nature
(*physis*); hence their name. Some years after Chalcedon they devel-

oped a new motto, which, they contended, would refine and soften the harsh declarations of that council: "One of the three persons [of the Trinity] has suffered in the flesh." This they proposed as an acceptable formula. The Byzantine emperor Justinian urged Pope John II to approve this so-called compromise formula. In effect, it was the old heresy camouflaged in a catchy phrase. (The orthodox position as determined by the earlier ecumenical councils) was that Jesus suffered only in his human nature, not in his divine nature.)

Pope John waffled on the issue, so the neo-Monophysites came up with a second plan. They sought an outright condemnation of three bishops, all enemies of the Monophysite position and all deceased for more than a hundred years. This, at least, they believed, would provide some legitimacy to their accommodated variation of the old heresy.

Largely for political reasons, Justinian asked the new pope, Vigilius, to approve the condemnation. Vigilius refused, so the emperor had him seized and transported to Constantinople in 548, where the pope, probably under force, consented to the condemnation of the dead bishops. On better reflection, he later repudiated what he had done and, in addition, called the "one of the three persons" formula heretical.

In 553 an angry Justinian summoned the Second Council of Constantinople and compelled Vigilius to attend. The bishops of the East were reportedly more than willing to accept the "one of the three" formulation, but Vigilius rose up and forbade them to proceed. Whereupon the council, under the direction of Emperor Justinian, excommunicated Pope Vigilius for defying their clear intent. The council then passed resolutions condemning the old foes of the Monophysites. No council has ever expressed its rejection of a pope's claim to authority more strongly.[9]

Nevertheless, both Justinian and the bishops still recognized the need for some kind of papal approval of the council decrees if they were to have widespread acceptance among the people, especially in Western Christianity. And they obtained it when the terminally harassed Vigilius issued a constitution seemingly supportive of the

Monophysite leanings of the council. And there the matter lay for many years.

Vigilius' successors in the papacy were reluctant to contradict what he had written, fearing a further loss of prestige and deeper rifts between the churches of the East and the West. But Christians remained irate at what they perceived as Vigilius' betrayal of the Council of Chalcedon; they wanted no part of any one-nature interpretation whether in new or old clothing or of any condemnations that would give comfort to neo-Monophysites.

Thus it happened that Constantinople II did not result in any resurgence of the old heresy; neo-Monophysitism simply faded away. Scholars later concluded that Pope Vigilius' constitution had not, in fact, subscribed to the new form of the Monophysitism but merely pointed out subtle deviations from orthodox doctrine in the three bishops of old.

Critics of papal authority have long argued that these events indicate the pope was not regarded as an approved arbiter, much less an infallible one. But defenders of papal primacy claimed that Vigilius did well, given the circumstances. Whatever approval of heresy he provided was probably forced, and his final resolution of the matter so ambiguous no heretical conclusions could be drawn. Regardless, some conclusions about the mind of sixth-century Christians can be gleaned from these chaotic events.

- The Church considered the pope's involvement—even his physical presence—extremely important for a council's validity.
- The pope thought he had authority on his own to contradict the clear intent of the gathered bishops.
- By seeking the pope's final approval of its actions, the council seemed to recognize that it had gone beyond its powers when it excommunicated him.
- The authority of this ecumenical gathering would be verified only in retrospect—when the bishops and the Church as a whole rejected the new version of an old heresy.

Nevertheless, the case of Vigilius survived for another thirteen hundred years and became one of those ancient embarrassments that would keep the bishops at Vatican I in heavy disagreement.

At the two councils following Constantinople II, in 680 and 787, the popes played significant roles, though it is not clear that their authority was regarded as above the council.

On the basis of salutary experience then, ecumenical councils came to be seen as sharing under certain conditions the high level of certainty that Christ had promised the Church as a whole. Says Sullivan:

> Perhaps it would not be an over-simplification to say that by the end of the first millennium a council's dogmatic decisions were recognized as infallibly true when it was certain that the council itself was fully ecumenical, and that a council was recognized as fully ecumenical when its decisions had been received by the universal episcopate. The basic supposition…was that the whole Church cannot be led astray in its faith, which it would inevitably be if the whole episcopate could err in what it solemnly obliged all the faithful to believe.[10]

PAPAL LIGHT IN DARK AGES

Meanwhile, in the latter half of the first millennium the papacy was growing in reputation, not so much for its doctrinal stands but as a political, moral, and even military power in the ages of overwhelming change: the Dark Ages settled over Europe, the barbarians were arriving, the old Roman Empire was in tatters, and European civilization appeared doomed.

Instead of despairing, a series of strong popes was instrumental in helping create a new Roman Empire—Christendom. Four instances of their interventions stand out. In the sixth century, Gregory I, later known as Saint Gregory the Great, used his diplomatic skills to prepare the way for the conversion of the invading Lombards; he established the popes as de facto rulers in central Italy and stabilized papal authority over the bishops of the West. In the eighth century, Boniface I, later Saint Boniface, forged a political alliance with the Franks through a series of meetings with their leaders and began the conversion of the tribes in Germany. Also in the eighth century, Pope Stephen II met with the powerful Frankish leader Pépin and named him and his sons "protectors" of Western Christianity. In turn, Pépin gave the papacy permanent constitutional control over what was to become known as the Papal States. This alliance of church and state was firmly consummated early in the ninth century, when Pope Leo III crowned Pépin's son Charles (thereafter known as Charlemagne) as "the great and peace-bringing emperor of the Romans."

The union of spiritual and temporal authority proved a mixed blessing for both sides for hundreds of years. The question of who was the final authority in individual disputes would lead to angry quarrels and bloody wars. Popes made great effort to establish their primacy—their spiritual authority over all Christendom—beyond question. And their mode of activity indicates they firmly believed they had such primacy by right, even if their subjects did not always agree. But there were no clear instances of any claim of infallibility in doctrinal matters, at least as it later came to be understood. The papacy was continually preoccupied with matters of state, and the distinction between spiritual and temporal became easily blurred or lost on many occasions.

Nevertheless, the popes' high profile in the medieval world and their knack for maintaining at least a modicum of stability in turbulent times earned the papacy legendary status by the end of the first millennium. This image helped pave the way for later claims of a still higher order.[11]

CHAPTER II

PAPAL
INFALLIBILITY
PROPOSED

*A concept of infallibility closely in accord with modern think-
ing appeared suddenly and almost full grown in the last quarter
of the thirteenth century.*

BRIAN TIERNEY

The thirteenth century was once labeled by Catholic apologists "the greatest of centuries." Such boasts are rare today in
view of some of that century's lesser claims to fame, like the Crusades and the beginning of the Inquisition. Yet the thirteenth century did see a remarkable blossoming of Catholic scholarship and
spiritual renewal. It is the century of the first universities—in Paris,
Oxford, Salamanca, Prague, and elsewhere. It is the century that
witnessed the founding of the Dominicans and the Franciscans,
the century of Albert the Great and Thomas Aquinas, of Bonaventure and Francis of Assisi. It is also the century when papal
authority rose to unprecedented levels, and it is the century when
the infallibility of the papacy was first clearly articulated.

Papal Power Dominant

In the eleventh century, the long festering disagreements between the Eastern (Byzantine) and Western (Roman) branches of Christianity had led to the Great Schism. Their languages (Greek and Latin) were different, their cultures were different, and so was their understanding of church authority and its relation to politics. Serious attempts to mend the widening cracks had occurred in the eighth and ninth centuries, but suspicion and hostility won out.

Following one more misunderstanding (over the necessity of using unleavened bread in the Eucharist, among other things), in 1054 legates from Pope Leo IX entered Constantinople's Church of St. Sophia and laid a papal bull on the altar excommunicating the patriarch, the Byzantine emperor, and all their supporters. The citizens of Constantinople rioted in the streets and publicly burned the bull. Hopes for a reconciliation lingered for a while, only to finally disappear, due in part to the various Crusades, which brought Western armies into the East bent on wresting control of the Holy Land from the Muslims. But Western crusaders treated Eastern Christians as badly as they treated the followers of Muhammad. During the Fourth Crusade, for instance, they ravaged the entire city of Constantinople and burned the churches.

With the split hopelessly beyond repair, the Western branch of Christianity proceeded on its own course. The blurred line between church and state had led to grave abuse on both sides of the line, and the eleventh-century Pope Gregory VII, described as a man of "colossal will power," entered a titanic struggle with the emperor, Henry IV, to wrest control over church affairs from political influences.

The most vexing problem was lay investiture, a system that allowed kings or secular princes to appoint bishops within their territories; these bishops owed their first loyalty to their sponsoring lords (to whom they had frequently paid a high price for their appointments). Henceforth, declared Gregory, bishops would be elected by local clergy and people. But resistance to his orders was so great and abuses so regular that Gregory and his successors often felt the need to intervene. Eventually, the appointment of bishops was reserved exclusively to the pope. Gregory VII also made celibacy mandatory for priests and bishops. The move (at the time some thought it would be temporary) was aimed at preventing clerics from handing over to their children the titles to church properties—an abuse common in that era.

To those who questioned his sweeping decrees, Gregory left little room for discussion:

> The pope can be judged by no one; the Roman church has never erred and never will err till the end of time; the Roman church was founded by Christ alone; the pope alone can depose and restore bishops; he alone can make new laws, set up new bishoprics and divide old ones....He alone can call general councils and authorize canon laws; his legates...have precedence over all bishops....A duly ordained pope is undoubtedly made a saint by the merits of St. Peter.[1]

The Gregorian reforms were gradually enacted by successive popes, and the papacy became for a time the dominant monarchy of Europe. More than one penitent emperor or king bent his knee to the pope and begged for absolution. The papal investiture ceased to be a simple ceremony and became a kind of royal coronation with the placing of the great tiara on the pope's head and his assumption of powers over the whole earth. No longer merely "first among equals," as many Eastern Christians were willing to regard him, the popes achieved a position of genuine sovereignty, with unlimited temporal and spiritual authority over church and state.

The popes played major roles in all seven of the general councils held in the twelfth and thirteenth centuries. Notes Francis Sullivan:

> From the time of Pope Gregory VII, it was accepted that the pope was the supreme legislator for the universal Church [identified with Western Christendom]. The decrees of these coun-

cils were promulgated as decisions made by the reigning pope "with the approval of the sacred council."…The unquestioned fact that the decisions were made "with the authority of the universal Church," combined with the axiomatic belief that the universal Church could not err in faith, justified the conclusion that when such conciliar decrees determined points of faith, they could not be erroneous.[2]

In other words, they were accepted as infallible.

A BOUNDLESS AUTHORITY

With the papacy exerting such tremendous power and influence, it would seem a small leap to claim that the pope alone, on his own authority, could also infallibly interpret the faith. Even the testimony of the important writers of that era suggests a common conviction that the pope had this authority.

Says Saint Thomas Aquinas in his *Summa*: "The Roman Pontiff can [interpret the creed] by his own authority, for it is by his authority alone that a council can be convoked and its decisions confirmed, and to him appeal can be made from a council." Elsewhere in the *Summa*, Aquinas cites the admonition of Saint Paul against schism in the community of faith and explains, "This same holy Roman Church holds the supreme and full primacy and sovereignty over the whole Catholic Church, which it…acknowledges it received from the Lord himself in blessed Peter, the prince and head of the apostles, whose successor is the Roman Pontiff."[3]

In the same vein, Saint Bonaventure writes: "The supreme pontiff alone has the whole plenitude of authority that Christ conferred on the church….From him all authority flows to all inferiors throughout the universal church…just as in heaven all the glory of the saints flows from that fount of all good, Jesus Christ."[4] Unfortunately, the lofty position that the papacy achieved was due in some measure to the so-called Pseudo-Isadore decretals, which had been written in the eighth century. These documents, purporting to come from the earliest centuries, exalted the popes as routinely setting norms for the universal Church. It was later established that some 150 such decretals had been in fact totally or partially forged.

Many Catholic historians and theologians have contended that the multiplicity of texts, genuine and forged, proves that the Church in the twelfth and thirteenth centuries acknowledged universally (at least in the West) not just the primacy but the infallibility of the Holy Father. Furthermore, they argue, that belief had always been an integral part of the Church's faith. For example, in his often-cited theology manual, *The Church of the Word Incarnate*, Charles Journet says Catholics could always have known of papal infallibility from the "ordinary magisterium"—the general agreement by bishops and theologians on the subject. During the early days, he admits, belief in papal infallibility may have been implicit or even "unconscious" among the faithful, but it was always present and conspicuously so in the early centuries of the second millennium.

However, the American historian Brian Tierney, in his articles and in his 1972 book, *The Origins of Papal Infallibility: 1150–1350*, argues that texts like those of Aquinas and Bonaventure, as well as declarations by the popes themselves, do not prove any assertion of papal infallibility. What they do show, he says, is a seemingly boundless exaltation of papal primacy, along with supreme confidence in the inerrancy of the Church.

More important, Tierney says, a belief in papal infallibility in Church tradition (even an implicit one) cannot be established from the historical record. He bases this view on his comprehensive study of the canonists and decretalists of the eleventh through the thirteenth centuries.

Scholars like Gratian and Huguccio had synthesized the myriad canons of belief, codes of church law, the declarations of councils and synods and the decrees of popes from the earliest days of the Church—in short, the extant written record of Christian belief and practice. Their examination of ancient, authoritative tests was exhaustive, observes Tierney, and their conclusions were amazingly consistent. The commentators "knew all the most important texts...relating to the pope and the...Roman church," he says. "What can be proved is that no public teaching affirming the infallibility of the pope was transmitted to the canonists of the eleventh, twelfth and thirteenth centuries in whose works, for the first time, abundant texts for the investigation of this whole question become available."[5]

Nor can it be argued, continues Tierney, that belief in papal infallibility was bubbling unconsciously just below the surface in those first twelve hundred years or that it is not mentioned explicitly in the canons and decrees because it was simply taken for granted. On the contrary, Tierney shows, the canonists repeatedly cited texts stating that individual popes could err and did err. Jesus' prayer in Luke's Gospel for Peter's perseverance hardly establishes his immunity from error, argued the canonists on the basis of their sources, because Peter's faith did fail in the denial of Christ before the Passion; and his judgment went awry in his ill-conceived attempt to obligate Gentile converts to all the prescriptions of the old law— an attempt for which he was rebuked by Paul a few years after the Resurrection.

To be sure, these medieval researchers did find a belief in infallibility present in the Church from the very beginning to their own day—but it was a belief in the Church's divinely guaranteed permanence, a rooted faithfulness to the genuine message of Christ. Tierney says the canonists "were not thinking of 'infallibility' in the modern sense but more strictly of indefectibility. Christ's promise to Peter was taken to mean simply that the church would always survive...."

Typical is this quote in the Gratian compilation: "For although the Roman pope has sometimes erred, this does not mean that the Roman church has, which is understood to be not he alone but all the faithful, for the church is the aggregate of the faithful."

The distinction we make today between official, infallible pronouncements and official but noninfallible pronouncements was apparently unknown to the students of canon laws and decrees.

Says Tierney: "They were content to distinguish between the pope who could err—and err in any of his pronouncements so far as they knew—and the universal church whose faith could never fail. Ideas akin to the modern doctrine of papal infallibility never occurred to them."

If then the idea of papal infallibility was so far submerged—even denied, in the Church's tradition for some twelve hundred years—how did it become such a tangible reality that it would pre-occupy the thinking of a great many Catholics for the next seven hundred years and beyond?

THE BIRTH OF A DOGMA?

According to Brian Tierney, a concept of infallibility, closely in accord with modern thinking on the subject, appeared suddenly and almost full grown in the last quarter of the thirteenth century, just a few years after the death of Thomas Aquinas.[6] It came from a most unlikely source—Pietro Olivi, an eccentric Italian theology teacher of the Franciscan religious order, who spent the better part of his career generating controversy. The charismatic Francis of Assisi, who died in 1229 when Olivi was a young man, not only founded a religious order, he almost single-handedly forced the Catholic world to take a fresh look at the radical nature of the gospel. Many saw his emphasis on simple living and voluntary poverty as a "new gospel," the definitive model for all Christians.

After Francis' death a division broke out among his followers over the implications of the Rule he left behind. One group, called the "Conventuals," said the essence of the Rule was renouncing ownership of all earthly goods, whether held individually or in common. The other group, the "Spirituals," insisted the practice of "severe frugality" in daily living was equally and perhaps more important. A life of consecrated poverty would be useless, said the Spirituals, if an abundance of food, clothing and other amenities was supplied to the friars by outside benefactors.

Olivi was a leader of the Spiritual school of thought, and he was adamant about frugality. This was largely a result of his resentment of the luxurious lifestyle of many members of the hierarchy and clergy of the day. He regularly expressed his views in no uncertain terms and in copious writings, which were, with equal regularity, received badly by bishops and clergy.

Olivi's thinking had been greatly influenced by the mystical ruminations of a visionary figure named Joachim of Fiora. Joachim, who had a sizable following in the twelfth century, taught that all history could be divided into two epochs corresponding to the Old and New Testaments, and each epoch could be further divided into seven stages, each related to one of the seven angels of the Book of Revelation. The sixth angel of the second epoch was critically important to Joachim, because that angel would open the sixth seal of the scroll of the Lamb; and that in turn would tear away "the veil" over the Scriptures and reveal the "spiritual meaning" until then hidden deep inside.

Olivi was absolutely convinced Saint Francis himself was that sixth angel, that his teaching on simplicity and poverty was the hidden message under the sixth seal, and that popular acceptance of the Franciscan way would lead to a new age, the opening of the seventh seal, and the end of the world.

Says Tierney: "Olivi saw the whole thirteenth century as a time of struggle between the forces of the sixth age, already heralded by Saint Francis, and the surviving evil forces of the fifth age typified in the abuses of the actual existing church. This conflict could also be described as a struggle between the 'true church' and the 'carnal church.'" Making sure that Francis' teaching was interpreted correctly was, for Olivi, no little thing; it was a matter of cosmic, apocalyptic importance.

So it was that Olivi and the other Spirituals rejoiced in 1279 when Pope Nicholas III issued the bull *Exiit*. The document not only reiterated earlier papal approval of Franciscan poverty, it called on the whole world to embrace Franciscan values and said this was the way of perfection Jesus personally taught his disciples "by word and example." And, added *Exiit*, the Franciscan way involves severe, daily frugality: "They shall not accept utensils or other things, which they can licitly use...for they ought not to have the use of things...in any superfluity or copiousness or abundance." In Olivi's view, this papal declaration paved the way for the final stages of world history and Christ's Second Coming.

But one roadblock remained, and the Spirituals could not rest easy. For the seer Joachim of Fiora had predicted that before these last days could occur, a mystical Antichrist, a "pseudo-pope," would appear; he would plot against the evangelical Rule of Francis and delude most of the world.

Notes Tierney, Olivi "was obsessed with the fear that such a calamity was about to happen. From his point of view, therefore, it was essential that the papal decrees already enacted to define the faith—the decrees of true, orthodox popes—should be regarded as not only authoritative for the present, but immutable, irreformable for all time." The coming pseudo-pope must not be allowed to betray the recent papal endorsement of true Franciscanism.

One year after the promulgation of *Exiit*, Olivi produced a series of questions and responses on Church teaching authority. In great detail, he explained that when a pope teaches definitively on a "matter or faith or morals," he has a guarantee of infallibility because he speaks as head of the Church and as Christ's vicar. Olivi makes it absolutely clear (as others had not) that he is not talking about papal primacy but about infallibility. "It would be impossible for God to give to any one the full authority to decide about doubts concerning the faith and divine law" and then permit that person to err, he says in one place. In another section, he says, "It is first necessary to consider the inerrancy of the church and secondly, to consider the particular inerrancy of the Roman see and of him who presides in it, namely the pope."

Olivi was fully aware that some popes had erred badly in times past, so he provided a series of subtle distinctions, some of which anticipated by six hundred years the arguments at Vatican I.

INFALLIBILITY AS LIMITATION

Clearly, Olivi's motive in developing a theology of infallibility was just the opposite of the intent of the bishops of 1870. Olivi wanted to limit papal power and sovereignty, while Vatican I wanted to extend it. If the official teaching of past popes must be accepted as dogma, Olivi reasoned, then all future popes are inhibited regarding what is already on the irreformable record; they may not contradict their predecessors. That being so, he argued, the doctrine of *Exiit* was fixed and definitive and could not be tampered with by any pope or pseudo-pope.

Recalling Joachim's warning about the imminent coming of a pseudo-pope, Olivi attempted to further shore up his defenses. Should anyone sitting on the papal throne ever contradict the truth of *Exiit*, he said, the faithful should recognize that person for what he is, "a pope only in name and appearance," and depose him from the throne as the Antichrist. Satisfied that he had done what he could to avert an apocalyptic disaster, Olivi died in 1298, just at the close of the thirteenth century.

Because of his penchant for combining detailed theological argumentation and wild flights of imagination, scholars have had a difficult time analyzing Olivi. After his death, some of his Spiritual associates said he might have been himself the angel of the seventh seal, while other observers said he was either crazy or the Antichrist himself. A new head of the Franciscan order sided with the latter group and ordered Olivi's writings burned, but many were salvaged by his supporters.

The Olivi saga took an exceedingly bizarre, posthumous twist in the 1320s, as the various factions of the Franciscan order continued their disagreement. A new pope, John XXII, authorized a debate on the subject of poverty and the frugal use of goods, but the Spirituals informed him a debate would be pointless; one of his predecessor, Nicholas IV, had already ruled definitively in *Exiit*, and John had no choice but to abide by that interpretation. John XXII was not impressed with that argument. He replied bluntly in a bull that as pope he could do whatever he chose to do: "There is no doubt that it pertains to the founder of the canons [the pope], when he perceives that statutes put forth by himself or his predecessors are disadvantageous rather than advantageous, to provide that they no longer be disadvantageous."[7]

Accordingly, in a solemn, dogmatic decree, the pope renounced the basic ideas of *Exiit,* called it heresy to insist that Jesus and his disciples had renounced all right to ownership, and labeled Olivi's ideas on infallibility "the work of the devil."[8]

This prompted veteran Spirituals, ever mindful of Joachim's predictions and Olivi's fears, to accuse Pope John of showing himself to be a pseudo-pope, an Antichrist and one unworthy to remain on the throne of Peter. Their attempt to oust him failed, and the old controversy between the Coventuals and the Spirituals eventually passed into history.

THE DOCTRINE GROWS

Such are the peculiar shifts of Providence that the essence of Olivi's doctrine—the explicit attribution of infallibility to the pope—would not only survive but flourish, accompanied, of course, by controversy and dispute.

One of the first to pick up the theme was an English Franciscan, William of Ockham, best known as the philosopher who favored the simplification of ideas and definitions (hence the term "Ockham's razor"). In the early years of the fourteenth century, he shaved from the doctrine all of Olivi's and Joachim's eccentric speculations. But he agreed that popes can speak infallibly and had done so. Ockham was the first to insist that tradition, as well as Scripture, is a valid source of revelation and therefore contains material about which popes might exercise their infallibility. In time this two-source theory would be used to refute the Protestant contention that only Scripture provides revelation. Like Olivi, Ockham called for a condemnation of John XXII as an a pseudo-pope. Ockham's logic on this point was impeccable, says Tierney: "If a

Catholic theologian believes that a true pope is infallible—and if he believes that the current occupant of the papal throne has erred in a solemn official pronouncement on faith and morals...then the theologian has no choice but to denounce the current occupant...as a pseudo-pope."[9]

An important refinement of all this came from a contemporary of Ockham's, the Italian Carmelite bishop Guido Terreni. Unlike Ockham and Olivi, he did not wish to harness papal authority but to expand it. He explained more clearly than the others that it is indeed the pope's prerogative to determine definitively questions of faith, and in this duty he cannot err. But Terreni went beyond that by distinguishing more carefully between the noninfallible opinions, orders, statements, and pronouncements of popes and the rather narrow area that rightly constitutes issues of "faith and morals." Only in a quite restricted sense, he argued, can a pope be said to speak infallibly. He also abandoned the idea of denouncing so-called false popes who, by some trick or treachery, might ascend to the throne of Peter. A biographer of Terreni said the writings of this fourteenth-century bishop on infallibility are so carefully nuanced that "hardly a word would have to be changed" to put them in total conformity with the doctrine of Vatican I.[10]

CHAPTER III

THE FALL AND RISE OF PAPAL POWER

We therefore declare...that for every human creature submission to the Roman pontiff is absolutely necessary for salvation.

POPE BONIFACE VIII

I f the political and cultural conditions of the thirteenth century had remained stable in the fourteenth century and beyond, the papal ascendancy might have continued indefinitely. The doctrine of papal infallibility, out in the open and the subject of scholarly discussion, could have become firmly established. But conditions did not remain stable, and the failure of the papacy to adjust to changed times signaled the rapid decline of its absolute status. A new political force was on the rise: nationalism. It would challenge the foundations of a unified Christendom with the revolutionary notion that a territorial or national state had a right to be an independent, self-regulated entity. In the spiritual realm, too, a new force would emerge to challenge the traditional top-down organization of the church.

The political trouble began in 1302, when Philip the Fair, the young, ambitious king of the rapidly coalescing Franks, imposed a host of unwelcome taxes on the clergy and bishops within his realm and attempted to depose a bishop. The pope, Boniface VIII, described as a tall, bald Italian with big ears and a ferocious temper, responded with the papal bull, *Unam Sanctam*. This document, arguably the most absolute (and bewildering) statement of papal supremacy ever formulated, declared:

> There are two swords in the control of the Church, the temporal and spiritual. Certainly he who denies that the temporal sword was under the control of Peter misunderstands the words of the Lord when he said, "Put your sword into the sheath." Therefore, both the spiritual and material sword are under the control of the Church, but the latter is used for the Church and the former by the Church. One is used by the hand of the priest, the other by the hand of kings and knights at the command and with the permission of the priest....We therefore declare, say, affirm and announce that for every human creature submission to the Roman pontiff is absolutely necessary for salvation.[1]

In a changing Europe, *Unam Sanctam* became a watershed document. And it has lived on since as one of those exercises in intemperate authority that is difficult to reconcile with the doctrine of infallibility. Instead of reacting in fear and trembling—as any leader of the Franks surely would have done fifty years earlier—Philip retaliated by sending a small army into a town near Rome where the pope was staying and kidnapping him. The stunned pope died within a year of his captivity.

Soon after, a Frenchman, the bishop of Bordeaux, was elected pope. Sensing he had gained the upper hand, Philip the Fair blackmailed the new pope into remaining in France instead of moving to Rome. Papal headquarters were set up in the town of Avignon on the border of Italy in 1305, and it was there the popes would remain for the better part of the century, until 1378, in what has been called the Babylonian captivity of the Church.

Papal prestige suffered irreparable harm in those seventy-three years. During the reign of one of the Avignon popes, John XXII (the pope who rejected Pietro Olivi's theories of infallibility), the Church began to undergo severe financial difficulties, along with a rash of new heresies and an unprecedented amount of clerical corruption. The popes tried, largely in vain, to halt the slide by appeals to sheer authority. The system of Church taxation, which had long supported the popes and their armies, did not work as it had in the past. On one occasion, John XXII announced he had just excommunicated forty-six abbots, thirty bishops, five archbishops, and one patriarch for failure to pay their taxes. Meanwhile, the heavy toll taken by the Black Plague made ordinary life in the 1300s bleaker still.

THE RISE OF CONCILIARISM

It was during these troubled times when doubts and misgivings concerning the very institution of the papal monarchy were seriously uttered by scholars that the concept of conciliarism began to receive serious attention. William of Ockham, who had been an early advocate of infallibility, suggested that papal claims to temporal authority violated the rights of free persons; diatribes like those uttered by Boniface VIII seemed to him delusions of grandeur that only worsened the problems. Another churchman of the day, Marsilius of Padua, argued that the Church is a spiritual community and should never have modeled itself on the pattern of civil governments in the first place. Moreover, he argued, if a general council is to represent the faith of the whole Church, it should include laypersons as voting members, not just bishops. The pope's major task, said Marsilius, is simply to carry out the council's directives.[2]

Some of these ideas reflected an approach to Church governance that had been first talked about by canonists in the twelfth century. It was called "conciliarism," and it had been first voiced by the canonists. With the unraveling of papal power, these old speculative fantasies had an interesting new appeal.

In its basic form it held that an ecumenical council, not the pope, is the highest teaching authority in the Church. Another form distinguished between the "universal Church," that is, the entire Christian community, and the "apostolic Church," that is, the pope, bishops, and other administrators of affairs. The apostolic Church, in this view, is subordinate to the wishes and directives of the universal Church, somewhat the way the chief executive officer and board of directors in a modern corporation are subject to the wishes of the stockholders. Conciliarism thus left little room for papal supremacy, much less for claims of infallibility, and it had never been taken seriously in the golden age of the papacy.

Then in the years after 1378, when the pope returned to Rome from Avignon, conciliarism suddenly seemed the only way to save the papacy from total collapse. The crisis that developed has become known as the Great Western Schism. First, the college of cardinals, dominated by the French, met in Rome and surprisingly elected an Italian as pope. Within a few months, the cardinals claimed that mobs of Roman citizens had compelled them to make that choice. They declared the election null and void and selected a French bishop as the new pope. But the first pope refused to step aside. Christianity was suddenly faced with two popes: an Italian, headquartered in Rome and backed by about half the cardinals and half the civil governments of Europe, and a Frenchman, who retreated to Avignon and was backed by the rest of the cardinals and the other civil governments. Nor did the death of these popes resolve anything, since both sides elected successors. This situation continued for thirty-one years, then got worse.

In 1409 the cardinals from both sides met together, summoned a council at Pisa in Italy, and invited the two popes to resign. Both refused, so the cardinals elected a third man as the valid pope. For the next five years, then, the Church had three popes—the Roman pope, the Avignon pope, and the Pisa pope—all issuing decrees, appointing bishops, collecting taxes, and battling continually with one another.

CONSTANCE: CONCILIARISM'S APPARENT VICTORY

Fortunately, the newly elected holy Roman emperor, Sigismund, intervened and persuaded the currently reigning Pisa pope, John XXIII, to summon an ecumenical council in 1414 at the city of Constance, renowned for its mild climate. So widespread was concern about the sad state of the Church that more than eighty thousand ecclesiastics from all over Christendom crowded into the city—including some seven hundred bishops and abbots. The Council of Constance lasted three years amid heated debate and constant frustration. John XXIII refused to step down, and so did the other two popes who refused even to appear at the proceedings. When John realized that the assembly was likely to depose all three of them, he fled from Constance, hoping that would shut down the council and preserve whatever vestige of authority he still had.

But the bishops, invoking the doctrine of conciliarism, acted on their own authority and deposed all three contenders. Faced with the inevitable, John accepted the verdict. Then the Roman pope, Gregory XII, quietly resigned. The Avignon pope, Benedict XIII, held out, though he had lost all his supporters. He fled to a fortress in Spain where he died, reportedly still "excommunicated and excommunicating."[3] A new pope, Martin V, was elected by the newly united college of cardinals, and in November 1417 the Western Schism was declared over.

Perhaps more significant than the removal of the three popes at the Council of Constance was the apparent victory of the theory of conciliarism. The assembled bishops had gone beyond stating that in a dire emergency (such as when the identity of the true pope is unclear) a council would be justified in taking action on its own. They declared openly in their fourth and fifth sessions that popes are subordinate to general councils as a general operating rule. The council's document, *Haec Sancta*, is explicit on this:

> This synod declares that being legitimately convoked in the
> Holy Spirit, forming a general Council and representing the

universal Church, it has immediate power from Christ, which every state and dignity, even if it be the papal dignity, must obey in what concerns faith, the eradication of schism...and the reformation of the Church....Likewise it declares that whoever of whatever state, even the papal one, refuses persistently to obey the mandate, statutes and orders...of this sacred synod and of any other general Council legitimately convened...will be penalized and duly punished.[4]

This solemn declaration of Constance would thus become one more chronic obstacle in the path of papal infallibility. Liberals rejoiced at the outcome: Church governance, they believed, would henceforth take a less monarchical, more parliamentary form, with pope and bishops working jointly on a regular basis; in order to prevent any future obstructionist pope from refusing to cooperate, the bishops at Constance also decreed that a general council be held every five years.

Conservative Catholics feared anarchy. There were already indications that secular princes welcomed the decentralized conciliar approach as a way of controlling church appointments and other ecclesiastical affairs within their own territories. In the aftermath of Constance, the papacy, so long the linch pin of Western civilization, seemed a shadow of its former self. The question wasn't, what are the limits of papal power, but will the papacy have any power or influence at all?

THE PAPACY REBOUNDS

Though the council did halt the Western Schism, it did little to correct the torrent of abuses in the wake of the schism. The exorbitant demands of rival tax collectors, the blatant simony, the absenteeism of bishops from their dioceses, the breakdown of Church courts, the ignorance of the clergy—all required decisive action. But little happened. Pope Martin's successor, Eugenius IV, a tall, austere Venetian, did convoke a council within five years (as Constance had required), at Basel in Switzerland in 1431. But he was no supporter of conciliarism and refused to attend the sessions.

While proceedings at Basel dragged on, leaders of the Greek Orthodox churches of the East, much besieged by the Turks and seeking alliances in the West, approached the pope and spoke of a possible reunion with Rome and Western Christianity. That schism was now almost four hundred years old, and an opportunity to end it was greeted with enthusiasm by many, especially Eugenius. Accordingly, he ordered the bishops at Basel to dissolve the council and join him in a new endeavor to reunite the whole Church. Already several years into their reform efforts, the bishops refused, instead passing legislation further curbing the power of the pope and Curia. But then bitter differences of opinion poisoned the atmosphere at Basel. Finally, in 1437, following a legendary fist-swinging melee (as several factions of bishops tried to seize the rostrum at the same time), the Basel sessions disintegrated.

Gradually, the disillusioned bishops left to join the pope and the Greek churchmen in Italy, first at Ferrara, then at Florence, for the reunification talks. These proved highly successful, at least at the hierarchical level, and in 1439, the East-West split was declared healed, with the bishops from both sides hailing Pope Eugenius as vicar of Christ and head of the universal Church.

In one fell swoop, it appeared at first, the pope had regained moral prestige, conciliarism as an effective method of governing the Church had been discredited, and the ancient schism had been healed. A mood of euphoria swept Christendom. It proved short-lived, however. When the Greek bishops and patriarchs returned home, their local churches flatly refused to ratify the Florence agreement. This strange, altogether disappointing manifestation of the sense of the Christian people proved decisive: The Eastern Schism wasn't over after all. The pope's status had indeed been raised in principle, but all the nagging problems remained untouched, not the least of which was rampant simony in the papal Curia.

In the late fifteenth and early sixteenth centuries, a well coordinated general council aimed at a sweeping reform might have provided the Church a second spring, and respected leaders like Bernardine of Sienna repeatedly called for one. But no council was

summoned. One reason, notes Church historian Thomas Bokenkotter, was the character of the papacy itself: "This was the period
of the so-called Renaissance papacy—a time when the Popes were
more concerned with Italian politics than with the interests of the
universal Church. Externally, it was a time of papal grandeur as the
Popes made Rome a foremost center of the Renaissance and inspired
imperishable works of art that to this day adorn the Vatican."[5]

An equally serious obstacle was the lingering confusion over the
relative authority of the pope vis-à-vis a general council. The Council of Constance said councils, by their very nature, were superior
to popes. The experience at Florence, where the pope seized the
initiative and held it, seemed to negate Constance. But that victory had been achieved through a series of fortuitous events and
did not repudiate conciliarism in principle. At that point in history, argues Yves Congar, there was unmistakably universal agreement among Christians that the Church was infallible; but "it was
not completely decided to which hierarchical person [or entity]
that inerrability is guaranteed."[6]

In 1460 the papal bull *Execrabilis* condemned conciliarism in
strong language. But its doctrine was spurned in France and Germany where the notion of a decidedly limited papacy still held
great appeal. Given that situation, the popes feared what another
council might bring. Says Bokenkotter, "In the minds of the popes...
the call for a council was often tantamount to a cry of revolt."[7]

Church historians are reluctant to speculate on whether the re-
form-minded popes of the late Middle Ages, such as Pius II, thought
they were speaking infallibly in their solemn utterances on faith
and morals. If so, they did not press the issue in so many words,
perhaps out of fear of triggering another catastrophe. But this time
it was their caution that helped trigger the catastrophe.

Trent Creates a "Bulwark"

The whole of Christendom from top to bottom seems to have been
caught unaware when the German monk Martin Luther nailed his

Ninety-Five Theses to the church door in Wittenberg in 1517. The split was sudden and sweeping in its effects. It almost seemed, says the historian J. Lortz, that "one day the great patrician families of Nuremberg were calmly donating new, wonderful costly altars and numerous splendid statues in honor of the saints; next day they were dragging out of the cloister the child whom they dedicated to the life of perfection as a nun under the seal of the threefold vows of the Church—rescuing her from the net of godless human ordinances, from the sacrilege of papistical idolatry."[8]

Many theologians today contend that Luther's concepts of grace, sin, merit, and justification are fully compatible with sound Catholic theology, but for many Christians of those times the critical ideas had been buried, Lortz notes, "in an externalism run riot: pilgrimages of all kinds, a superstitious cult of relics of the saints, a semimagical and materialistic view of the efficacy of the Mass—all giving the impression that heaven was something you could buy, like anything else."[9]

Luther's conception of the visible Church, however, differed radically from traditional Catholic doctrine. In his epic debate with John Eck at Leipzig in 1519, Luther made it clear that he did not view the Church as divinely founded, did not accept the authority of popes or bishops as derived from Christ's promise to the apostles or to the Church, did not accept the distinction between the laity and the ministerial priesthood, did not believe that general councils could be considered to speak infallibly in any sense, and most assuredly did not accept either the primacy of the pope or any theory of papal infallibility. For Luther, sacred Scripture was the supreme and only authority.

Official Church reaction was hesitant at first. Calls for a general council were opposed by the Curia, fearful as always that the hard-won prerogatives of the papacy might be threatened. By the time the Council of Trent finally met in 1545, twenty-eight years after Luther's original challenge, the most powerful and populous countries of Europe (with the exception of France) were all well along the way of becoming officially Protestant.

The council, which itself lasted eighteen years (with many long interruptions) condemned Luther's innovations one by one with absolute rigor. The divine institution of Church, papacy, episcopacy, and priesthood were upheld. A theology of the Mass and sacraments was spelled out. Firm steps were taken to end simony and other abuses, and a uniform, disciplined education of all clergy and seminarians was established. In so doing, Trent set the stage for a centralized, disciplined, tradition-minded church for at least the next four hundred years.

No hint of conciliarism intruded at this council. With the Church in such extreme distress, the bishops seemed to gravitate toward a single leader—a general—to head the Counter-Reformation. And the cardinals provided a series of such leaders—like Pius V and Gregory XIII—during the council's protracted life. The pope was clearly in charge of the proceedings; all decisions were submitted to him for his personal confirmation. And to him was entrusted responsibility for carrying out all the council's directives. The ties binding bishops to the pope were tightened, though at the same time bishops were granted absolute control within their own dioceses.

In their zeal to set church authority on an unshakable base, a sizable contingent of bishops at Trent stated that now was an opportune time to define the doctrine of papal infallibility. But bishops from France, Germany, and the Scandinavian countries protested that such action would amount to a gratuitous slap at the Protestants. Besides, the council had already vindicated papal power, raising it to a level it hadn't enjoyed since the thirteenth century. Others contended the Church was not in universal agreement on the subject, and any attempt to define it would divide the council and the Church. Accordingly, the subject was shelved.

Beneath the debate, everyone realized, conciliar ideas and visions of a limited papacy still survived; in the next two centuries these ideas would rise up again in a determined struggle for respectability.

CHAPTER IV

CHALLENGES FROM
WITHIN AND WITHOUT

In questions of faith the Pope has the chief part...yet his judg-
ment is not irreformable unless the consent of the Church be
given to it.

FOURTH GALLICAN ARTICLE

The reenergized Catholic Church that came to life after the
Council of Trent confounded skeptics who thought the old
institution terminally impotent and moribund. Intellectually, cul-
turally, spiritually, the Church rebounded, thanks to decisive leadership in Rome, the general renewal of the clergy, and a rising level
of morale among the laity. Extremely important was the work of
the Society of Jesus. This new religious band, which grew to fifteen
thousand members by the end of the sixteenth century, became a
kind of backbone of the Counter-Reformation. Jesuits led the way
in scholarship, education of the young, and missionary work. Its
members took a special vow of loyalty to the pope, thus providing
the papacy of the time with an added measure of legitimacy and
respectability.

Thirty years after the conclusion of the council, in 1586, the
renowned Jesuit scholar Cardinal Robert Bellarmine published the

first volume of his epic work, *Controversies Against the Heretics of Our Times*. It contains a strong defense of papal primacy and the first clearly stated argument for papal infallibility. "The government of the Church is not a democracy, nor an aristocracy," says Bellarmine, "but a monarchy....The Roman bishop has succeeded not only to the See, but to the primacy and prerogatives of Peter, and this by divine ordinance....not by ecclesiastical law.

"The Pope is supreme judge in deciding controversies on faith and morals. When he teaches the whole Church in things pertaining to faith, he cannot err. Nor can he err in moral precepts prescribed for the whole Church and relating to things necessary for salvation."

Bellarmine then indicates where ecumenical councils fall in his construction:

> It belongs to the Pope to convoke a General Council or to sanction its being convoked by another....But if it neither be convoked, nor approved, nor its acts confirmed by him, it is no true General Council but a conciliabulum....It is the Pope's confirmation that gives to decrees of General Councils their authority and authentication as free from error in faith and morals. General Councils may err before the Pope's confirmation has been given....The decrees of particular Councils, if confirmed by the Pope, are thereby stamped as free from error.[1]

Bellarmine was among the very first to speak of supreme papal teaching as coming *de* (or *ex*) *cathedra,* that is, "from the chair," meaning with the highest level of authority.

Bellarmine's works made a profound impression. For the first time, papal infallibility became a subject of discussion and comment both in academia and among the educated public. The idea had a certain fascination for churchmen of the seventeenth century. For Europe was entering the period known as the Enlightenment. It would be an era that stressed reason over faith, freedom over authority, and innovation over tradition. Great thinkers like Galileo, Newton, Descartes, and Diderot would challenge all the old certitudes that had always been the province of the Church—

in science, philosophy, art, music. The Bible itself would be subjected to criticism and interpretation, and the Church as an institution would be ridiculed and mocked by rationalists like Voltaire. With the old certainties under attack, the concept of a single spokesman who could speak the truth—and speak it with such godly authority that every believer would know it to be true beyond the shadow of a doubt—held a powerful appeal.

THE BIRTH OF GALLICANISM

For others, the image of an absolutely certain monarch, whose utterances demand automatic submission, was anything but appealing. And the image was becoming even less enticing in a world rapidly losing confidence in secular monarchies. So it was that a new variation of conciliarism, the old nemesis of absolute papal supremacy, emerged—this time in very complicated form. It was called Gallicanism, and its principal site of origin—as in many earlier variations of conciliarism—was France (*Gallica* being the Latin word for French), though it found support in other countries as well, most notably Germany.

Gallicanism has received a decidedly bad press in church history because it tends to be identified almost exclusively with efforts by secular governments to subordinate the Church and make it a creature of the state. In fact, the French government had claimed for centuries the right to supervise papal decrees and appointments within its boundaries to ensure they did not interfere with the legitimate rights of the king. The claim, generally referred to as "political Gallicanism," had been tolerated by Rome for the most part, though it was a source of chronic abuse and argument. But Gallicanism also has a theological and ecclesial aspect distinct from political interference, and in this sense it has more to do with the relationship between popes and councils.

In the last quarter of the seventeenth century, France enjoyed something of a golden age under Louis XIV, the so-called "Sun King." According to historian Bokenkotter:

> Louis was the greatest monarch of the time and carried France
> with him to the pinnacle of European power. After finally strip-
> ping his nobles of their power, he brought them to Versailles
> to ornament his grandiose palace....He succeeded in greatly
> strengthening the national economy, establishing sugar refin-
> eries, iron works, glass factories and textile industries to enrich
> his nation of twenty million people....In his foreign policy Louis
> was intent on extending the frontiers, with the ultimate aim,
> it seems, of restoring the Holy Roman Empire, with himself
> wearing the imperial crown.[2]

Reveling in his eminence, the king began extending his involvement in the church of France beyond the prerogatives he already
enjoyed as monarch. He appropriated the revenues of dioceses that
were awaiting the appointment of new bishops and claimed the
right to accept or reject any directives from Rome concerning the
French Church. This produced a long, bitter conflict with the
austere, but unyielding Pope Innocent XI. The Sun King's preten-
sions can only be called a gross manifestation of political
Gallicanism, and they nearly provoked a war between France and
the papacy.

The French clergy, under the charismatic leadership of Bishop
Jacques Bossuet, were hardly elated over Louis' wholesale intrusions into Church affairs, but many believed that the greater danger at this point lay in Rome. If papal claims to unlimited spiritual
authority, solidified by the Council of Trent, went unchallenged,
they feared, the papacy would become an absolute one-man
dictatorship, with no possibility of appeal or recourse to checks
and balances. Mounting enthusiasm for the doctrine of infallibility provided ample evidence of the way public opinion was moving, at least in the Catholic world outside France and parts of Germany.

To be sure, no one knew exactly what papal infallibility meant.
Would every directive, every opinion, of an infallible pope require
total acceptance by loyal Catholics? And if not, who would decide
which of a pope's utterances were infallible and which were not—

other than himself? And what of the historical record, with its ample evidences of papal fallibility? To the French clergy, some variation of conciliarism seemed the safe and sane solution: Accept without question papal primacy, but reserve infallibility only to general councils.

In late 1681, King Louis, under threat of excommunication by the pope, called an Assembly of the Clergy, which met on and off for six months. His aim was to get the pope off his back; the clergy's aim was to set some restraints on papal prerogatives. The result, finally agreed to after considerable debate, was an odd mixture of political and theological Gallicanism known as the Four Articles of 1682:

1. "We reject the deposing power [the right of a Pope to oust a civil ruler] and the right, direct or indirect, of the pope or the ecclesiastical power to interfere in civil and temporal affairs."
2. "We assert the full validity of the decrees of the fourth and fifth sessions of the Council of Constance on the authority of General Councils over the Pope."
3. "We declare that the exercise of the Apostolic power is to be regulated by the canons of the Church, and in France by the laws and customs of the Gallican Church."
4. "In questions of faith the Pope has the chief part, and his decrees apply to all the churches and each church in particular; yet his judgment is not irreformable unless the consent of the Church be given to it."[3]

Pope Innocent was outraged, declared the articles null and void and refused to install any of the nominees for bishop presented to him by the king. Louis threatened to invade Italy and did seize the papal property at Avignon. He ordered that the Four Articles be taught in all the universities and seminaries of France as official Church doctrine. Yet in the end, neither war nor schism occurred. Both sides backed off just enough to maintain very strained, suspicious relations. Rome consented to some continued oversight by the Crown in Church matters, and Louis withdrew his demand that the Articles be taught everywhere. Nevertheless, concepts embedded in the Four Articles took deep root in France. (They would remain alive for 120 years before finally withering, only to reappear in somewhat altered form at the First Vatican Council.)

On the basis of the Four Articles, the French government tended to treat Rome more as an advisor in matters of church and state throughout the eighteenth century. French bishops and the French Church rallied behind the Articles, promoting the superiority of council over pope as a needed antidote to growing Roman authoritarianism. None did this more persuasively than Bishop Bossuet, the leading French theological mind of the seventeenth century. His immense volume *A Defense of the Declaration of the Assembly of French Clergy* is a veritable cornucopia of citations from Church Fathers, councils, theologians, and historians of all ages—all of it aimed at supporting the infallibility of councils and the fallibility of the papacy.

The Articles' fundamental ideas took deep root also in Germany, where the movement was called Febronianism, after its chief popularizer, Johann Nikolaus von Hontheim, who wrote under the pen name Febronius. It also flourished in Austria, where it was sometimes called Episcopalism, sometimes Josephinism (after the emperor Franz Joseph).

To its credit, Gallicanism prompted a wave of scholarly inquiry into the history of the papacy, and it aroused ecumenical interest among Protestants, since it claimed to represent church governance in its primitive form before the accretions of the Middle Ages. There is much in the Gallican position that has a ring of moderation and reasonableness, and that is one reason why it flourished among Catholics during the Enlightenment. For in principle it seemed compatible with the trend of the times to loosen state and society from severe ecclesiastical controls and to encourage governments that were more parliamentary, more participatory, less absolutist.

THE ESSENCE OF GALLICANISM

A balanced summary of the Gallican position, as it developed in the hundred years after the Four Articles, appeared in the 1768 manual of Catholic doctrine intended for an educated French readership by the Benedictine writer Dom Jamin.

- *On the papacy*: "The Church must have a visible Head because she is one, and her unity cannot be preserved without a common centre. But this Head is the Roman Pontiff, who has...the primacy of honour and of jurisdiction...
- *On the hierarchy*: "The bishops are bishops by divine right: they hold their power immediately from Jesus Christ, and not from the Sovereign Pontiff whose equals they are, except in the primacy..."
- *On the extent of infallibility in the Church:* "We must recognize in the Church an infallible authority which terminates disputes that arise concerning the faith. If there is not in the Church a living infallible oracle, then believe what you please. But if there is in the Church a living oracle, an infallible authority, there is no liberty of choice— one must hold without questioning to the teaching of the Church. Infallibility in dogmatic judgments has been given only to the body of bishops. No particular bishop, not even the Bishop of Rome, may attribute to himself this glorious privilege. Jesus Christ spoke to all the apostles in common and in their persons to all the bishops, the promise, 'I am with you'..."
- *On the powers of the pope*: "The dogmatic constitutions of the Sovereign Pontiffs, although they are not irreformable except by the consent of the body of the bishops, are for all that of great authority, and merit on the part of the faithful great respect. If the presumption ought to be in favour of the superior, it is especially in favour of the com-

mon Father of Christians: it is therefore criminal inso-
lence to take occasion of his fallibility to despise his decrees."

- *On appealing papal decisions*: "It is permitted without doubt
  in certain cases to appeal from the Roman Pontiff to a
  General Council, as from a lower to a higher tribunal....To
  propose to the faithful a bull of a pope as having by itself
  and of its own nature the force to subject to it all minds...is
  to profess openly the dogma of the infallibility of Popes,
  unknown to the ancient Fathers and to destroy the rights
  of the episcopate, reducing the bishops to the simple role
  of executors of the decrees of Rome."

- *On the relations of church and state*: "The union of the two
  powers can never be on the principle of the subjection of
  the one or the other. Each is independent, absolute in
  what concerns it....It is not for Popes to give Kings to the
  earth, nor for Kings to give Bishops to the Church: If Kings
  enjoy the right of nominating those to be raised to prelate, this is not a primitive right but a concession from the
  Church."[4]

Despite its tone of moderation and tolerance, Gallicanism was
forever plagued by an inherent weakness—the tendency of political bodies to dominate the affairs of the Church. Ironically, it was
a most extreme manifestation of such domination, the French Revolution, that would, for practical purposes, doom Gallicanism.

A MOVEMENT GONE WILD

It began innocently enough in the spring of 1789, when Louis XVI
summoned twelve hundred delegates from all over France to Ver-
sailles to help solve a vexing financial problem. The assembly was
quickly dominated by the six hundred commoners in attendance,
the representatives of the Third Estate. Influenced by the Enlightenment, they wanted far more than fiscal reform; they wanted an

end to the privileges of the nobility, an extension of real political power to the masses, and a pledge from the king that he would cease operating as a supreme monarch. When it became clear this group would not cease or desist, Louis allowed them to form an ongoing National Assembly and promised to cooperate.

This he failed to do, angering the assembly by bringing in foreign mercenary troops, thus setting the stage for the storming of the Bastille and his own quick demise. At first, France's estimated one-hundred-thousand clergy, the First Estate, remained uninvolved in the revolution, though many supported its initial goals. Then the National Assembly determined to reform the Church, too—seizing some of its extensive land holdings and abolishing special clerical privileges. In 1790 the assembly went a step further when it denied to the papacy any voice whatsoever in the affairs of the Church and demanded that all clergy take an oath of compliance with the new order. Those who refused could be considered guilty of disloyalty and treason.

The pope, Pius VI, condemned the oath and forbade the clergy to sign. The assembly, already deep into organized violence, deported some forty-five thousand priests and bishops who refused the oath and ordered the death sentence on any who dared to return. More than anything else, this oath decimated the French Church, dividing it into two competing camps. Priests who signed, the "constitutional" clergy, were installed in their parishes after election by the people. Those who declined, the "nonjurors," were harassed and pressured to step down; some were hunted down as traitors. During one four-day frenzy in 1793, 220 noncooperating priests were executed.

Soon National Assembly leaders tried to turn the Revolution into a religion by "de-Christianizing" the nation. The standard, twelve-month Gregorian calendar was suppressed; the seven-day week was extended to ten days; all religious holidays and feasts including Christmas were suppressed, and parents were urged to name their babies after non-Christian revolutionary heroes like Brutus. In many places, churches were turned into "temples of reason." At Notre

Dame Cathedral, an actress dressed as the Goddess of Reason was enthroned on the high altar.

Between 1791 and 1794, some twenty thousand French priests and bishops ceased functioning as clergy altogether. Those who remained active either worked quietly with small congregations in rural areas or tried to find some way to accommodate the gospel message to the bizarre theology of reason. The "new religion" displayed a chameleonlike ability to change colors, appearing first as the worship of reason, then as an exaltation of atheism, finally as the official installation of something called "philanthropic deism."

THE FALL OF ANCIENT REGIMES

By 1795 the enthusiasm was mostly spent. The new trends in religion prompted little enthusiasm, especially among the commoners, and the successive beheadings of political leaders had become a bloody, tragic farce. The National Assembly passed a decree guaranteeing freedom of religion, and churches in areas where priests were still available quickly reopened. But nothing would quite be the same again in France, traditionally renowned as "the Church's eldest daughter." French culture would be marked by a distinctive anticlericalism and a certain cynicism toward political movements or promises of reform.

In fact, nothing would be the same anywhere in Europe. As if lit by a long fuse from France, revolutions would break out all over during the next twenty years—in Germany, Spain, Holland, Italy, Greece, Belgium, and Poland.

In 1797 Napoleon, France's new, aggressive military leader, invaded Italy, set up several puppet republics in northern Italy, then kidnapped the pope, who died soon after. He decisively defeated Austria, which was also contending for parts of Italy and thereby claimed absolute control over the entire country, including Rome and the Papal States. But Napoleon wanted to be seen as a reasonable conqueror, one representing the best of the European revolutionary movement, and he realized the new pope, Pius VII, could be helpful in stabilizing the troubled Church conditions in France.

Accordingly, he and the pope signed the Concordat of 1801, which restored the Papal States to Rome and recognized Catholicism as "the religion of the great majority of the French people." It also required all French bishops, whether signers of the oath or not, to turn in their resignations to the pope; henceforth, episcopal appointments would be subject to confirmation by the pope. Some historians contend this last provision effectively killed political Gallicanism by placing the French episcopacy directly under Roman jurisdiction.[5]

The cooperative spirit between throne and altar quickly deteriorated, but by a twist of fate this provided the papacy with a long-term advantage. In 1808, when Pius VII refused to allow the Papal States to join Napoleon in a military blockade of England, Napoleon, now the newly crowned emperor, seized the papal states again, arrested the elderly pope, and imprisoned him in France until he would agree to follow orders. The pope refused, enduring six years of hard captivity rather than allow the most powerful figure in Europe to control him.

Suddenly, in 1814, their roles were reversed. Napoleon was by then surrounded by his enemies and approaching his Waterloo. He saw no further purpose in keeping the pope, so he released him. A pale, gaunt Pius VII entered Rome to be greeted by a huge throng hailing his heroism. This was no arranged celebration; there was a popular perception that this ordeal had vindicated papal resistance to the Revolution and the forces of modernism that spawned it.

The next year, the Council of Vienna established general peace throughout Europe. It restored all the old monarchs to their thrones (at least in principle) and gave the Papal States back to the pope one more time. Of course, the previous twenty-five years could not be washed away so easily. The foundation on which stood the ancient regimes, the privileged nobility, the casual intermixing of spiritual and temporal authority, had been cracked beyond repair.

In their place would come, in time, constitutional governments, the notion of equality for all citizens, and the ideal of separation of church and state.

Still, the image of the despoiled, imprisoned old pontiff standing up to all these new ideas—and the excesses that had come with them—stirred Catholics. They would remember that image as they faced a frightening, hostile world. So would the popes of the nineteenth century. They felt called to hold firm, to make no concessions to theories that challenged tradition. And they would seek ways to enhance that authority, to enable the papacy to speak with a voice that could never be muffled or disputed.

CHAPTER V

THE ERA OF
ULTRAMONTANISM

It is the nature of this government to be infallible.
JOSEPH DE MAISTRE

During the brief conservative backlash following the Council of Vienna in 1815, the Church experienced another period of renewal. The monarchy was restored in France, and political leaders elsewhere seemed bent on wiping out every vestige of the Revolution. In Spain, for example, all the Church and feudal property that had been confiscated was restored, the Inquisition was reestablished, and prominent advocates of the new order were arrested. In Austria, Prussia, and Italy, governments treated the upheaval as a bad dream from which the world was awakening. The Church assisted in supporting the illusion. Especially in France, the restored clergy attacked the ideas of the Enlightenment, sometimes burning the books of Voltaire during parish missions. Without strict obedience to authority—civil and religious—society would crumple again, they warned. And many French Catholics, disheartened by the excesses of liberty, fraternity, and equality, believed this to be true. During this interlude, Catholic devotionalism experienced a resurgence, and a large number of converts entered

51

the Church. Catholic identity and Catholic loyalty became important and proudly displayed values.

DE MAISTRE THE PROPHET

A movement that came to be known as Ultramontanism developed. The word means literally "beyond the mountains," and for Europeans that referred to Italy—Rome in particular, and the Vatican most specifically. People looked to the pope for inspiration, and an unshakable loyalty to the papacy, unknown in earlier times, rose up almost spontaneously among refugees of the Revolution seeking solid ground.

Ultramontanism's most powerful boost came from a book called *Du Pape* (*The Pope* in the English translation) by Count Joseph de Maistre of Savoy, published in 1819. An international bestseller, it went through forty editions in the next forty years and was translated into six languages. De Maistre, a lawyer and layman with no formal theological training, managed to argue his case, using the sort of clear, nontechnical terms that ordinary people understood. The book became a major force in the movement for papal infallibility and was still being discussed by the participants at the First Vatican Council, though de Maistre himself had died almost fifty years before the assembly met.

De Maistre was of a noble family of Savoy, a French-speaking province of Italy. Serving in the Savoy legislature in the years before the French Revolution, he had extensive experience with political Gallicanism: No papal documents could even be published in the province until the legislature made certain they did not contradict the rights of the government. He came to detest the procedure as political interference with the rights of religion. Then, during the Revolution, de Maistre and his family were forced to flee into exile several times as the marauding French Army invaded and annexed various territories. He hated the "satanic" Revolution and what it stood for.

In Switzerland de Maistre associated with French priests deported by the Revolutionary government, and it was there in his writings that he portrayed the Revolution as God's scourge on Europe for the pride and disobedience of the French people. Later he served as an ambassador in St. Petersburg, where he wrote most of *The Pope*. Unlike most historical or theological works on the subject, this book attempted to establish infallibility largely on the basis of reason and common sense. While its argumentation may seem simplistic and somewhat arrogant today, its rhetorical flourish and self-confident style caught public attention. The thesis of the book comes down to this: There can be "no public morals nor national character without religion, no European religion without Christianity, no true Christianity without Catholicism, no Catholicism without the Pope, no Pope without the supremacy which belongs to him."[1]

The credibility of the argument hangs precariously on de Maistre's supposition that the sovereignty of temporal rulers and the infallibility of popes are closely linked companion ideas. "Infallibility in the spiritual order of things and sovereignty in the temporal order are two words perfectly synonymous," he says. "The one and the other denote that high power which rules over all other powers—from which they all derive their authority."[2]

SOVERIGN KING, SOVERIGN POPE

If order is to be maintained in either realm, he insists, an absolutist form of government is required, and that fact should be self-evident to any thinking person:

> Sovereignty indeed has different forms...but once it has spoken, there can be no appeal....The case is the same in regard to the Church. It must be governed like any other association; otherwise there would no wholeness, no unity. It is the nature of this government therefore to be infallible—that is to say, absolute—else it would no longer govern....Let us view it as we will, let us give to this high power whatever name we please, there must always be one to whom it never can be said...You

> have erred!....It is absolutely the same thing in practice not to
> be liable to error and to be above being accused of it.[3]

Even if Jesus had not promised Peter and his successors immunity from error, de Maistre contends, the pope would still be infallible because it follows from the very nature of his spiritual office. The Protestant churches erred, he argues, by attributing infallibility to the Bible or to the members of the Church as a whole, while the Orthodox have strayed by regarding all the patriarchs including the pope as equally supreme; yet in all cases confusion will reign without a single, final arbiter.

In de Maistre's analysis, general councils resemble advisory bodies or think tanks for the pope; yet in practice they have often created more problems than they have solved. He quotes with approval the opinion of Saint Gregory Nazianzen: "I never saw a council assembly without danger and inconvenience. To speak truly, I must say I avoid them as much as I can. I never saw so much as one concluded in a happy and agreeable manner."

Whatever force a council has, says de Maistre, comes exclusively from the papal authority. "To the Sovereign Pontiff alone belongs essentially the right of convoking general councils....He alone is judge of the circumstances which require this extreme remedy.... The Pope, in order to dissolve the council, in as far as it is a council, has only to leave the room, saying 'I am no longer of it.' From that moment it is no longer anything but an assembly, and an unlawful one if it persists."

He makes quick work of Gallicanism: "I never could understand the French when they affirm that the decrees of a general council have the force of law independently of confirmation by the Sovereign Pontiff."

No one, he says, neither a general council, a smaller body of bishops, or an individual Catholic, has the right to question decrees pronounced *ex cathedra*. "But since no right to judge, why discuss? Is it not better to accept humbly and without previous examination a determination which it is not entitled to contradict?"

Like other tributes to infallibility of the time, *The Pope* set no real limits on its scope. There is no fudging here, no nitpicking or introduction of subtle distinctions, and this may be one reason for its longevity: The pope is infallible and the case is closed.

No one early in the nineteenth century seems to have objected that the book's foundational supposition—the intimate link between sovereignty and infallibility—has a major flaw. The two ideas are not synonymous at all, as historian Brian Tierney has pointed out:

> It would be more true to suggest that the ideas they express are intrinsically incompatible with one another. It is of the essence of sovereignty...that a sovereign ruler cannot be bound by the decisions of his predecessor. It is of the essence of infallibility...that the infallible decrees of one pope are binding on all his successors since they are by definition irreformable.[4]

In fact, some six hundred years before de Maistre's time, the Franciscan Pietro Olivi had made this point when he argued for the infallibility of a papal bull precisely in order to tie the hands of any future pontiff who might want to contradict its doctrine. Whatever its logical limitations, de Maistre's book served to insert the concept into the public forum as no other document had done before.

PAPAL ENTHUSIASM

Toward the middle of the 1800s, it was clear that the restoration of the monarchies in the earlier years had been nothing more than a last hurrah; one by one constitutional forms of government embodying some of the democratic ideals of the French Revolution replaced nearly all. This did not, however, noticeably stem Ultramontane enthusiasm for the papal monarchy. A host of influential publications, many of them exceeding de Maistre's book in zeal, determination, and wordiness, furthered the campaign.

In France Louis Veuillot, editor of the widely read *L'Univers*, envisioned a messianic age strewn with mixed metaphors:

Society is in a sewer—it will perish—with the debris of the
Vatican God will stone the human race. These stones of the
Vatican will roll through the world, crushing thrones and dwell-
ings, even to the tombs....Peter has heard the voice—"Launch
out into the deep!" The fisher of men will cast his great nets.
The multitude of the nations will form one universal confed-
eration under the presidency of the Roman Pontiff, a holy
people, as there was a Holy Empire.[5]

In Rome, the Jesuit publication *Civiltà Cattòlica*, a kind of semi-
official predecessor of *L'Osservatore Romano*, minced no words in
defining its editorial position: "The infallibility of the pope is the
infallibility of Jesus Christ himself."[6]

In England, W. G. Ward, a convert from Anglicanism, presented
an all-encompassing view of infallibility in his magazine, the *Dublin
Review*. According to Vatican I scholar Cuthbert Butler:

[Ward] held that the infallible element of bulls, encyclicals,
etc., should not be restricted to their formal definitions but
ran through their entire doctrinal instructions; the decrees of
the Roman Congregations, if adopted by the Pope and published by his authority, thereby were stamped with the mark
of infallibility; in short, his every doctrinal pronouncement is
infallibly directed by the Holy Ghost....He utterly rejected the
idea that infallible pronouncements are few and far between
or need to be marked by the solemnities and conditions laid
down by the theologians or require any theological tribunal to
declare them ex cathedra or interpret their meaning. On the
contrary, they bore their ex cathedra character on their face,
and any man of good will and ordinary intelligence could recognize them and understand their import and was immediately bound in conscience under pain of mortal sin to accept
their teaching with full interior assent.[7]

Minority Voices

To be sure, extreme Ultramontanism and its fascination with absolutist governments did not totally dominate Catholic thinking. A
group of prominent intellectuals argued that the Church was mak-

ing a mistake in taking a defensive posture toward the emerging modern world. A leader of the movement was Felicite de Lammenais, a priest-publisher, whose daily newspaper, *L'Avenir*, represented a viewpoint diametrically opposed to that of Veuillot's *L'Univers*. His motto was, "Let us not tremble before liberalism, let us Catholicize it."[8] The experience of the Revolution and its aftermath should convince society that the union of church and state— any union of these two, no matter how benign—must be abolished forever, said de Lammenais; only by a complete divorce could the Church gain the freedom it needs to preach the gospel. He thus anticipated by more than one hundred years a doctrine the Church would finally embrace at the Second Vatican Council.

Absolute separation, he contended, should necessarily lead to freedom of conscience, freedom of the press, and freedom of education, because the only sort of submission worthy of a human being is a free submission. Censorship and compulsion, he insisted, had never led anyone to the truth. In addition, de Lammenais "moved a half century ahead of his times—even beyond most liberals—by espousing complete democracy, demanding universal suffrage as the only way of achieving these freedoms. This was in accord with his doctrine of the universal consensus of mankind as the basis of religious certainty." Casting off the age-old reliance on the monarchies, institutions of government, he believed, must now trust the people.

Yet de Lammenais, along with such other leaders of the movement as Lacordaire and Montalambert, did not apply their theories about the demise of monarchies and the value of new ideas to the institutional Church. They promoted a strong papacy and refrained from speaking against infallibility; they just wanted the papacy and the whole Church to present a friendlier face to the secular world. Their influence might have been wider if Catholic intellectualism had a greater presence and influence in the great centers of higher learning. Unfortunately, notes historian John Tracy Ellis, it did not, so that even the scientific achievements of Catholics like Mendel and Pasteur went virtually unnoticed. Meanwhile,

Church education was stubbornly committed to the methods of scholasticism from the thirteenth century; as late as 1820 a book that said the earth went around the sun was denied the Church's imprimatur at Rome, although that view had been generally accepted for more than two hundred years.

When French bishops and clergy opposed de Lammenais's ideas, even banning sales of *L'Avenir* near churches, de Lammenais and his associates prepared a lengthy summary of their thought and submitted it directly to Pope Gregory XVI in 1831. The pope's response some six months later was the encyclical *Mirari Vos*, a scathing denunciation of every proposal. Liberty of conscience was labeled "sheer madness," liberty of the press as "abominable and detestable," the separation of church and state as "nonsense." Gregory demanded unqualified acceptance of his positions. De Lammenais, who thought times had changed, was devastated by the rebuke. After a year of spiritual and intellectual torment, he decided the cause was hopeless and abandoned Catholicism. "The hierarchy has divorced itself from Christ the savior of the human race, in order to fornicate with its enemies," he wrote.

THE LIBERAL POPE

In 1846 the election of Cardinal Giovanni Maria Mastai-Ferretti as pope provided a surge of hope among those with liberal views. The new pontiff took the name Pius IX in honor of his heroic predecessor, Pius VII, who had endured years of confinement rather that submit to Napoleon. But unlike Pius VII, this handsome, outgoing, witty man gave evidence of a willingness to accommodate himself and the Vatican to a changed world—at least to some extent. He had a commanding presence and enjoyed conversing jovially with visitors during papal audiences. He surprised his cautious advisers by insisting on visiting hospitals, even conversing with strangers during long walks on the streets of Rome. Stories similar to those that were told many years later about Pope John XXIII circulated concerning this pope's human touch. On one occasion when he encountered a distraught girl who had dropped and broken a bottle of wine she had purchased for her family, the pope reportedly went to a store and bought her another.

Just six months after the papal election, Roman visitor Frédéric Ozanam, founder of the St. Vincent de Paul Society, wrote to a friend:

> This pontiff whom one encounters on foot in the streets, who this week went one evening to visit a poor widow and to aid her without making himself known, who preaches each fortnight to the people assembled at San Andrea della Valle, this courageous reformer of abuse in the temporal government, seems truly sent by God to conclude the great affair of the nineteenth century, the alliance of religion and liberty.[9]

And Pius immediately began fulfilling these lofty expectations. He announced a general amnesty for more than two thousand political prisoners held in Roman jails. He ordered the construction of railroads in the Papal States and introduced gas lighting. He founded an agricultural institute and called for reforms in taxation policy and in criminal justice procedures in the Papal States. One year after his coronation, Pius IX announced the government of the states and of the city of Rome would be henceforth in the hands of predominantly lay councils of ministers, supported by elected representatives from every sector.

Everyone was astonished. "Pio Nono," as he came to be known, grew so popular so quickly that he was deluged by cheering crowds everywhere he went. Popular pressure began to develop for him to use his amazing charismatic presence for the good of all Italy. Politically, the peninsula was in the midst of the so-called *"Risorgimento,"* a popular movement to unite the whole country into one, independent nation and to drive out the Austrians who still occupied two northern provinces. But the movement was badly splintered by factions battling one another. Who had better credentials to pull it all together than this beloved leader? He stoutly resisted the pressure to insert himself into the political arena, but the scene all over Italy was so volatile and unstable that something had to yield.

When Piedmont, an Italian province, declared war on Austria in 1848, the Roman council of ministers, the pope's own appointee, voted to send a contingent of troops to assist the campaign against Austria. Pius was appalled at the prospect of war between two Catholic countries, one of which was within his own domain. He repudiated the military action in an allocution, adding that he had no intention of leading any move for a united Italy, either.

Almost overnight his popularity with the fickle Roman citizens plummeted. Riots fomented by nationalist agitators broke out, and the pope found himself a virtual prisoner in his own palace, with a handful of Swiss Guards between him and the angry citizens who had trained a canon on the front door. Always adept in crisis situations, he executed a getaway by disguising himself as a simple priest, sneaking out a side entrance at night, getting into an unobtrusive carriage, and fleeing to the neighboring province of Gaeta, where he lived in exile for over a year.

In his absence, the Risorgimento forces of Giuseppe Garibaldi entered Rome, set up a legislative body, and declared Italy a united Republic. From a distance, the pope denounced the treachery and appealed to France to intervene. Though hardly a champion of the Vatican, the French government feared further intrusions of its old enemy Austria in Italy. A small army was dispatched, and it quickly routed the Republican hordes and restored the original status quo.

No More Concessions

The pope returned to his rightful place, but he was a different man. He had dallied with the principles of liberalism and democracy, and he had learned his lesson. Subsequently, through his thirty-one years as head of the Church—the longest papal reign in history—he would emulate the intransigence of old Pius VII: no more concessions to progress. He denounced the democratic reforms he had inaugurated, swore to defend even unto death the Papal States, and condemned the movement for a united Italy—though by then it was clearly irresistible. A similar attitude colored his oversight of the institutional Church. Concerned about the spread of liberal doctrines (and the continuing influence of Gallicanism) among the hierarchy in countries like France and Germany, he forbade the formation of national episcopal conferences and inaugurated the practice of regular, required (*ad limina*) visits to the Vatican by individual bishops in order to keep a closer watch over his flock. Without a strong, authoritative center of gravity, he worried, the Church would quickly adopt the chaotic pattern of the secular world.

From a distance of more than one hundred years, it is tempting to deride the reactionary posture that prevailed in the Vatican throughout the nineteenth century. But as John Tracy Ellis notes, these popes had face-to-face encounters with the fierce anti-Catholic, antireligious animosity of so many advocates of democracy and liberalism. That deeply affected their world view: Says Ellis:

> The failure of the pontiffs...to comprehend, much less to accept, the fact that the day of the absolute monarchs was over, that the era of parliamentary rule had come to stay, and that such was the type of government that was winning more and more of their spiritual subjects throughout the western world— this was a barrier that tended to separate the popes, not only from their contemporaries outside the Church but even from many Catholics.
>
> Having experienced harsh, at times brutal, treatment at the hands of men who, ironically enough, liked to style themselves disciples of the liberal creed, it was altogether understandable that the pontiffs should have fought to prevent what they regarded as an evil revolutionary inheritance from taking lodgement in their own domain. But where Rome's lack of political realism unwittingly inflicted injury on the Catholic name was its refusal to distinguish between the principles of philosophical liberalism...in many aspects totally unacceptable to Catholics, and the perfectly legitimate aspirations with which many of the Holy See's spiritual subjects supported freedom of conscience, of assembly, of speech and of the press.[10]

PART TWO

The

DOCTRINE DEFINED

CHAPTER VI

THE CALL
FOR A COUNCIL

The Roman Pontiff cannot and ought not to reconcile himself...with progress, liberalism and modern civilization.

SYLLABUS OF ERRORS

When Pius IX returned to the Vatican in 1850 from the humiliation of his exile in Gaeta, he began to work toward making papal infallibility an explicit dogma of the Church. In a history of the council approved by the pope himself, Bishop Claude Plantier said Pius saw himself on a mission from God and believed the definition of infallibility would be the climax of his pontificate.[1] To prepare the way for this historic achievement, he worked quietly with the Curia, Jesuit theologians like Clemens Schrader and John Baptist Franzelin, and the editors of *Civiltà Cattòlica*, the Jesuit publication in Rome recognized as the informal voice of the Vatican. In 1851 that publication declared the time was ripe for Catholicism to become forthright and aggressive—first, regarding its own teachings by proclaiming the doctrine of the Immaculate Conception, and second, in relation to the outside world by condemning the "pernicious heresies of the day."

Mary "Immune From All Stain"

The idea that Mary, the mother of Jesus, was preserved from original sin from conception was not universally agreed on throughout the ages. Thomas Aquinas, for example, argued that it would impinge on Jesus' unique position as savior. Nevertheless, the Immaculate Conception had maintained a long history as a pious opinion among the faithful. The doctrine received a boost in the sixteenth century when some Jesuits in Spain uncovered tablets that traced the belief back to the time of the apostles. The tablets were later found to be forgeries, and the belief floundered. Then, in 1830, popular devotion revived when Catherine Labouré reportedly had a vision in which the Blessed Virgin told her to have a medal struck depicting her standing on a globe with the words "O Mary conceived without sin, pray for us who have recourse to thee." The spread of the Miraculous Medal devotion increased Marian interest, and some devotees called for an official declaration from the Church.

In 1846, the year Pius was elected, another appearance of the virgin, to two children at La Salette in France, elicited widespread interest; Mary reportedly provided a secret message to be sent to the pope. Its contents were never made public, but in writing out the secret, one of the children asked how to spell the words "infallibility" and "Antichrist."[2]

Pius himself exhibited a lifelong fascination with miracles and prophecies. He had reportedly been cured of epilepsy as a boy when he drank "water of Jesus of Nazareth" supplied by a visionary of the day, Elizabeth Canori-Mora. During his pontificate, he frequently referred to the sayings of another seer, Anna Maria Tiagi, herself an outspoken advocate of infallibility. After her death, he raised her to the ecclesiastical rank of Honorable.

With devotion to Mary growing throughout the world (La Salette became a place of pilgrimage much like Fátima in later times), the pope deemed it appropriate to affirm the Immaculate Conception of Mary publicly and officially. The obvious way would have been during an ecumenical council, but he indicated he would prefer to proclaim the doctrine in his own name. He consulted with some 603 bishops worldwide, of whom only 56 opposed the idea of a definition. A number of others, however, reportedly expressed reservations because the Immaculate Conception lacked a foundation in Scripture. Its sole claim to authenticity was derived from tradition—a somewhat shaky tradition at that.

On December 8, 1854, Pius IX issued the bull *Ineffabilis Deus*, which stated that "the most Blessed Virgin Mary was, from the first moment of her conception, by the singular grace and privilege of almighty God and in view of the merits of Christ Jesus the savior of the human race, preserved immune from all stain of original sin." The language indicated that this teaching was clothed in the highest possible authority of the Church: "If therefore any persons shall dare to think—which God forbid—otherwise than has been defined by us, let him know that he certainly has abandoned the divine and Catholic faith."[3]

The proclamation set a genuine precedent: On his authority, the pope had created an article of faith, obligating the universal Church's acceptance. According to his adviser Schrader, the definition was "an act to which no former pontificate can show a parallel; for the Pope defined the dogma of his own sovran authority, without the cooperation of a council; and this independent action involves practically, if not formally, another dogmatic definition, namely that the Pope is infallible in matters of faith in his own person and not merely when presiding at a council."[4]

Protestant reaction was overwhelmingly negative in view of the absence of biblical confirmation, while Catholic response was almost universally positive. Devotion to the Blessed Virgin was so strong at the time that the unusual manner in which the doctrine was promulgated went largely unnoticed.

A Harsh Syllabus

Pius IX's rejection of "certain erroneous doctrines" was likewise intended to establish the papacy as a strong, authoritarian voice, in this case against the rising forces of liberalism. Preparations involved the work of several theological commissions over a four-year period. The result was a virtual creed of extreme Ultramontane thinking. It was published in December 1864 as the encyclical *Quanta Cura*, with a separate attachment identifying eighty false teachings of the age; the latter document quickly became known as the *Syllabus of Errors*. The encyclical, which condemned in general what the *Syllabus* condemned specifically, spoke of "the impious and absurd principle of naturalism" as the root of modern evil. Those who believe the highest interests of society demand that government take no regard of religion or that it make no distinction between true and false religion are deluded, said Pius.

The overall argument of *Quanta Cura*, according to historian J. B. Bury, comes down to this:

> The State must recognize a particular religion as regnant, and submit to its influence, and this religion must be the Catholic; the power of the State must be at its disposal, and all who do not conform to its requirements must be compelled or punished. The duty of governments is to protect the Church, and freedom of conscience and cult is madness. Not the popular will, but religion...is the basis of civil society, otherwise it will sink into materialism. The Church is superior to the state, and therefore the state has no right to dictate to her....The family and the education of children belong to the Church, not to the State. The Pope can decree and prescribe what he chooses, without the State's permission, and his authority is not limited to doctrines and morals.[5]

The propositions in the *Syllabus* are presented as errors. Therefore, the Vatican counseled readers, it is best to state them in contradictory form in order to grasp what the Church is really teaching. So stated, many of the propositions in the *Syllabus* are relatively indisputable and hardly controversial. For example: "The Church has an innate and legal right to acquire and possess property"..."The method of studies in clerical seminaries is not subject to state supervision"..."The violation of oaths is absolutely unlawful, even when done from patriotic motives."[6]

But large portions of the *Syllabus* were quite controversial. With numbing repetition, the Church set its face like flint against every vestige of liberalism.

Some declarations opposed freedom of conscience, e.g.: "It is not lawful for the individual to accept and profess that religion which, guided by the light of reason, he considers true"..."The Church has the power to decide dogmatically that the religion of the Catholic Church is the only true one"..."It is still expedient in our days that the Catholic religion should be treated as the only religion of the state, to the exclusion of all other worship."

Others insisted on the Church's superiority over the State, e.g.: "The Church has the power to employ external force; she also possess a direct and an indirect temporal power."

Still others were so sweeping in scope or so defensive regarding the Church that they appeared almost ludicrous: "The sons of the Christian and Catholic Church are not divided in opinion as to the compatibility of the temporal sovranty with the spiritual"... "Arbitrary acts on the part of the Roman pontiff have not contributed to the schism of the Eastern and Western churches"..."The decrees of the apostolic chair and the Roman congregations do not hinder the free progress of science and learning."

The last of the eighty declarations was a summary of everything that went before: "The Roman pontiff cannot and ought not to reconcile himself and come to terms with progress, liberalism and modern civilisation."

Scholars have long wondered what purpose Pius IX had in proclaiming theories modern society was in the process of forgetting and what value he saw in provoking old antagonisms between church and state. The answer may be that, along with the Ultramontane advisers in the Curia, he really believed that liberal notions of freedom and democracy were passing phases doomed by their materialistic foundations, and a well-aimed blow might hasten their inevitable collapse. This was unquestionably the position of Louis Veuillot and others who praised the *Syllabus*; they believed participatory and parliamentary systems rested "on an heretical principle" and would fail as every heresy must fail.[7]

These two documents also served as an exercise of unilateral, high-visibility papal authority, a kind of test case to further set the stage for the great event Pius IX was pondering. When his immediate predecessor condemned the liberal views of de Lammenais thirty-one years before, there was no great protest in the Catholic world. But a generation had come and gone since then, and in countries like the United States, England, and Belgium freedom of worship and freedom of conscience had been integrated into the political system. The *Syllabus* provoked loud protest, not just from Protestants and identified liberals, but from ordinary Catholics who saw it as reactionary and medieval. The *Civiltà Cattòlica* found it necessary to assure enraged Belgians just two months after publication of the *Syllabus* that the Church did not intend to interfere with their new constitution or civil liberties.

Errors Seen "in Context"

The most concerted effort to defend *Quanta Cura* and the *Syllabus* against its critics came from Félix Dupanloup, the bishop of Orléans and the most influential prelate in France. In a widely circulated pamphlet, he explained that each of the condemned errors had a context, and placing the statements in context mitigated their bluntness. For example, he noted that the final claim—that the pope ought not to reconcile himself with modern civilization— had originally been stated in an allocution chastising the Italian province of Piedmont for trampling on Church rights. In its original form, it stated the pope should not accommodate to modern civilization "if by 'civilization' is meant a system invented on purpose to weaken and perhaps overthrow the Church."[8] Furthermore, said Dupanloup, a distinction must be made between thesis—that is, certain principles that would prevail in an ideal society, and hypothesis—that is, adaptations to meet conditions the church cannot control. No need for panic, said the French bishop, because there is no chance the ideal society will be realized soon, if ever.

Dupanloup's defense had obvious limitations. Putting *Syllabus* statements in context was certainly helpful, but it was the pope who took them out of context. Besides, it was not particularly consoling to constitutional governments to learn the pope would refrain from imposing absolutist claims only because he lacked the opportunity to do so. Nevertheless, Dupanloup's effort earned him letters of appreciation from more than six hundred bishops and from Pius himself.

In the years preceding Vatican I, Dupanloup became a valued presence in the hierarchy—a French bishop who was greatly respected by his peers and unquestionably loyal to the papacy. His skills might have made him a major architect of the council itself (as Cardinal Leon-Joseph Suenens was at Vatican II), but as it turned out, he would become one of the pope's most determined opponents.

PROVIDING FOR "EXTRAORDINARY NEEDS"

In December 1864, just two days before the *Syllabus* was published, the pope told selected members of the Congregation of Rites that he had been thinking of convening an ecumenical council to provide for the "extraordinary needs of the times," swore them to secrecy, and asked their opinions. After deliberation, thirteen wrote in favor of the idea, while eight were opposed or had grave doubts. Some suggested the council should consider relaxing Church discipline due to changed times, others advocated a stronger affirmation of Church doctrine, still others wanted the council to work for the reunification of Christians. None mentioned infallibility. Four months later, the pope shared his idea—again confidentially—with thirty-four selected bishops from around the world. The majority favored a council, and eight mentioned a declaration of infallibility among the possible outcomes.

That was enough outside encouragement for Pius. But due to world events, notably a war between Austria and Prussia, he did not announce his intention publicly until June 1867, when a body of five hundred bishops was in Rome for a special commemoration of St. Peter's. He made no mention of infallibility in his talk, nor did any mention appear in the papal bull one year later summoning all bishops to Rome. The purpose of the event, he said, would be to provide "what in these hard times may promote the greater honor of God, the purity of the faith, the dignity of divine service, the salvation of souls, the discipline of the secular clergy, and the common peace and concord of the whole world."[9]

Dupanloup had at first opposed holding a council because its stated purpose seemed so vague. But he soon warmed to the idea, believing it might precipitate an ecumenical movement among Christians. Like others outside the Roman inner circle, he seemed unaware that a declaration of infallibility was the major goal. The more determined Ultramontane bishops held high hopes that infallibility would be the final outcome and worked diligently to further the cause. More than a year before the official announcement, Archbishop Henry Edward Manning of England and Ignatius Senestréy of Bavaria had taken an oath together to do all in their power to promote infallibility.

After the pope read the bull of announcement, protocol required the gathered bishops to prepare a public address thanking him and pledging support. It was here the first lines of division appeared. Manning wanted a "fighting manifesto" condemning modern ideas and "wounding in order to strike home."[10] He also wanted a mention of infallibility in the text of the address. Dupanloup objected that the pope had not taken such an aggressive position and claimed that bringing up infallibility would only create division. Manning then said that if infallibility was not explicitly mentioned, reference in the talk must at least be made to the Council of Florence, the fifteenth-century convocation that opposed conciliarism. Manning and the many he spoke for wanted papal superiority over council—even independence of council—affirmed from the start. They suspected there were remnants of theological Gallicanism in Dupanloup and other French and German bishops wary of Roman centralization. Harsh words were exchanged between the two leaders on this occasion, but Manning got his way. The congratulatory speech contained these words: "We fully accept what the Fathers of the Council of Florence defined in the decree of union—that the Roman Pontiff is the Vicar of Christ and head of the whole Church, and Father and Teacher of all Christians, and to him in Blessed Peter has been given by Jesus Christ full power of feeding, ruling and governing the universal Church."[11]

A Dogma to "Conquer History"

During the following months, the planning of the council was undertaken by a central commission of cardinals who oversaw the work of five subsidiary commissions. These groups were manned almost exclusively by members of the Curia, two thirds of whom were Italians living in Rome. Their activity drew little attention until February 1869, when the *Civiltà Cattòlica* hinted broadly at what lay ahead. In a much-discussed article, the publication stated that "Catholics hope that the council...will proclaim the doctrines of the *Syllabus* [as infallible]...and will accept with joy the proclamation of the dogmatic infallibility of the sovereign Pontiff...[and] will define it by acclamation."[12]

The article did not say these were Pius's own wishes, but those who knew the publication's quasi-official status with the Vatican immediately took that to be the case.

Reaction was instantaneous from Germany. Using the pseudonym "Janus," the man widely considered the leading theologian in Europe, Johann Joseph Ignatius von Döllinger of the University of Munich, launched a series of articles attacking papal infallibility in the Augsburg publication, *Allgemeine Zeitung*. His own intensive studies of the subject had transformed him from a mild Ultramontane priest into a fire-breathing theological Gallican: that is, he endorsed papal primacy but did not view the pope as above a council and favored a degree of independence from Rome for national churches. Döllinger feared that the world's bishops, uncertain how to proceed in a new age, would yield all their authority to the papacy and thus destroy the collegial nature of the hierarchy. In one article, he noted:

> In 449 a synod was held which got the name of the synod of robbers; the Council of 1869 will be the synod of flatterers. If the Council allows itself to be used to bind the wreath of Infallibility round the Pope's brow...there will be no great and sudden rebellion, no insurrection in the grand style; all will remain quiet, only too quiet. The Jesuits and their pupils will sing Hosannah, draw some inferences from the dogma and use it for their purposes; and the world will look on indifferent. But a deep antipathy against the [papacy and the] Italian priesthood will gradually grow.[13]

Döllinger was not a diplomat. His articles were strewn with sarcasm and invective; he regularly impugned the sincerity of anyone who would dispute him. But his knowledge of history was prodigious. "We are standing here on the solid ground of history, of evidence of facts," he wrote. And these told him that infallibility had a basis neither in the Bible nor tradition; therefore it was simply not the raw material out of which a dogma could be shaped. "Before I could ever inscribe this modern invention on the tablet of my mind," he said, "I would first have to plunge my 50 years of theological, historical and patriotic studies into Lethe [river of forgetfulness] and then draw them forth like a blank sheet of paper."[14] In the months before the council, he maintained a continuous barrage of articles, many of which were published in a book, *The Pope and the Council*. The work was promptly put on the Index of Forbidden Books.

Döllinger's was not the only voice raised against the doctrine at this early juncture. In England, Lord John Acton, a former student of Döllinger's in Munich, argued that modern ideas could not be put to flight by attributing quasi-divine powers to the pope. (It was in reference to the papacy that Acton delivered his famous quote: "Power corrupts and absolute power corrupts absolutely.") The Church, he wrote, "must meet its adversaries on grounds which they understand and acknowledge...answering the critic by a severer criticism, the metaphysician by closer reasoning, the historian by deeper learning."[15]

Proponents of infallibility like Louis Veuillot called Döllinger a heretic and accused him of trying to precipitate "a 1789"—that is, a French Revolution within the Church. Archbishop Manning attempted damage control with a long pastoral letter. As a body, the Church is infallible, he explained, and the pope is the head of the Church; but an infallible body without an infallible head is absurd; therefore the pope is infallible. Instances from history in which popes acted in a decidedly fallible manner should not be taken too seriously, said Manning: "The appeal to antiquity is treason because it rejects the divine voice at this hour. The dogma [of infallibility] must conquer history."[16]

A "HOODWINKED" PUBLIC?

Meanwhile, at the political level the subject of infallibility caused considerable tension. In a letter to international diplomats, Prince Hoenhole, the Bavarian foreign minister, wrote:

> The only dogmatic thesis that Rome would wish to be proclaimed at the Council is papal infallibility. It is evident that this pretension raised to a dogma would pass beyond the purely spiritual domain, and would become a question eminently political, raising the power of the Pope, even on the temporal side, above all princes and people of Christendom....Governments should ask themselves if it be not their duty to call the serious attention of their bishops and of the Council to the disastrous results that would follow from such a disturbance in the actual relations of Church and State.[17]

Political reaction caused more than passing interest because by 1869 Rome and the Papal States were confronted by an otherwise fully united Italy under the head of the newly crowned king, Victor Emmanuel. Only the continued presence of French troops in papal territory guaranteed the pope's safety and independence. Should France pull out, there would most certainty be no council. But France decided to maintain its protective stance—for the time being—while urging the pope to proceed cautiously. In an instruction submitted to the Vatican, the foreign minister wrote, "For some years past there has been a movement in the Catholic Church aiming at augmenting unduly the prerogatives of the pope....There is no doubt that the doctrine of the pope's infallibility speaking ex cathedra admits many subtle distinctions, and we...hope that if a statement on this matter must be made, the expression will be chosen with extreme discretion."[18]

The council was scheduled to begin in December 1869, and preparations were especially intense during that summer and fall. In addition to the Curia members working on the agenda, a number of theologians from various countries had been invited to contribute. Döllinger was not one of these. John Henry Newman, the much esteemed English churchman, was invited but declined the invitation. One who did attend was Joseph Karl Hefele from the University of Tübingen; his reputation as a Church historian was almost the equal of Döllinger's. While in Rome he came to believe the agenda and the final outcome of the council had already been decided by a group surrounding the pope.

He wrote to a friend:

> The longer I stay here, the more clearly I see the duplicity behind my appointment as a consultor to the council. That was just Rome's way of hoodwinking the public with an appearance of neutrality. In reality I have no idea what I'm supposed to be doing here....The only job I've been assigned is to excerpt the ceremonial portions from the acts of the Council of Trent....I think the sly Jesuits are laughing up their sleeve at the way the Tübingen professor has been so neatly paralyzed.[19]

# HAPTER VII

——

OPENING SESSIONS:
CONTENTION AND
CONFUSION

What have we done to be treated as the faithful were never treated before?

JOHN HENRY NEWMAN

T he council began on December 8, 1869, with a solemn Mass in St. Peter's. The 719 cardinals, bishops, and abbots in attendance heard the pope dedicate the proceedings to the Mother of God. One third of the voting members were Italians, one third from other European countries, and one third from the rest of the world, including 113 from the United States and Canada. The major meetings, called general congregations, were all held in the right transept of St. Peter's, which had been set up as an aula, a kind of auditorium with the president's chair at one end and a speaker's podium in the center. Bishop William Ullathorne of England, who wrote extensively on his experiences, described the scene during a typical meeting:

> The circle of cardinals round the apse, the inner circle of patriarchs, the long protracted lines of bishops in red copes and

white miters, interspersed with orientals in their many coloured robes and crowns, for they all seem to have a taste for Joseph's coat, and the officials at the tables between. Eight rows ascended on one side, eight on the other, face to face with a considerable space of green cloth covering the marble floor between.[1]

ALIGNING ON THE ISSUES

Problems developed almost from the start. Acoustics in the aula were extremely poor, causing complaints and an air of general dissatisfaction from beginning to end. On some roll calls, disgruntled bishops were inclined to vote against a proposal (*non placet*), adding "because we haven't understood the question." The pope, however, preferred the location because it was closer to Saint Peter's tomb. Especially disturbing to some attendees was the announcement that the pope had reserved to himself the right to propose questions to the council. If anyone else wished to do so, he would have to submit his proposal to a committee appointed by the pope, and the pope would then determine if it was appropriate. The ruling was in clear contrast to the procedure at the Council of Trent and at earlier general councils. In addition, Pius IX imposed strict secrecy on all present—which meant each bishop could confer only with the one theologian he had been allowed to bring with him. "This foresight is highly necessary at the present time," said the pope, "when godlessness equipped with a thousand weapons of destruction, is on the watch to lose no opportunity of stirring up odium against the Catholic Church and its doctrines."[2]

The bishops were also forbidden to write or print anything about the conciliar speeches and debates. To prevent abuses of the rule, the papal post office was instructed to intercept suspicious letters and send them to a censor for review. The aim was to shroud the whole event in a veil of secrecy. But judging from the amount of material published and disseminated by various bishops during the proceedings, the plan proved largely ineffective. One added touch of early gloom was the death of the president of the council, Cardinal von Reisach, just a few days before the opening.

Though the word "infallible" appeared nowhere in the preliminary speeches or in the documents circulated for discussion, practically everyone knew this was the *raison d'être* for the gathering. Accordingly, the bishops began to align themselves on that critical issue. Polls were forbidden, but it soon became evident that if the question were put to an early vote, infallibility would win by a margin of four to one or better. Yet many still believed a dogma could not be imposed on the faithful without near unanimity among the council fathers. That had been the tradition in earlier councils, and a break from precedent here on such a volatile issue would surely create a stir.

The 20 to 25 percent of the bishops who opposed the definition felt the stringent control measures served to curb free discussion and to prevent the world from seeing the very real division in the world's episcopate. The majority, who favored infallibility (or who were indifferent), accepted the controls as a necessary means of keeping discussion within bounds.

Opponents of the definition were often referred to as "Inopportunists," though their numbers included both those who thought this was not an appropriate time and place to define infallibility as a dogma and those who held that it should never be defined. Proponents of the doctrine were called "Infallibilists."

THE INOPPORTUNISTS

A standout among the Inopportunist leadership was Félix-Antoine Philbert Dupanloup of Orléans. A man of great charm and incredible energy, Dupanloup, who was sixty-eight at the time of the council, was the recognized spokesman for most of the French episcopacy. Throughout his career, he had defended papal prerogatives, and more than anyone else he was responsible for persuading the French government to drive Italian nationalists out of Rome and to set up a military guard over the Papal States. Pius IX repeatedly expressed his gratitude and would surely have relied on Dupanloup to use his persuasive powers at the council. But Dupanloup was adamantly opposed to a definition of infallibility, and he used his skills to fight the proposal from the start. He brought six secretaries with him to Rome and turned out a continuous series of articles and pamphlets that were published and widely distributed, somehow bypassing the watchful eye of the papal censors at the post office.

Dupanloup said he believed in the concept of papal infallibility yet feared a conciliar definition would give the pope a kind of "separate infallibility," distinct from the infallibility that has always been in the Church. His seven-point summary of the case against is similar to the position of most of the Inopportunists:

- There is no need to define papal infallibility; the Church's infallibility has sufficed for eighteen centuries.
- The Council of Trent, which had more reason to define the doctrine, did not do so in order to avoid division among the bishops.
- A definition will create new barriers against the return of the Orthodox churches and the Protestants.
- Making the pope officially infallible will antagonize secular governments; they will see it as Boniface VIII's *Unam Sanctam* all over again.
- There is no consensus among theologians or bishops as to the precise meaning and limits of infallibility; the concept is vague and should be left so.
- Numerous events in history suggest that popes are not infallible, even in matters of faith and morals; no adequate response to these objections has ever been offered.
- A definition of infallibility will "depress" the position of the bishops in the eyes of the faithful; they will look exclusively to the pope and expect the hierarchy to simply endorse the judgments of the supreme judge.[3]

Dupanloup was never content to provide only principles. He regularly responded to the Ultramontane position of *L'Univers* and *Civiltà Cattòlica*, thereby earning the opprobrium of these journals and their readers. The ongoing debate served to bring the great issue of the council before the general public. Noted Emile Ollivier, a French statesman, "Discussions began in the market-place and everyone took part, even society ladies between the acts at the opera."[4]

If Dupanloup was the most articulate Inopportunist, Joseph Karl Hefele was the most scholarly. The author of a definitive history of ecumenical councils, he had been called in from Tübingen as a consultor during council preparations and was consecrated the bishop of Rottenburg, Germany, just before the opening session. His opposition to the proposed dogma was based on historical instances in which popes like Vigilius and Honorius apparently spoke authoritatively on matters of faith or morals and were later found to be wrong. Without an adequate explanation of these lapses, he did not believe infallibility ought to be submitted to the vote of a council.

Unlike Dupanloup, the sixty-year-old Hefele was not a gripping speaker. Though packed with scholarly insight, his presentations before the full body were more like classroom lectures and left many bishops twisting in their chairs. After the council, few bishops had more difficulty accepting the doctrine in good conscience than Hefele.

By far the fiercest Inopportunist in the debate was Joseph George Strossmayer, fifty-five, the bishop of Bosnia. Though of German ancestry, his family had lived in Croation territory for generations; Strossmayer was particularly interested in efforts to restore unity with the Eastern churches and had labored for years to lessen tensions. He believed a definition of infallibility would undo that work and perhaps establish a permanent barrier to reunion. Strossmayer became something of a storm center at the council. He resented the seemingly restrictive procedures imposed by the pope and his Curia advisers as contrary to the spirit of a free and open assembly; and he was candid about his views.

THE INFALLIBILISTS

The Infallibilist majority was no less equipped with leaders passionate about their cause. Henry Edward Manning, sixty-one, the archbishop of Westminster, England, was recognized as the "chief whip" of that group. Manning had been a highly regarded Anglican churchman before his conversion to Catholicism in 1851. He was ordained a priest ten weeks later and began a meteoric rise in the Catholic Church, attaining the prestigious position of Westminster archbishop four years before the opening of the council. Manning's gaunt, almost emaciated appearance belied his unlimited energy and facile mind. The only convert among the bishops at Vatican I, he was absolutely committed to the rights of the papacy and found it nearly impossible to understand how anyone could oppose infallibility. As priest and archbishop, he had been an effective apologist for Catholic views in Britain, but he never got along well with John Henry Newman, whom he regarded as too theoretical and abstract a thinker. Manning did not get along well either with the Jesuits, whom he once described as "a mysterious permission of God for the chastisement of England."[5]

With scholars like Hefele who argued against infallibility, Manning had little patience. "It is time for historical science and the scientific historians, with all their arrogance to be thrust back into their proper sphere, to be kept within their proper limits," he said. "And this Council will do just that, not with controversies and condemnations but with the words, 'it has pleased the Holy Spirit and us.'"[6]

His tireless behind-the-scenes work to put down dissent and bring the burning issue before the council earned him Pius's gratitude and continual opposition from Dupanloup. Their swords crossed continually in articles and pamphlets published during the council.

Working closely with Manning was Victor August Dechamps, sixty-four, the archbishop of Malines, Belgium, a skilled theologian. He repeatedly addressed the fears of the Inopportunists that

papal infallibility would set up the pope as an omniscient author-
ity who can proclaim definitively on whatever subject he chose.
Replying to Dupanloup's concerns about a "separate infallibility,"
Dechamps wrote:

> If by the term "separate infallibility" people mean to say
> that...the pope does not always need to convoke Councils or
> even to consult bishops...they mean to say what is true, but
> they say it very badly. The Church is a living body, and in
> order that the infallibility of the head could be separate, it would
> be necessary that the head itself could be separated from the
> body....It is not to the private person, but to the public person
> that infallibility is promised, and only for the exercise of his
> supreme charge, the conservation and definition of the Faith.
> There is no infallibility in acts which are not definitions of
> faith, or which do not lay upon the whole Church the obliga-
> tion of believing. All *ex cathedra* definitions have this three-
> fold character: they come from the Pope as Pope; they are ad-
> dressed to the Universal Church; and they are proposed to it...as
> a dogma of faith....Pontifical documents which have not this
> threefold character are not definitions *ex cathedra*.[7]

Unfortunately, Dechamps' calm, relatively conservative interpretation tended to get lost as the council fathers were buffeted by
the near hysterical commentaries of Ignatius von Döllinger on the
one hand and Louis Veuillot on the other.

A more sweeping and argumentative approach was that of
Ignatius von Senestréy, bishop of Regensburg, Bavaria. A relatively
youthful fifty-one at the time of the council, he was always Manning's companion in arms. He proved a capable organizer of the
majority, and his house in Rome became their information center.
Unlike Dechamps, Senestréy believed infallibility must be extended
to papal encyclicals and accompanying documents (like the *Syllabus of Errors*), to the canonization of saints, to virtually any opinion of the pope that touched on religion, and even to papal inter-
jections in the political realm. It was precisely this far-flung net of
inclusion championed by the more vocal Infallibilists that created
panic and near hysteria among Inopportunists; they could not

imagine how the rest of the civilized world, the leaders of the great nations in particular, would ever be able to countenance such extremism.

Pius at first refrained from taking a public position, but few could be unaware of his conviction. When Cardinal Friedrich Schwarzenberg, a staunch Inopportunist, presented his objections in a private audience, the pope reportedly declared "I, Giovanni Maria Mastai, believe in infallibility. As Pope I have nothing to ask from the Council. The Holy Ghost will enlighten it."[8]

JOCKEYING FOR POSITION

Even as the sessions began, a mention of infallibility was not to be found anywhere in the two major documents submitted by the preparatory commission: the schema on Catholic doctrine and the schema on the Church. Yet the subject remained always present just under the surface. Noteworthy events of these first months of the council can perhaps best be presented in chronological fashion.

December 17: The results of votes for membership on the all-important Committee on the Faith were announced. This would be the body overseeing any new declaration of Catholic belief (infallibility, for example) to be presented to the assembly. All twenty-four bishops elected were strong Infallibilists, including Manning and Senestréy. This prompted an immediate protest from the minority; complaints were voiced that the election had been rigged. And indeed, evidence of that emerged after the council. Bishop Plantier, the Vatican I historian approved by Pius, wrote:

> Among the bishops of the minority, there were men of prominence who had deserved well of the Holy See and the Church, men distinguished for learning and eloquence. They had a right to be included on the Commission's....But their writings and speeches...show that in the great question of infallibility they held stubbornly to views that were obsolete....They had announced they would oppose any decree which contradicted

> those views. That was enough. They were inexorably excluded
> from committees which were open to men of less reputation,
> but who represented a purer faith, a sounder theology. Certain
> elements, in short, were mercilessly excluded.[9]

Also on this date articles about events within the council chambers began appearing in the Augsburg *Allgemeine Zeitung*. They were titled "Letters from the Council" and bore the pseudonym "Quirinus." In fact, as everyone assumed, they were compiled and put in final form by Döllinger. The amazing accuracy of his information about council regulations, speeches, and rumors made it clear there was a leak among the gathered hierarchy. Greatly offended at this internal leak, the pope released Manning and several others from their vow of secrecy in order to investigate. Suspicion centered on Cardinal Gustav Hoenhole, a brother of the Bavarian foreign minister, but he flatly denied the charge. The source was never identified, but it is well known that Lord John Acton was in contact with the leak and largely responsible for relaying information to Döllinger.

December 28: Formal debate began on the lengthy schema of doctrine, which contained condemnations of modern heresies and an explanation of divine revelation. Critics argued that it was too negative and too abstract. "Words, words, words," said one bishop, "nothing but words." Said another: "This schema should not be redone, it should be buried." Archbishop Peter Kenrick of St. Louis, the first American to address the council, said the document was simply too long and urged that it be returned to the commission for a total revision. Another American representative, Augustin Verot, the French-born bishop of Savannah, Georgia, said the council would do well to ignore "the obscure errors of German idealists" and wrestle with "real" heresies. In his diocese, he noted, some still hold that black people do not have souls. He urged the bishops to anathematize that position but got no response. Verot was to gain considerable notoriety as the enfant terrible of the council for his frequent and imaginative interventions.

A few days later, as discussion continued, Bishop Strossmayer objected to the introductory words of the schema: "Pius, bishop, servant of the servants of God, with the approval of the council...." In effect, said Strossmayer, the pope appears to be making himself the legislator of the assembly, with the bishops in a subordinate position. As he explained his reasoning, several bishops began calling for him to "come down!" He tried to continue but finally stepped from the podium when the council president said that wording was contained in a papal brief and subject to alteration under no circumstances. Soon after, the entire schema was sent back to the drawing board.

January 1: With the council in recess, the pope met with diplomats and said, "A great noise was made about the *Syllabus*, but the ecclesiastical world has now acquiesced in its principles. It will be just the same with the decrees of the Council."[10]

January 2: Manning, Senestréy, and Dechamps began gathering signatures from council members supporting the addition of infallibility to the schema on the Church: "The undersigned Fathers humbly and earnestly beg the Holy Ecumenical Council to decree clearly and in words that cannot be mistaken, that the authority of the Roman Pontiff is supreme and therefore immune from error, when in matters of faith and morals he lays down...what is to be believed and held."[11] It was later revealed that the pope hoped the petition could amass four hundred signatures. Thanks to the organizational skills of Manning and Senestréy, it did have that many by the end of the month. Caught by surprise, the poorly organized Inopportunists drew up a series of manifestos seeking to table the doctrine. In this effort, they got 140 signatures, mostly from French, German, American, and English bishops.

January 21: Dupanloup spoke to the council about the rights of bishops, urging that they not be relegated "by dogma or discipline" to the level of legates answerable to an all-powerful monarch. He did not mention infallibility explicitly, but his meaning was obvious. Commenting on the speech, Bishop Ullathorne noted in one of his letters that Dupanloup "was the only man to whom many bishops...paid the compliment of crowding around down in the middle, and there standing as close as they could to hear him more perfectly....It was much observed that his recent adversary in polemical warfare, Archbishop Manning, stood in front of all the listeners who had left their places for the purpose of hearing better."

On this day, an especially scathing attack on infallibility, outlining the historical obstacles in detail, was published in the *Allgemeine Zeitung*. Such was Döllinger's reputation, that it created an uproar as copies circulated among the bishops. The minority admired Döllinger's scholarship and his skill in cutting to the bone, but most were reluctant to identify with his radical rhetoric.

Manning was irate that so much detailed information about the proceedings was in the hands of the enemy. Senestréy forbade theology students from his diocese to attend any of Döllinger's lectures in Munich. And the pope gave *Civiltà Cattòlica* permission to respond to the attack.

Several days later, during a discussion of Church discipline, Bishop Verot returned to the podium with a plea that clerics be forbidden to hunt with guns. "It is a disgraceful spectacle," he said, "to see a man of God going about the roads and fields shooting birds and beasts." Verot also called for a wholesale reform of the breviary, which, he confessed, he could never read without major distraction. His views provoked momentary release from the gathering tension in the assembly, but no action.

DOGMAS "MANUFACTURED IN ROME"

January 28: John Henry Newman, who chose not to attend the council as a consultor, wrote a letter to his bishop, Ullathorne of Birmingham, in which for the first time he shared his views on the mounting campaign for infallibility. Intended as a private reflection, the letter somehow was leaked to the press, creating yet another uproar. Wrote Newman:

Is this the proper work of an oecumenical Council? As to my-self personally, please God, I do not expect any trial at all; but I cannot help suffering with the various souls which are suffer-ing, and I look with anxiety at the prospect of having to de-fend decisions which may not be difficult to my private judg-ment, but may be most difficult to maintain logically in face of historical facts. What have we done to be treated as the faithful never were treated before? When has a definition of a doctrine *de Fide* been a luxury of devotion and not a stern prac-tical necessity? Why should an aggressive, insolent faction be allowed to "make the heart of the just to mourn"...? Why can't we be let alone, when we have pursued peace and thought no evil?[12]

Because of Newman's reputation, the letter received international attention and gave the Inopportunists a momentary lift in morale. Coming as it did from his more famous countryman and fellow convert, Manning found the assessment an especially bitter pill to swallow.

February 18: Archbishop George Darboy of Paris authored a pow-erful article in the French publication, *Monteur Universal*, in which he charged that bishops like himself found at Rome "a Council already constituted by theologians and canonists who had been selected on exclusive principles and had framed resolutions which the bishops were expected to sanction."[13] He claimed the Inoppor-tunists, though representing less than a quarter of the episcopacy were for the most part from the populous dioceses and therefore represented about half of the Catholic world. Essentially, charged Darboy, the council was not a free, open forum.

February 22: Meanwhile, in order to speed up deliberations, the pope revealed a new order of procedure. Anyone objecting to a proposal must submit his views in writing along with proposed amendments for each objection. More important, debate on any issue might be closed at any time if ten or more members of the council moved for closure and the majority agreed. The order contradicted the traditional conciliar practice of keeping a discus-sion open until there was moral unanimity that it be closed. This meant, in effect, that the vocal minority could be silenced at any time.

More than one hundred bishops signed a letter of protest, and many came close to leaving at that point. They stayed, however, partly because of rumors that the governments of France and Germany were so seriously disturbed about the political consequences of an absolutely infallible papacy that they might move diplomatically or even militarily to halt the proceedings. Some members of the minority were reportedly trying to promote such an intervention. Their efforts, however, did not reflect well on their cause because this was little more than a naked appeal to political Gallicanism in more modern dress.

March 7: The assembly was informed that the upcoming schema on the Church would be amended to contain the draft of a definition of papal infallibility "in answer to the petition of a large number of fathers." They were provided with a draft copy for consideration. Moreover, they were told, Pius IX hoped the dogma could be officially proclaimed on March 19, the feast of Saint Joseph, just twelve days away. If an attempt to steamroll the matter through so quickly were made, Dupanloup informed the council president, he and most of the French hierarchy were determined to depart the council and reveal "how dogmas are manufactured in Rome." Kenrick of St. Louis said he and three other American bishops were similarly prepared to leave the assembly and inform the public what was occurring. The council leaders quickly backed off the timetable, allowing a "sufficient interval" for discussion and debate.[14]

Also on this day a letter that Charles Montalambert, the veteran liberal, had written to Döllinger was published in France. In it he blamed reports of government intervention on the pope. "I once said Gallicanism is dead," he wrote, "but it has risen again. It is due to the prodigal encouragement of extreme doctrines in the pontificate of Pius IX, doctrines which insult both same common sense and the honor of the human race." Montalambert died six days after publication of the letter. A memorial service in his honor was scheduled in Rome but was forbidden at the last moment.

Pius IX told a papal audience that Montalambert had one great enemy—pride. "He was a liberal Catholic," he said. "That is, he was a half-Catholic."[15]

March 9: Darboy of Paris, in a letter to the French premier, made a bald-face appeal for governmental intervention: "It is a true revolution to place the absolute government of consciences in Italian hands, under the name of personal, absolute and separate infallibility....Can the government of France...take upon itself...the responsibility for a Council which...will let loose religious storms for years to come? All legitimate means should be used to prorogue [terminate] the Council. Send an extraordinary ambassador to explain reasons and induce other governments to do the same."[16] His plea might have borne fruit, but the French foreign minister resigned soon after and was replaced by a man more sympathetic to the majority members of the council. The French defense of the Vatican remained intact. Other European governments expressed concern about the implications of the discussions in Rome—Austria, England, and Spain in particular—but refrained from action.

"NOTHING COULD BE MORE DANGEROUS"

March 18: The schema on Church doctrine that had been rejected three months before it was submitted to the council in new form—which proved even more objectionable to some than the original. Protestants were characterized in the Introduction as the root of all modern evils, including rationalism, pantheism, neutralism, and atheism. Equally disconcerting was the mode of address: "We [the Pope] by our apostolic authority have summoned this ecumenical Council in order, from our *Cathedra,* to prescribe and condemn these errors."[17] Distraught at what they perceived as another expression of unilateral papal authority, the minority refused to participate in the debate, then decided they could not allow the document to go unchallenged.

March 22: Tensions between the antagonists burst forth at last in full view when Bishop Strossmayer labeled the attack on Protestants unfair and untrue. The outspoken bishop of Bosnia expressed his belief that "there are among Protestants many grave men who are a great help to Catholics...who love our Lord Jesus Christ...."

Some in the assembly began to murmur in protest. The council president cautioned Strossmayer to refrain from words "that might cause scandal to some fathers." He continued anyway, defending the positive contributions of Protestants, while the murmers grew louder.

The president, Cardinal Annibale Capalti, interrupted, imploring the bishop to stick to the schema. "There is no mention in it of Protestants," said Annibale Capalti, "only of the sects condemned at Trent. Therefore it seems to me there is no offense given to Protestants. And so I beseech you to desist from such speech."

"I finish," said Strossmayer, "but I know...." He was again reproved. Cries from the floor of "Fie!" "Heretic!" and "Sit down!" made it difficult to hear for some moments.

When the noise subsided, Strossmayer declared what was really on the mind of the minority: "I attribute this outburst to the deplorable conditions of the Council"—more shouts and boos—"and I make another observation— short, very short— but which I hold touches the essence of things and so moves my conscience....In the recent regulation it is laid down that questions are to be settled by a majority of votes. Against this some bishops have put in a statement asking if the ancient rule of moral unanimity...." A thunderous interruption occurred here. The president was ringing his bell, struggling to regain control, while some of the bishops were rising from their seats, shaking their fists, and yelling.

Strossmayer. "I protest against every interruption!"

Bishops: "We protest against you!"

Strossmayer: "I respect the right of the Presidents. If that former..."

More cries from the assembly: "He is Lucifer!" "Let him be cast out!" "Anathema, Anathema!" Some irate fathers had left their places and were approaching the podium in menacing fashion—at which point Strossmayer finally did step down.[18]

Council historian Cuthbert Butler described this emotion-laden scene as "unfortunate" and "scandalous" and lays much of the blame on Strossmayer, since the proper topic was not the necessity of moral unanimity in decisions to close off discussion. What it may more clearly reveal is the sheer frustration of the minority, which felt helpless to implement any of their ideas and the impatience of the majority at continued resistance to the pope and his plan. In any event, the bishops returned the next day in a more sober state of mind. The offensive comments about Protestants were removed, and the statement about papal authority was softened. A month later, the full schema on doctrine, titled *Dei Filius*, was approved by a 667-0 vote. Strossmayer was the only bishop who did not attend that session.

April 23: Dupanloup became aware of a move by the Infallibilists to suspend the order of procedure so infallibility would be discussed and voted on ahead of everything else in the schema on the Church. He sent a letter to the pope that began:

> Most Holy Father: My name is not pleasing to you. I know it and it is my sorrow. But for all that I feel authorized and obliged...to open my ear to you at this moment. The report is confirmed that many are soliciting your Holiness to suspend suddenly our important works and invert the order of the discussions in order to bring before the Council on the spot, abruptly, before its time and out of place, the question of infallibility. Allow me to say...nothing could be more dangerous.

Dupanloup then urged the pope to call together in his presence representative bishops of the different countries and urge them to speak freely. "It is the only way you can get to know the realities, he said."

Pius IX quickly replied:

> Venerable Brother: Your name is no less pleasing to us now than in the past, nor do we love you less or esteem you less

than formerly the gifts God has bestowed upon you. But our paternal affection for you compels us, when you are stiffly dissenting from most of your venerable brothers...to warn you not to be wise in your own eyes or to rely on your own prudence; for you know that all errors and heresies have arisen from the fact that their authors thought they were wiser than others and would not acquiesce in the common opinion of the Church....[19]

April 29: At a general congregation the president announced that the body of the schema on the Church would be set aside for a time so the Fathers could discuss and vote on the matter of papal primacy and infallibility immediately. The Committee on the Faith immediately set to work. Sixty minority bishops sent Pius a letter objecting to this procedure. By placing infallibility before other matters on the schema, they said, it appeared the pope was promoting a separate and personal infallibility for himself—distinct from the council and from the bishops. They feared what this might mean in practice. They were, as always, upset about the apparent manipulations of the proceedings. "This is not a petition," they said, "but a remonstrance against the mode of transacting business which is injurious both for the Church and the apostolic see."[20]

CHAPTER VIII

THE VIGOROUS
DEBATE

Is power arbitrary because it is supreme? Are civil govern-
ments arbitrary because supreme?....Let all this confusion of
ideas go!

BISHOP CHARLES FRAPPEL

On May 13, 1870, the pope's seventy-eighth birthday, discussion and debate commenced on what Bishop Ullathorne labeled "the great question": the schema concerning papal primacy
and infallibility. A preliminary draft had been given to the bishops
in March, and it had elicited 147 written observations and suggestions for change. These had been wrestled with for over two months
by the twenty-four member Committee on the Faith, consisting
entirely of infallibility supporters. Finally, a new draft was now in
the hands of the bishops. This version of the schema contained
four chapters—three relating to primacy, the fourth to infallibility.
The council rules called for debate first on the schema as a whole,
followed by debates on the particular chapters.

The sessions got off to a somewhat bewildering start when French
bishop Louis Pie presented, by way of clarification, a bizarre anal-
ogy. Saint Peter, he noted, had been crucified upside down, so that

his head had to bear the weight of his whole body; in the same way, it is the pope, Peter's successor, who bears the weight of the Mystical Body, the Church; as a result, infallibility belongs principally in the head, only secondarily to the body. The comparison left even some Ultramontane bishops muttering and shaking their own heads.

However, there was rapt attention when Archbishop Manning made his sole public speech at the council. He left no doubt as to his sentiments: "The Pope's infallibility *is* Catholic doctrine of divine faith, and all are already obliged to hold it; to question it is at least material heresy, for it is not an open theological opinion, but a doctrine contained in the divine revelation. In no way is there any doubt as to the Catholic doctrine of the Pope's infallibility. Does any one of us present here doubt the doctrine? I have not heard any such word...."

As far as England is concerned, he said, papal infallibility would be a "powerful attraction" for non-Catholics. The progress of Catholicism in England, he noted, should be measured, not so much by the number of converts, as by the "progressive penetration of the whole English people by Catholic ideas and Catholic truth." Nothing, he said, is so injurious to this penetration of Catholicism as the doubts and controversies among Catholics concerning infallibility. "The shelving of this question at Trent has had disastrous results; worse will follow should the Vatican Council, after facing it, fail to speak with a decisive voice."[1]

Manning regarded this talk, which lasted just short of two hours, as a major triumph of his life, and even anti-Infallibilists like Kenrick of St. Louis, congratulated him for his "lucid organization of ideas," his "delightful choice of words," and his "singular eloquence."

In contrast to many speakers before and after him, Manning concentrated on the pastoral effects of the doctrine rather than on history or theology. His presentation was therefore viewed as an apt expression of his much-repeated motto, "Dogma has conquered history."

OBJECTIONS FROM HISTORY

History was the realm of Karl Hefele. He presented a panoply of instances over the centuries in which the Church did not appear to regard a reigning pontiff as infallible or when a pope clearly erred on a doctrinal matter. He gave extended attention to the Council of Chalcedon, held in 451, when the Monophysite heresy was battling for recognition as official Church teaching. Prior to that council, Pope Leo I had written a long letter, known as "the Tome," to the Patriarch Flavian, stating in no uncertain terms that Christ had two natures, not one, as the Monophysites insisted. If ever there was an *ex cathedra*, dogmatic statement, said Hefele, the Tome was it. Nevertheless, when the council met, the pope insisted that all the bishops read the letter and declare under oath whether or not the doctrine in it conformed to dogmas approved at earlier councils. "They were called on to judge its orthodoxy," said Hefele, "and the Fathers of the council subjected the Letter to an examination....It was not said to the Bishops, 'Here is a dogmatic letter of the Pope; hear it and submit'; but rather, 'Hear it and judge!' Some of the bishops thought it suspect of heresy in three places. But no one said they were rash for doubting. No one questioned their right to doubt."[2]

After the reading, the bishops at Chalcedon had unanimously agreed with Pope Leo, shouting, "This is the faith of the apostles and fathers—Peter has spoken through Leo!" That final, great acclamation was not the significant point, noted Hefele; rather, it was the pope's submission to the decision of the bishops. If Leo considered himself infallible, why did he act that way?

Hefele then recounted in detail the strange case of Pope Honorius I in the seventh century. By then, almost two hundred years after Chalcedon, several variations of the Monophysite heresy were still circulating in the Eastern Church. In an attempt to find a compromise between Monophysitism (one nature in Christ) and the Orthodox doctrine of the early general councils (two natures), the patriarch Sergius came up with the idea that Christ did, indeed, have two natures but only one "will." The doctrine was called Monothelitism. Sergius asked Pope Honorius for a judgment, and the pope, who regarded all the disputants on this matter as "croaking frogs," wrote a letter agreeing with the one-will theory. Some forty years later, the Third Council of Constantinople flatly condemned Monothelitism and declared Honorius (who was deceased by then) a heretic. It was Hefele's contention that Honorius was exercising his full teaching authority on a matter of faith in his letter to Sergius, yet both an ecumenical council and Catholic tradition have since agreed he was wrong. Where is papal infallibility here? he asked.

And where is it to be found, he asked, in the case of Pope Vigilius, who was excommunicated by the Second Council of Constantinople and who later appeared to approve certain Monophysite teachings? How explain the decree of the Council of Constance, which said popes are always subject to the decisions of ecumenical councils? How regard the ruling of the Council of Florence, which contradicted the decision of Constance? And how was one to handle *Unam Sanctam*, the solemn bull of Boniface VIII, which claimed papal supremacy in both spiritual and temporal matters over all peoples and nations and declared salvation cannot be found outside membership in the Catholic Church?

Ever the scholar, Hefele did not say these events positively rule out the concept of infallibility, only that he did not think a satisfying reconciliation of history and dogma was possible at this time. "I yield to no one in reverence for the apostolic see and the Holy Father," he said, "but I did not think it lawful to proceed to a declaration of infallibility."

In the following days, several bishops attempted to rebut Hefele. His interpretation of Chalcedon was badly skewed, said one, who argued that Pope Leo, far from seeking the council's approval, had in fact forbidden the bishops to alter in any way the wording of his Tome.

Unfortunately, few rebuttals of this kind occurred during general sessions of the council. Instead, a bishop would read his speech, perhaps raise several interesting issues, and sit down. The next bishop or even the next ten bishops would deliver talks and never touch on the points raised, so that very few back-and-forth exchanges of opinion enlivened the proceedings. The real exchanges and debates occurred in the pamphlets and papers written by men like Manning and Dupanloup, circulating daily among the council fathers.

By now even Pius IX had discarded any mantle of neutrality and was wading into the midst of the battle. Virtually every commentator on Vatican I speaks of his vigorous, almost daily, campaign to gain support both inside and outside the council hall. Pius dispatched a veritable flotilla of personal letters expressing gratitude to those approving his quest.

To a chapter of clergy in Avignon, he wrote: "Your letter has given us clear proof of your veneration and love of this Holy See. For from it we know how desirous you are that the irreformable judgment of the Roman Pontiff...may be decreed at the council...."

To a priest who had published a contradiction of Dupanloup's position: "The Holy Father...has much enjoyed the manner in which...you...refute the vain, hostile sophisms, which are the one and only cause of the trouble that has arisen in consciences...."

To Abbot Prosper Guéranger for his refutation of Inopportunists' arguments: "You have done a great service to the Church in...showing up their hatred, violence and artifices...with such solidity...that in a word you have taken all prestige of wisdom from those who have wrapped up their opinions in words of ignorance...."

To H. G. Ward, the English proponent of extreme infalliblism: "Go on fighting the battle of the Lord."[3]

THE CLOSURE OF DEBATE

At this juncture, the bishops were not supposed to discuss specific passages of the draft document, but it was becoming clear that minority fears centered mostly on the prospect of a totalitarian definition of infallibility, an infallibility set apart from the body of the Church—a "decapitated" infallibility, as one bishop put it. More and more often in council speeches and in discussions outside the sessions, the Inopportunists expressed resistance to a "personal, separate, and absolute" understanding of infallibility. They did not see how there could be checks and balances in such an interpretation, and they feared its effects inside and outside the Church.

Meanwhile, the majority concentrated almost exclusively on the benefits of a strong, reliable, central source of stability in a world beset with relativistic ideas and lowered moral values. Following Manning's lead, many predicted a great gravitation of non-Catholics to the Church in the wake of an authoritative definition: If history presented obstacles to the dogma, then historians would have to work them out; the present, perilous situation is more important than past confusion and misunderstanding.

Several bishops suggested that now might be the time for the two sides to sit down and try to create a formula tolerable to both camps. The proposal was ruled out of order by the president, Cardinal Capalti, since the Committee on the Faith had exclusive authorization to draw up and present drafts on this matter to the council. The fact that the Inopportunist minority had no representation on that body was regrettable since it seemed to effectively rule out any possibility of compromise.

The dilemma was expressed by Paris archbishop Darboy, who viewed the inevitable Infallibilist victory with grave misgiving:

> [Infallibility] was not named in the bull of convocation or in the official documents of the Council but was introduced by a demagogic agitation outside, so that the hands of the bishops have been unduly forced. Say what they may, the infallibility proposed is personal, absolute, independent, separate. The terms of the definitions are vague and uncertain. The definition will not cure the ills of society and of the world.[4]

The irrepressible Verot provided a momentary diversion during his long speech opposing the council's momentum. Infallibility is almost impossible to define, he said. "It is true that the Irish believe in the Pope's infallibility," he said, "but they also believe in the priests' infallibility—and not only do they believe it, but they beat with sticks any who deny it!" He noted that Cardinal Paul Cullen of Dublin had given a ringing endorsement of papal infallibility, claiming the Irish had always believed in the doctrine. "But," he asked, "will the Cardinal say...the Irish believed Pope Hadrian IV was infallible when he handed over Ireland to the King of England [in the twelfth century]?"[5]

On June 3, after three weeks of talks, Bishop Joseph Fessler, council secretary, announced that he had received a petition from 150 of the fathers stating that further discussion of the schema as a whole would be a waste of time and result only in useless repetition. Invoking the regulation imposed on the council in February, they asked for a vote from the full body on closing debate at this time and moving on to particulars of the schema. This marked the only time during the council when the controversial closure rule was employed, and it was seen by many in the minority, especially those who hadn't yet had a chance to speak, as a violation of their rights. The majority voted for closure, and some eighty minority bishops filed a protest the next day, claiming the vote prevented many speakers from stating their case: "From the very nature of Councils it follows that the faculty of adding to one's vote the reasons on which it is based, is not the privilege of some but the common right of all....The discussion cannot be closed by the vote of a majority without violating the right of those who were going to express their opinion."[6] Especially upset was Archbishop Peter Kenrick of St. Louis, who had prepared a speech for general discussion and was now prevented from delivering it. He had the talk published in Naples, and it proved a withering retort to the Manning camp.[7]

The majority bishops pointed out in response that sixty-five speeches had already been given (thirty-nine favoring infallibility, twenty-six against) and that most of the Inopportunist leaders had spoken to the full assembly, including Hefele, Darboy and Strossmayer. Besides, summer was approaching, the aula was becoming warmer and more uncomfortable by the day, and many were getting itchy to return home.

THE PAPAL PRIMACY

Discussion of the first three chapters of the schema, all concerning papal primacy, began on June 9 and occupied only four days. There was not a great deal to argue about here because an aggregation of Roman Catholic bishops would not be expected to deny that the pope is the head of the Roman Catholic Church. Nevertheless, a dispute did arise. The first chapter presented key Scripture quotes concerning Saint Peter's prerogatives. "To secure in his Church perpetual unity in faith and in communion, Christ established in Blessed Peter a perpetual principle and visible foundation of this twofold unity, as He immediately and directly promised and conferred on him a primacy of jurisdiction over the universal Church."[8]

The second extended this notion of jurisdiction to the popes through the ages: "It is necessary that what Christ instituted in Peter should also continually endure in the Church. Up to the present time and always he lives and presides in his successors, the bishops of the Roman See."[9]

The third claimed "immediate and ordinary" jurisdiction for the pope "over the pastors and faithful of every rite and every rank...by the duty of hierarchical subordination and of true obedience." In an effort to entomb theological Gallicanism once and for all, this chapter cited the Council of Florence's rejection of conciliar ideas and said the pope's judgment "can be revised by no one and judged by no one; therefore, those depart from the way of truth who affirm that it is lawful to appeal from his judgments to an Ecumenical Council as to an authority superior to his."[10]

A major criticism of these decrees was the absence of any reference to the special place of bishops in the Church, and it came from both the Infallibilist and Inopportunist sides. The term "immediate and ordinary" jurisdiction rankled in particular, because it suggested to some that the pope all by himself runs the Church, leaving bishops as mere vicars, legates, or branch managers. Several bishops suggested the term should be changed to "extraordinary" jurisdiction or "super-ordinary" jurisdiction; this would imply that papal involvement in a local situation would be extremely unusual.

Others called for an explicit mention in the text that "ordinary" simply means the pope's authority is his by right and not delegated from someone above him. They also sought a notation that bishops, too, have "immediate, ordinary" jurisdiction in their own dioceses and do not serve only at the pleasure of the pope.

Said Dupanloup, "That the Pontiff has ordinary and immediate power...is true and not open to doubt, in the sense that this power is his own and not delegated, and certainly may be exercised of itself and directly. But it should not be brought into play usually, so as not to interfere with the bishop's immediate and ordinary jurisdiction."[11]

Verot then came forward to propose wording that he believed might have a more universal appeal: "If anyone says that the authority of the Pope in the Church is so full that he may dispose of everything by his mere whim, let him be anathema!" His proposal was not well received by the president, who accused him of "buffoonery" and making "absurd statements."

No changes were authorized by the council on the original wording, and the text, lacking qualification or explanation, bears some responsibility for the exaggerated concept of papal power that developed after Vatican I. The issue would be remedied somewhat at Vatican II, which spoke specifically of the rights of bishops.

The third chapter also received sharp criticism from Eastern rite bishops who thought the language of papal authority was needlessly offensive to Orthodox congregations and, therefore, a further bar to unity. The Rumanian rite archbishop of Transylvania, Vansca, fairly pleaded for change in the text: "For the sake of Reunion, I am compelled to declare solemnly and with the utmost urgency to beg of you, Rt. Rev. Fathers, that the things contained in the second and third chapters be cut wholly, or at least that another formula be used....I beg humbly....I wish to hurt no one,

God forbid, but I pray that you grant me this, for otherwise I could not set foot in my diocese again."

French bishop Charles Frappel argued there was no need to modify the text. "Ordinary" and "immediate" are not new terms, he said. "Every legislator is bound to observe the laws he has made or confirmed unless and until they are lawfully abrogated, this by natural and divine law," he said. "This distinction excludes the fantastic despotism or absolutism that we have heard spoken of....Who has ever said that the Roman Pontiff should govern the Church according to his sweet will, by his nod, by arbitrary power, by fancy—that is, without the laws and canons. We all exclude mere arbitrary power, but we all assert full and perfect power. Is power arbitrary because it is supreme? Are civil governments arbitrary because supreme?....Let all this confusion of ideas go! Let the doctrine of the schema be accepted in its true proper, genuine sense." Frappel received sustained applause, and his recommendation was followed. Discussion of the primacy concluded on June 13.

AN APPARENT CONCESSION

Given the makeup of the Committee on Faith, the Inopportunist minority expected the wording of the fourth chapter, the one specifically on infallibility, to be severely Ultramontane. Some were therefore surprised and others confused at the draft that was placed in their hands. In its preliminary form, issued in March, the fourth chapter said in part, "The Roman pontiff cannot err when, exercising the office of supreme teacher of all Christians, he defines with authority what in matters of faith and morals must be held by the universal Church. And this prerogative of inherence or infallibility...reaches to the same object as the infallibility of the Church extends to."

Between March and May the committee had sifted through the bishops' comments and substantially altered the text. In the new form, which the bishops would now debate, the chapter declared in part, "The Roman Pontiff, by the power of divine assistance promised to him, cannot err when...he defines...what in matters of faith and morals must be held by the universal Church as of faith, or is to be rejected as contrary to faith...."[12]

At first glance, the wording appears clumsy and redundant, with the word "faith" appearing twice in the same sentence. But the repetition was deliberate, and it was fraught with meaning. Committee members Manning and Senestréy, it appears, preferred to keep the sense of the original draft, since it gave wide latitude to objects of papal infallibility. "Matters of faith and morals" could mean almost anything "related" to faith—papal censures, for example, the approval of religious orders, the canonization of saints, the condemnation of books, the interpretation of certain historical facts that have a bearing on Church teachings. All this was the province of the Church, and therefore the province of its infallible head.

However, others on the committee, notably Dechamps and Cardinal Luigi Bilio, the chairman, opposed so broad an interpretation. They had heard the debates of the past six months and they believed insistence on an absolutist definition would provoke a divided vote, perhaps even a schism in the Church. Dechamps believed more moderate members of the minority would surely yield for the sake of the Church if a more restrictive formula was presented.

Thus was created the seemingly awkward text that said the pope cannot err in matters of faith and morals when he presents these matters "as of faith" or rejects them "as contrary to faith." With this wording, one could understand the pope's infallibility as extending only to objects of faith strictly speaking—that is, only to what can be found in Scripture and tradition and not to all "matters" of faith. Historian Butler said Manning fought any such limitation: "Manning's whole mentality was different: As always, his own view was simply *right*, and he wanted it defined in the most absolute way, opponents to be crushed. And so he proposed various formulae stretching the doctrine to extreme limits, and to be enforced by stringent canons under anathema."[13] Senestréy was of the same mind.

Yet the more moderate wording prevailed on the second draft. It appeared as if the Committee on the Faith, at least for the moment, had acquiesced to Bishop Verot's proposal: the pope cannot just pronounce definitively on anything he chooses.

CHAPTER IX

DECISION AND DEFINITION

As we believe the pope is by divine assistance infallible, we thereby believe also that the assent of the Church can never be lacking.

BISHOP VINCENT GASSER

There was more than a little interest in the proposed formula of definition when discussion began in a general congregation of the bishops on June 15. More than 120 wished to speak, offering amendments and suggestions. By now the minority had pretty well come to terms with the fact that some kind of papal infallibility was inevitable, and their efforts henceforth were in trying to avert, insofar as possible, a definition conferring the feared "personal, separate and absolute" power on the pontiff.

The minority got off to a flying start when Cardinal Joseph Arthur Rauscher of Vienna urged that the definition should incorporate the fifteenth-century formula attributed to Saint Antoninus: "The successor of Saint Peter, using the counsel and seeking the help of the universal Church, cannot err." If the word "help" seemed too restrictive, said Rauscher, "testimony" might be more acceptable— or at least some expression that unambiguously requires the involvement of the larger church in a papal declaration that is considered infallible.[1] Several other minority members followed up with similar proposals based on Saint Antoninus.

Then, on June 18, came another prelate to the cause, Cardinal Philip Maria Guidi, the archbishop of Bologna. He was a Dominican and a Thomistic theologian of some repute, whose views on conciliar issues remained largely unknown. His long talk represented an effort to bring together the factions by stressing the strong points of both camps.

As to the problem of "personal" infallibility, said Guidi, it should be recognized that it is not the pope who is infallible, strictly speaking, but the truth about which he is speaking. In Guidi's view, the assistance given to the pope by the Holy Spirit under certain conditions guarantees that what he says is free from error; that is what infallibility is all about. It does not make the pope permanently or personally infallible, as if he were some omniscient, supernatural being. Guidi urged an alteration of the title on the chapter under discussion from "The Infallibility of the Roman Pontiff" to "The Infallibility of the Pope's Dogmatic Definitions."

Concerns about "separate and absolute" infallibility are unfounded, he said, because a pope simply cannot use the gift rashly; rather, he is obligated to use "ordinary human diligence in arriving at a right judgment," and that normally means studying the tradition of the Church and consulting "with a greater or lesser number of bishops" since they are the witnesses of the faith of the Catholic people. That being the case, argued Guidi, the formula approved by the council should conclude, "If anyone says that the Roman pontiff, when he issues dogmatic decrees…acts by his mere will and by himself, independently of the Church, that is separately, and not by the counsel of the bishops manifesting the tradition of the Church, let him be anathema."

Murmurs of disapproval had been growing during much of the talk, but this last proposal revealed the deep cleavage between the factions. Some rose up shouting, "No, no!" Others cried, "Good!" or "Excellent!" and crowded around the cardinal afterward, kissing or shaking his hand and offering congratulatory words. Strossmayer embraced him.

Then came an extremely important moment in the history of Vatican I, though few realized it at the time. Cardinal Cullen of Dublin, a member of the Committee on the Faith, came forward to present another formula of definition. It was similar to the one the council fathers were now discussing, but that one left far more ambiguous (and far more open) the matters about which the pope could speak infallibly. Cullen began with a kind of preface that revealed the rationale behind the new wording: "Christ did not say to Peter 'Thou art the rock,' provided you consult bishops or theologians; 'I give you the keys of the kingdom of heaven,' but on condition you hear others before you use them....He does not receive his authority from the Church, but from Christ."

Cardinal Cullen then read the suggested formula: "The Roman Pontiff, when he speaks *ex cathedra*, that is, when in discharge of the office of pastor and doctor of all Christians...he defines a doctrine regarding faith or morals that must be held by the universal Church, by the divine assistance promised...is possessed of that infallibility with which the divine Redeemer willed that his Church should be endowed for defining doctrine regarding faith and morals." As events turned out, this is almost the exact wording that the council would finally adopt.

The key words here are "must be held" (*tendenda* in Latin). If the formula had read "must be believed" (*credenda*), it would have been clear that infallibility was extended only to matters of belief—matters of faith, strictly speaking—that is, only to what is found in Scripture and tradition. The new variation left entirely unclear the extent of this infallibility "with which the Divine Redeemer wished his Church to be endowed." Manning and Senestréy obviously wanted it extended to papal encyclicals and a whole body of Church-related directives and statements that "must be held." Others wished it extended only to the deposit of faith, and the formula the council had been discussing did just that with its reference to those things that must be held "as of faith."

This new proposal was, in fact, the result of further discussions within the Committee on the Faith and represented a kind of concession to the Manning-Senestréy camp, which regarded the currently debated formula as "not reformed but deformed." Under pressure, the committee was now leaning heavily toward advocating this Cullen formula. But they decided to wait until after the debate on the prior version was completed. The council fathers were not informed of the committee's view, however, and so spent three weeks suggesting variations on a formula of papal infallibility that would quietly be discarded in the end.

NO COMPROMISE POSSIBLE

Meanwhile, Cardinal Guidi was summoned by the pope on the very day he spoke and scolded severely for his speech on the council floor. Guidi said he only wished to make clear that the statement of definition mention the bishops as witnesses to Church tradition. To which the pope reportedly lashed back, "Tradition? There is only one. I am tradition!"[2]

This remark immediately gained a wide circulation. Guidi supposedly related details of his meeting and conversation to others, who spread it. The pope's comment was viewed by opponents of infallibility as an indication that Pius IX was in a state of near frenzy and becoming unbalanced in his zeal for the dogma. Guidi himself never affirmed publicly that the quote was accurate, but never denied it, either, when pressed for comment.

Adding to the intrigue were rumors that this relatively unknown Cardinal Guidi was, in fact, the illegitimate son of the pope! The claim was made in several dispatches sent by a Polish count to the Italian foreign minister. Aside from a slight facial resemblance and some confusion about Guidi's place of origin, nothing was ever unearthed to support the claim or to link the pope with the cardinal. Yet the image of a father-son confrontation over ultimate authority has served to intrigue commentators on the council ever since.[3]

In the next few days, several informal meetings between majority and minority representatives took place. Dechamps, a member of the Committee on the Faith, and Darboy, the often explosive critic of infallibility, explored possible compromises based on Guidi's outline. Both felt that here was a basis for achieving common ground.

But as the debate proceeded, many speakers attacked Guidi, calling his idea a resuscitation of theological Gallicanism. It's worse, said one bishop, because Gallicanism requires the consent of the bishops after a papal declaration in order to stamp it as infallible, while Guidi seems to require the consent beforehand.

By the last week of June, the heat was taking its toll; the debate, as well as the participants themselves, was coming unraveled. A continuous battery of alternate formulas was proposed by the minority, all pressing to involve the larger Church in infallible definitions. Among them: The pope is infallible in matters of faith and morals—"after he has learned in his wisdom the faith of his brethren in the episcopate" or "having used the counsel and assistance of the Church" or "having ascertained the views of the cardinals of the Roman Catholic Church" or "when rooted and fixed in the ecclesiastical tradition."[4]

There were in addition long, sometimes rambling speeches analyzing the views of Polycarp, Iranaeus, Robert Bellarmine, and Augustine, most claiming these giants of the faith were committed to infallibility. One bishop became so overwrought with emotion that he accidentally spit out his false tooth; the proceedings came to a halt while he searched for it and reinserted it in place. The council presidents were repeatedly ringing their bell and pleading for brevity. A bishop who joined in this appeal to his colleagues spoke so long that the president recommended he follow his own advice. On the rare occasion when a scheduled speaker announced he would yield or forgo his time, great numbers shouted "Good!" or "Bravo!"

Eventually, leaders from both sides urged an end to the discussion. Among those who resigned their right to speak were Dupanloup, Strossmayer, and Verot. On July 4, when the president announced no one else was waiting to address the council, the assembly broke into shouts of jubilation. Some fifty-seven speakers had pressed their case (thirty-five for a definition, twenty-two against).

At this point, the Committee on the Faith went to work on the approximately 150 recommendations and amendments to the chapter on infallibility. Actively assisting the committee were advisers from the Curia, notably the Jesuits Schrader and Franzelin. Within a few days, most of the suggestions had been weighed and rejected, though the title of the chapter was recommended for change from "The Infallibility of the Holy Father" to "The Infallible Magisterium [teaching authority] of the Roman Pontiff"—a small concession to Guidi's concerns about "personal" infallibility. In the chapter on infallibility, some words were changed and new phrases added, but the formula of definition finally agreed on by the committee was essentially the one that Cullen had presented in mid June but that had never been debated in the assembly; it was the ambiguous one that equated the pope's infallibility with that of the church.

The fathers were then given, on July 9, the reworked and now recommended chapters, along with the definitions and concluding canons. Particularly disconcerting to the minority bishops was their inability to get any reference to the bishops or to church tradition into the proposed definition on infallibility.

GASSER'S DISCOURSE

On July 11, Bishop Vincent Gasser of Austria, secretary of the Committee on the Faith, delivered the longest speech at Vatican I— nearly four hours. It was a detailed apologia for the recommendations of the committee and an explanation of some of the more obscure changes in the text. A theologian and a particularly mild-mannered man, Gasser tackled one by one the objections that consumed the minority:

1. *Papal infallibility will make future general councils unnecessary:* "They will be as necessary in the future as in the past; absolutely, they never were necessary in order that the faithful who were of good will might know the truth with certainty; for this they could always know from the ordinary magisterium of the Church—the bishops in union with the Roman Pontiff....Nevertheless, the most solemn judgment of the Church in faith and morals is and always will be the judgment of an ecumenical Council, in which the Pope pronounces judgment, the bishops of the Catholic world sitting and judging along with him."[5]

2. *General councils will no longer be free:* "They will be as free as they were in the past." If the pope leaves a dogmatic matter to be dealt with by a council, "then the Council will use its liberty freely in the Lord. If a dogmatic definition has preceded a Council, it will act as the Third Council of Constantinople acted in the face of dogmatic letters" from the pope (an intriguing statement in view of Hefele's speech against papal infallibility on the basis of this council).

3. *The definition gives the pope personal infallibility:* "It is personal in that it belongs to the Roman Pontiff, not the Roman Church or the Roman See. The infallibility is personal in as far as it belongs to each legitimate occupant of the Roman see. But it is not personal as belonging to the pope as a private person."

4. *The definition makes the pope separate:* "It may be called separate or rather distinct, because it is founded on the special promise of Christ, and on the special assistance of the Holy Ghost, which is not the same as that enjoyed by the whole body of the teaching Church joined with its head. The relation of Peter and his successor to the Church is quite special, and to this special and distinct relation responds a special and distinct privilege....But we do not thereby separate the Pope from his ordinated conjunction with the Church....He can no more be separated from the Church than

the foundation can be separated from the building it bears....As we believe the Pope is by divine assistance infallible, we thereby believe also that the assent of the Church can never be lacking to these definitions."

5. *The pope's infallibility will be absolute*: "In no sense is it absolute because absolute infallibility belongs to God alone. The Pope is restricted by limitations and conditions as set forth in the definition."

HOW "WIDE" AN INFALLIBILITY?

Gasser then went into an analysis of the minority position. Their argument, he said, is based on three axioms: first, "the members should be joined to the head and the head to the members"; second, "as the bishops can do nothing in making dogmas of faith without the Pope, similarly the Pope can do nothing without them"; third, "the consent of the Church is the rule of faith, which even the Pope should follow." Gasser's response to all this is that no one can prove an absolute need for the pope to depend on the bishops in every situation, because his authority is of a different order: "It is true that the Pope in his definitions *ex cathedra* has the same sources as the Church has (Scripture and tradition). It is true that the agreement of the present preaching of the whole magisterium of the Church united with its head is the rule of faith even for definitions by the pope. But from this can by no means be deduced a strict and absolute necessity of inquiring about it from the bishops....That strict necessity, such as would be necessary for inclusion in a dogmatic decree, cannot be established. There may be a case so difficult that the Pope deems it necessary for his information to inquire from the bishops—such was the case regarding the Immaculate Conception—but such a case cannot be set up as a rule." To hold otherwise, he said, is to yield to theological Gallicanism.

Gasser defended the committee's rejection of some specific minority recommendations. The formula of Saint Antoninus, requiring the pope to use the "counsel" of the "universal Church," was found to be "vague and indefinite." It could trigger controversies, he said, about what kind of counsel is necessary, whether it actually took place, and if it was in fact used by the pope. Other limiting formulas were rejected for similar reasons, said Gasser.

He then turned to the Cullen formula of definition, copies of which the bishops had received two days previously. This was the formula that referred to doctrines that "must be held." Gasser said, "Without any doubt this infallibility, whether in pontiff or in teaching Church, reaches to those things which in themselves make up the deposit of faith, namely to the defining of dogmas and the condemning of heresies."

Finally, he touched on a most sensitive issue: to what else does the pope's infallibility extend? Many theologians agree, he said, that the Church's infallibility extends to "other truths which though themselves not revealed, yet are required for guarding intact the deposit of revelation, rightly explaining it and efficaciously defining it." (He did not provide examples of these truths.) To deny infallibility to these truths would be "a most grave error," said Gasser. But, he explained, others maintain that such a broad extension of infallibility is at best only "theologically certain"—a fairly low level of conviction in doctrinal matters. Therefore, he concluded, the committee decided unanimously to recommend that the council not specify as a dogma just how far this infallibility extends, "but to leave it in the state in which it is." So it was left unclear whether only matters in the deposit of faith can be infallibly defined, or whether "other truths" could also be the object of infallible declaration.

The presentation swayed few Inopportunists. They found Gasser's interpretation of infallibility questionable; they still wanted some kind of recognition—a hint, a suggestion, a token—that the pope in his definitions reflects the mind of the Church or is functioning as the mouth of the Church. At this point, notes council historian Butler, "they would have been satisfied with very little." To be sure, the Committee on the Faith had incorporated into the preamble of the definition a paragraph intended to allay minority concerns. It stated in part: "The Roman pontiffs according to the exigencies of the times and circumstances, sometimes assembling 'ecumenical Councils or asking for the mind of the Church spread throughout the world, sometimes by particular synods, sometimes using other helps which divine Providence supplied defined things conformable with the Holy Scriptures and Apostolic Tradition.'"[6] Still, this was part of the Introduction, not a component of the defining formula itself.

After the presentation, the council fathers voted by overwhelming voice majorities to adopt the few amendments endorsed by the committee and to reject the rest. Thus was the foundation laid for the final six days of Vatican I.

A DIVIDED VOTE

July 13: Some seventy-six bishops were conspicuously absent from the general congregation when the vote was taken on the whole constitution concerning primacy and infallibility as recommended by the Committee on the Faith. Some just stayed away for the day, others were reported to be preparing to leave Rome. This was a trial ballot, a preparation for the grand public session scheduled for five days later; it therefore had no binding effect. The bishops could vote *placet* (approve), *non placet* (disapprove), or *placet juxta modum* (approve with reservations). The results were not surprising.

Of the 601 present, 451 approved, 88 disapproved, and 62 approved with reservations. Those with reservations were required to provide a written statement of their position, and these would be considered by the committee before the next and final congregation three days hence. Some 140 bishops had signed a petition in January opposing infallibility, and their numbers had obviously dwindled somewhat. The largest cohort of *non placets* was the French (24), followed by the Hungarians (15) and the Germans (11). Of the North American petition signers (24 in January), only 9 voted *non placet* on this ballot, including Verot, Kenrick, and Edward Fitzgerald of Little Rock.

Interestingly enough, a few who voted *placet juxta modum* were the strongest Infallibilists. They objected to the Preamble's mention of general councils in the same sentence with the popes; this seemed to them a concession to Gallicanism. Other Infallibilists were disturbed that the wording did not state explicitly that the Church's infallibility is derived from the pope's infallibility. But the bulk of reservations came from minority members whose concerns about "personal, separate and absolute" would not go away.

"GOOD FATHER, SAVE US!"

July 14: The Committee on the Faith waded through the two hundred new recommendations and comments received from the *placet juxta modum* voters and turned down all but two. One called for the removal of a citation of Saint Augustine in one of the chapters on primacy. The other was far more significant: the addition of a short clause at the very end of the formula of definition. In the form voted on by the council the day before, the formula ended: "definitions of the Roman pontiff are irreformable in themselves." To this, the commission recommended the addition of the words: "and not, however, from the consent of the church."

To ardent Inopportunists, this represented an ultimate slap in the face—this explicit, unambiguous exclusion of the Church's participation in defining dogma, even though there was nothing anywhere else in the text that would lead a reader to think the Church did participate. Cooler heads, however, saw the addition as a repudiation of any strains of theological Gallicanism that might still be lurking in the hierarchy. As such, it was meant to deny that a retroactive approval by the full Church is what makes a papal decree infallible. The source of this last-minute amendment appears to be Pope Pius himself. On this date, he sent to the Committee on the Faith copies of majority recommendations seeking such an amendment, along with a note saying, "Let Cardinal [Luigi] Bilio [chairman of the committee] read the enclosed comments and try to make use of them."[7]

July 15: The minority realized their battle was lost, but they also knew a repeat of the heavily split vote at the public session would create a tremendous scandal and thoroughly embarrass the Church. This was a far cry from the moral unanimity some claimed was a prerequisite for a conciliar definition. The minority members met and authorized a six-member committee, including Darboy and Bishop Wilhelm Ketteler of Mainz, Germany, to meet with Pope Pius and present a proposal. At this hastily arranged audience, Darboy told the pontiff that the minority bishops could guarantee a virtually unanimous *placet* at the public session if the pope would allow two small changes in wording in the constitution. They wanted the third chapter to state that while the pope holds the most important part of power in the Church, he does not hold "the whole fullness of power." And they begged that the definition include some reference that the pope defines dogmas "relying on the tradition of the churches" or in some other way is connected with the larger Church. It was reported that Ketteler fell to his knees at one point saying, "Good Father, save us and save the Church of God!"[8]

The pope's reaction is disputed. One version claims Pius remained unmoved, said it was too late to change anything, and told them in any event it was the council, not he, to whom they should appeal. According to another version, the pope, seriously concerned about the prospect of an embarrassing vote, was inclined to authorize these small changes but was quickly talked out of his inclination by a follow-up visit from Manning and Senestréy. Manning later did acknowledge, "When they [the minority] went to Pius IX we went also; it was a running fight."

July 16: At this last general congregation, 552 bishops were in attendance. The Committee on the Faith ran quickly through the amendments they had discussed, then explained their support of two. The elimination of Saint Augustine in one paragraph was passed by the council almost unanimously. The addition of the clause at the end of the definition on infallibility also passed, though there was a sizable number of dissenting votes.

A statement was read deploring "the false and calumnious things" said in pamphlets and newspapers against the pope, the Holy See and the council during the past nine months. Döllinger's works were not cited specifically, though they were in the minds of many. Particularly heinous, said the statement, were claims that, given the conditions present at this council, the bishops lacked the freedom to define a dogma. The president asked all who agreed with the statement to stand, and all did—except one. When several bishops cried out, "One did not rise!" there were several moments of muttering and much craning of necks. Finally, the holdout, whose identity was never made public, stood up, too. All were urged to prepare prayerfully for the public session and the formal declaration of the dogma in two days.

"WE HAVE DECIDED TO BE ABSENT"

July 17: On this Sunday, the eve of the public session, the minority was perplexed and divided on what to do. Some disgruntled members had already left Rome. Archbishop Darboy believed the rest should attend the public session and vote *non placet*. An informal poll indicated they could count on at least 140 votes, including the *non placets*, many of the *placets juxta modum*, and most who had declined to attend the earlier general congregation. This opposition, he said, would constitute more than 20 percent of those likely to be in attendance. Minority members also discussed a proposal to place a solemn protest on the table of the council after the vote, asserting the minority did not feel bound by the outcome, in the absence of moral unanimity.

At a final, decisive meeting of minority leaders on this evening, Archbishop Ludwig Haynald of Hungary gave a moving speech recommending Darboy's strategy; the bishops, he said, could do no other than to obey their consciences. We should "go to the public session and with clear and distinct voice, in face of pope, of Europe, of kings and people, of the future, close this dolorous discussion with a resounding negative vote."[9] The great majority of those present agreed.

Darboy, who was ill, did not attend this meeting, and Dupanloup arrived late, after Haynald had finished. Dupanloup—the most visible and persistent opponent of infallibility for the past nine months—stunned the group by stating vociferously that this was not the way to proceed. "We cannot vote *placet*," he said, "for none would believe us; we cannot vote *non placet*, for the Catholic world would not understand us and would be scandalized."

The only alternative for those who opposed the dogma was to stay away the next day, said Dupanloup. A long discussion and argument ensued. In the end, the leaders voted 36-28 to abide by Dupanloup's counsel. They then sent a letter to the pope signed by 55 minority members:

> Most Holy Father: In the General Congregation held on the 13th...we gave our votes on the...Constitution....Your Holiness is aware that 88 Fathers urged by conscience and moved by love of Holy Church gave their voice in the words *non placet*; 62 others in the words *placet juxta modum*; finally about 76 were absent and gave no vote. Others had returned to their dioceses....Our votes are known to your Holiness and manifest to the whole world; it is well known how many bishops endorse our view....Confirming our votes by this present document, we have decided to be absent from the public session the 18th....For the filial piety and reverence which very recently brought our representatives to the feet of your Holiness, do not allow us in a cause so closely concerning Your Holiness to say *"non placet"* openly and in the face of the father. We return therefore without delay to our flocks...grieving that in the existing sad conditions we shall find...consciences disturbed.

News of the decision traveled fast. A British diplomat in Rome sent a note to Manning: "The whole opposition, for reasons unexplained, have decided NOT to attend tomorrow, at the suggestion of the bishop of Orleans! A unanimous vote is therefore certain!... How curious the history of the last few days has been." He told Manning he saw some twenty bishops waiting at the railway station later that evening, including Haynald, Ketteler, and Dupanloup. At least another twenty were expected to leave the next morning, he said, and a similar number during the day—even as the pope's infallibility was being solemnly proclaimed to the world.

A LITANY OF PLACETS AND THUNDER

July 18: The doors of St. Peter's opened at 7:30 A.M., and the session began at 9:00. The crowd, probably held down by the inclement weather, was smaller than the one at the opening ceremonies in December. So was the number of bishops, almost two hundred fewer. After a votive Mass of the Holy Spirit (with no singing), a bishop received from the hands of the pope the constitution, titled *Pastor Aeternus,* and read from it the chapters on primacy and infallibility, concluding with the statement of definition:

> Therefore, faithfully adhering to the tradition understood from the beginning of the Christian faith, we, for the glory of God our Saviour, the exaltation of the Catholic Religion, and the salvation of Christian peoples, with the approval of the sacred council, teach and define that it is a dogma divinely revealed that the Roman Pontiff when he speaks *ex cathedra*, that is, when in discharge of the office of Shepherd and Teacher of all Christians, in accordance with his supreme apostolic authority, he defines a doctrine regarding faith or morals which must be held by the whole Church, by the divine assistance promised him in blessed Peter, is possessed of that infallibility with which the divine Redeemer willed that his Church should be endowed in defining doctrine regarding faith and morals; and that therefore such definitions of the Roman Pontiff are irreformable of themselves, and not from the consent of the Church. Now if anyone, God forbid, shall presume to contradict our definition, let him be anathema.[10]

The roll call began, and along with it the storm. For some ninety minutes the voting proceeded—a nearly unanimous litany of *placets* accompanied by great rolls of thunder and bolts of lightening illuminating the stained-glass windows. When the voting was finished, the tally was handed to the pope, who read it aloud: 533 *placet*, 2 *non placet*. After a candle was brought forward so the pope could see in the dense darkness, he read, "These things which have been read We define and We confirm by apostolic authority, with the approbation of the Council."[11]

The two who voted non placet left their places and came forward to the throne. The first, Fitzgerald of Little Rock, said, "Now I believe, holy father." The second, Luigi Riccio of Naples, knelt and declared simply, "I believe."

A veteran Inopportunist, Fitzgerald never explained his action. One theory held he was unaware of the minority decision to absent themselves from the session, another that he merely intended to be there as a spectator but changed his mind, a third that he really said *nunc placet* (now I agree) during the roll call but was misunderstood by the secretary struggling to hear amid the thunderclaps. Riccio, whose views on council issues were never clear, also declined to talk about the incident.

The pope intoned the *Te Deum*, the grand Church anthem of triumph. At the end, he spoke final words to the assembly:

> This supreme authority of the Roman Pontiff, venerable Brothers, does not destroy but builds up, confirms in dignity, unites in charity and strengthens and protects the rights of his Brethren, the Bishops. Therefore, let those who now are judging in commotion of mind know that the Lord is not in commotion....May God enlighten minds and hearts...that all may come to the bosom of their Father, Christ's unworthy Vicar on earth, who loves them and longs to be one with them; and thus being joined together in the bond of love, we may fight the battles of the Lord, so that our enemies may not mock us but rather may fear; and finally the arms of malice may yield to the view of truth and all may be able to say with St. Augustine, "Thou hast called me into thy admirable light, and lo I see."[12]

July 19: As the bishops dispersed to the four corners of the world, they heard the news that France had declared war on Prussia. This resulted in the almost immediate withdrawal of the French garrison guarding Rome and the Papal States. The forces of King Victor Emmanuel, long awaiting the opportunity to unite all Italy under one banner, moved in. The pope ordered his hopelessly outnumbered army not to resist, though there were a few skirmishes. The king guaranteed Pius personal immunity from harm, allowed him to keep control over much of what is now Vatican City, a diplomatic corps, an independent post office, and the Swiss Guard. The regular operations of the Curia also remained undisturbed.

The Papal States were lost forever, and Pius IX saw himself ever after as a prisoner of the Vatican. He regarded the new government as illegal and refused to cooperate with it. Thus, the Roman papacy achieved its highest level of juridical-spiritual authority in history at the same time it was forced to relinquish its last vestige of temporal-political authority. The council, which was slated to resume in the fall to take up its unfinished business, would not be reconvened. (Since it was not officially declared over, many came to regard Vatican II, ninety-two years later, as the completion of Vatican I.)

CHAPTER X

CONSENT
AND DISSENT

*I believe today in infallibility as thoroughly as I disbelieved
in it yesterday.*

BISHOP FÉLIX DE LAS CASES

What would happen now? Given the controversy that had attended almost every session of the council, the acrimony at some sessions, and the dramatic boycott by a substantial number at the very end, no one knew for sure. Both in Europe and North America the press had kept tabs on major developments and the ongoing debate, thanks to substantial leaks within the council and the stream of pamphlets and papers issued by both sides.

Would the pope use his newly defined charism to wield unprecedented power over Catholics and perhaps even try to interfere anew in world affairs? Would ordinary Catholics go along with this new dogma, whose meaning they could scarcely understand, or would they reject it as beyond belief? And would the minority bishops, who had fought the doctrine so strenuously, now quietly embrace it, or would they continue their dissent, perhaps triggering a great schism in the Church?

The first two questions were quickly answered. Pius IX, the prisoner of the Vatican, was in no position to gloat over his triumph or attempt incursions in the temporal order. The aged pontiff had his hands full dealing with the secular takeover of papal properties and the humiliation of his losses. Meanwhile, the governments of Europe had their hands full as the Franco-Prussian War threatened to spread; a papal power play was the least of their worries.

The response of Catholics to the new doctrine was generally enthusiastic, especially in countries like the United States where Catholicism was a minority religion subject to bigotry, even persecution; infallible leadership provided a measure of assurance and confidence. And if Pius IX was now himself a victim of unjust persecution, their identification with him was all the greater, their respect for his prerogatives all the stronger.

The third issue—the reaction of the minority bishops—was more complicated. At first glance, it seemed that the overwhelming number accepted the doctrine with scarcely a whimper. In fact, as Infallibilists were happy to report, not a single bishop publicly denounced the doctrine, initiated a schismatic movement, or left the Church. But a closer look reveals much soul-searching, great mental anguish, and a generous reliance on mental reservation beneath the compliance.

SUBMISSION REQUIRED

Every bishop who did not attend the last session on July 18 was informed by the Curia that the pope expected him to submit a formal declaration of acceptance of the doctrine of *Pastor Aeternus*, and he expected it quickly. Submissions did come with extraordinary dispatch. (Feisty Bishop Verot had sent his before he left Rome to return to the United States.)

In an exhaustive study of the reactions of the French minority bishops, historian Margaret O'Gara says the compliance in France (likely in many other countries, too) stemmed from a simple notion of religious obedience compounded with a dread of instigating trouble in the Church. Said Cardinal Jacques-Marie Mathieu, head of the French delegation, soon after the council adjournment, "The French bishops will not go so far as to protest subsequently to either the Pope or the Council regarding the decisions of July 18. They accept without reserve what has been done and would not wish to begin...any discussion which might bring about greater difficulties."[1] That meant, added Mathieu, there would be no "manifestation of feelings" or personal reactions to the doctrine even when pressed by newspaper reporters.

Bishop Charles-Philippe Place said freedom of conscience is not diminished by legitimate subjection to superiors—"a child to his father and mother, a subject to the laws of his country, a parishioner to his pastor, a Catholic to the infallible oracle of truth."

According to Bishop William-Rene Meignan, "The council has spoken; all must submit to its decisions in word, in mind and in heart." And Bishop Etienne Ramadié said he would rather die than separate himself "from the unshakable rock on which rests the holy Church, the faith of Peter...the apostolic see, separated from which salvation is impossible."

Other French bishops were less effusive but nevertheless dutifully obedient. Said Dupanloup simply, "I adhere to the doctrine." And Darboy declared, "I accept the doctrine pure and simple."[2]

This prompt conformity stemmed in part from Gallican esteem for the authority of ecumenical councils. Notes historian Roger Aubert: "Even if the procedure followed by the Council had been illegal, as some thought, it had to be recognized that the affirmation of pontifical infallibility had been ratified at Rome itself by a significant proportion of the episcopate and that, by adding to this subsequent individual adherents, moral unanimity was rapidly approaching."[3]

O'Gara finds the bishops' unnuanced understanding of obedience perplexing. After the council, she says, it seems there was no more room for judgment on the part of these men, only the obligation to contribute to the growing moral unanimity. The minority bishops left the council early, she notes, because they did not want to break the "unanimity" of the vote. They were "clear on the principle that infallible teaching must express the faith of the entire church"…yet "failed, as it were, to count themselves among the church whose faith the council was called to express."[4]

For them, at least outwardly, obedience included the sacrifice of personal conviction, the end of doubts and discussion, and the kind of sudden and total transformation described by Bishop Félix de Las Cases: "I remained fixed in my opinion so long as the council had not pronounced; but on the morrow of the definition God gave me the grace to be able to say with entire truth, in the fullness and calm of my faith, 'I believe to-day in infallibility as thoroughly as I disbelieved in it yesterday.'"[5]

A similar mind-set was evident among minority bishops elsewhere. In August 1870, seventeen German bishops (not including Hefele) met at the city of Fulda and issued a joint statement:

> As long as the discussions lasted, the bishops…expressed their views plainly…and as was only to be expected in an assembly of nearly 800 fathers, many differences of opinion were manifested.…These differences can in no way affect the authority of the decrees themselves.…Wherefore, we hereby declare that the Vatican Council is a legitimate General Council; and moreover, that this Council…has [not] propounded or formed a new doctrine at variance with the ancient teaching.[6]

Council historian Cuthbert Butler finds this ready acceptance healthy and proper: "That is what it is to be a Catholic. When the teaching Church finally and formally declares a belief to be an article of Catholic Faith, it is the part of every Catholic to give up private judgement and accept the judgement of the Church."[7]

Still, it was difficult to determine what "acceptance" meant. For Manning, the mantle of infallibility covered "the whole…doctrinal authority of the Pontiff as the supreme Doctor of all Christians… And also all legislative or judicial acts…all judgments, sentences and decisions.…Under this will come laws of discipline, canonization of saints, approbation of religious orders, of devotions and the like, all of which intrinsically contain the truths and principles of faith, morals and piety."

To which Newman replied, "The Archbishop only does what he has done all along—he has ever exaggerated things....The Pope is not infallible in such things as he instances....You may dismiss all such exaggerations from your mind, though it is a cruel penance to know that the Bishop [Manning]...puts them forth. It is an enormous tyranny."[8]

A "CONDITIONAL" ACCEPTANCE

For many bishops, there was a marked distinction between formal acceptance and interior conviction. O'Gara notes that some French minority bishops followed up their public submission by never mentioning *Pastor Aeternus* in their dioceses for the remainder of their careers; a few refused to even publish the text. And those who did write about or discuss infallibility tried to interpret the doctrine in the most benign light—not an easy task in view of their fierce resistance to the various formulas of definition. When someone suggested to Dupanloup that his acceptance meant the minority was in fundamental agreement with Manning and other Infallibilists, he replied, "Fundamental agreement! Don't say that; we never were!" Darboy also asserted that his understanding of the doctrine differed from that of the majority. He claimed that, "as a theologian," he had always believed in some form of papal infallibility, but "as a man," found both the wording and the timing of the dogma at the council "inept." Darboy's participation in the postconciliar debate was tragically abbreviated; he was arrested in the takeover of Paris by Communists in 1871, imprisoned, and executed by firing squad one year after the cessation of Vatican I.[9]

Bishop Charles Maret was especially candid about his very conditional acceptance of infallibility. "I adhere to the decree purely and simply, because I can give *only one meaning* to it, a meaning which preserves the true character of the constitution of the Church," he wrote. In his judgment, the decree of July 18 does not include "the doctrine of absolute, separate, personal, pontifical infallibility." The aim of the Ultramontane school, he said, was to give the pope that kind of unreserved infallibility, to make him entirely independent, "but this end was not obtained, God has willed it otherwise."

Maret, Dupanluop, and others who gave a decidedly conditional approval of the decrees could draw some consolation from a paper published in 1871 by Austrian bishop Joseph Fessler. He had been the secretary of the council, and his paper inspired a letter from Pius himself thanking him for "having brought out the true meaning of the dogma of infallibility." Unlike Bishop Gasser, who saw a somewhat wide orbit for infallible decrees in his long talk during the final week of the council, Fessler provided a narrower ambit: The utterances of the pope are to be received as infallible only under the very rigid conditions stated in the definition; nothing is to be presumed infallible except that which is explicitly stated as *ex cathedra*; the pope is limited to those matters that have already been revealed as necessary for salvation; and he cannot "by his own fancy" extend infallible definitions to matters unrelated to divine revelation.[10] This restricted understanding of infallibility would appear in more developed form at Vatican II, though opinion about what can and cannot be declared an infallible dogma remains divided to this day.

Some bishops in Europe delayed making a formal submission in hopes that the council would be reconvened within a few months. This was clearly the position of Joseph Rauscher in Austria, Karl Hefele in Germany, and Joseph Haynald in Hungary. Under the leadership of Cardinal Friedrich Schwarzenberg of Prague, they intended to lobby for new regulations that would guarantee freedom of expression to the full assembly, a more balanced group of outside theologians working with the council committees, and, finally, a rewording of the definitions on primacy and infallibility. The complications of the war disabused them of these hopes by early 1871.

PRESSURE FROM ROME

Those who put off their submissions, either in anticipation of a reconvened council or because of conscience difficulties, felt strong pressure from Rome. Especially intriguing was the situation of Hefele, who agonized for months over what to do. As a historian, he could find no justification for papal infallibility in past ages, and unlike de Las Casas, he could not affirm today what he denied yesterday. "I'm sitting on a volcano," he wrote a few months after returning to his diocese in Austria. The Vatican was flatly refusing to grant any dispensations for mixed marriages submitted by his chancery, and Hefele was acquiring a backlog of angry would-be brides and grooms. Hefele contemplated stating his views publicly. Yet, he wrote to a friend, "The position of a suspended and excommunicated bishop strikes me as something terrible. I could hardly bear it."[11]

Nor, he believed, could the Church bear the scandal of a possible schism over his convictions. That, he reasoned, would be a disaster even worse than the doctrine. So Hefele, more than a year after the declaration of the dogma, sent in his written submission, burned all the papers he had written on the council, and asked his friends to return his letters so he could burn them as well. He called it "a sacrifice of the intellect."[12]

The irascible Bosnian bishop Strossmayer also remained adamant for a time. "I'd rather die," he told a friend in March 1871, "than go against my conscience and my convictions. Better to be exposed to every humiliation than to bend my knee to Baal, to arrogance incarnate."[13] But pressure from Rome eventually wore him down, too. He published the text of *Pastor Aeternus* in his diocese in 1872, which allowed relations with the Vatican to return to normal. However, his personal acceptance of the doctrine came only in 1881, some eleven years after the council and three years after the death of Pius IX.

Haynald finally yielded when he saw the crumbling of minority resistance. Had others, like Hefele and Darboy, held out, he said, he would have endured the pressure, but "as the Vatican decrees have been accepted almost without exception by all the bishops of the Catholic world, every Catholic, no matter what may have been his personal scientific conviction, is bound in conscience to look on these doctrines as teachings which Jesus Christ has delivered."[14]

Among those who experienced the gravest difficulties of conscience was Archbishop Kenrick. He did not return to St. Louis immediately after the council; instead he traveled around Europe for more than five months, sorting out his convictions. On his return home in January 1871, he immediately stated publicly his acceptance of infallibility. "The motive of my submission is 'simply and singly' the authority of the Catholic Church....I yield obedience and give full and unreserved submission to the definition, concerning the character of which there can be no doubt as emanating from the Council."[15]

Kenrick was soon afterward informed that a paper known as *Concio*, which he wrote and published at the council had been examined during his travels by the Sacred Congregation of the Index and been condemned due to "grave errors." The condemnation was personally approved by the pope, but it had not yet been publicized, pending Kenrick's retraction of his views. Without a retraction, said the congregation, the condemnation would be made public. Kenrick was infuriated with the threat. In *Concio* he had stated his belief that papal infallibility could not be established by historical proofs and was not a doctrine of faith in Church tradition; its argumentation was no stronger than that presented by Dupanloup or other minority members involved in the debate.

Kenrick refused to retract the paper. In a long letter to Lord Acton, he reiterated that his acceptance of infallibility was "purely and singly" on the basis of obedience and "was not grounded on the removal of my motives of opposition to the decrees." Kenrick said he was worried about the future of the episcopacy within the increasingly defensive structure erected in Rome. "It is evident that there can be no liberty in future sessions of the Council, with this example to warn bishops that they must not handle roughly the delicate matters on which they have to decide."

In June 1871, when Catholics in St. Louis celebrated the silver anniversary of Pius IX's pontificate with a four-mile procession through the central city, Kenrick was out of town. In fact, he virtually disappeared from sight for the next ten years, leaving arch-diocesan affairs in the hands of his coadjutor bishop. He did not retract *Concio*, nor did Rome press the matter to the limits. Kenrick returned to full, active duty in 1881, when he was named arch-bishop of Philadelphia by Pius IX's successor, Leo XIII.

In the aftermath of Vatican I, there were reports of other so-called revenge actions against minority members. A French bishop, Francis Lecourtier, who left the council early and threw his papers in the Tiber in disgust, was removed from his diocese three years after the council. Some minority bishops retired early, others grew uncharacteristically silent, opting for what was labeled at the time as "the emigration inwards."[16]

DÖLLINGER AND THE OLD CATHOLICS

Neither silence nor acceptance was the strategy adopted by a cote-rie of German theologians. On his return to Munich, Archbishop Gregory Scherr interviewed the University of Munich religion fac-ulty headed by Döllinger, the dean. "We are now going to work anew for holy Church," said the archbishop optimistically.

"Yes," replied Döllinger," for the old Church....They [the coun-cil and pope] have made a new one."[17] Along with a fellow Munich professor, Johann Friedrich, Döllinger met with eleven other dis-senting academics in Nurenberg in August 1870. They drafted a declaration that called the council's decisions invalid because the bishops lacked freedom, and they appealed to a future council (one held outside Rome) to set matters right.

In September when Scherr demanded that the theological fac-ulty at Munich accept the Vatican decrees, all did except Döllinger and Friedrich. Scherr, who had long supported Döllinger, gave them time to reconsider. Then, in March 1872, Döllinger explained his refusal to conform in an incendiary article in *Allgemeine Zeitung*: "The Pope by the one word 'Orbi' (to the whole world), may now make an article of faith of every sentence, every doctrine, every command. There is no right of opposition to his will; there is neither individual nor corporative liberty. God's tribunal and the Pope's are identically the same....As Christian, as theologian, as historian, as citizen, I cannot accept this doctrine." It had all come to pass, he surmised, because "the vast majority of bishops from the Latin countries lacked the will or the intelligence to distinguish truth from falsehood."

Scherr excommunicated Döllinger and Friedrich in April—an act that sent shock waves through the entire Catholic world, despite Döllinger's well-known antipathy for the doctrine. For over twenty-five years, he had been the outstanding defender of Catholic rights against aggressive monarchs on the Continent, the boldest and most articulate apologist for Catholic doctrine. His ouster, many predicted, marked the prelude of massive dissent. When similar excommunications were leveled against nonconforming professors at other academic centers, at Cologne, Langen, and Breslau, it appeared a revolt was inevitable.

Gathering in Munich in May, many of the ousted leaders formed a Committee of Action, which called on the king of Bavaria to forbid the teaching of *Pastor Aeternus* in public universities and to personally head a movement against "Roman impudence and ignorance." In June the formal organization of the Old Catholic Church got under way under the direction of Johann von Schulte, a layman and professor of canon law from Prague, and Paul Reinkens, a German theologian who was promptly consecrated the bishop of the church by a schismatic, Jansenist bishop from Utrecht, Holland.

The new Church experienced early growth since its beginnings coincided with the Prussian military victory over France. Otto von Bismarck, the "iron chancellor" of the new union of Prussia, Bavaria, and other Germanic states, openly supported this new ecclesial enterprise as a model national Church. Rejecting papal infallibility and the *Syllabus of Errors* as the ultimate in unwarranted Roman centralization, Old Catholicism still claimed a relationship with the universal Catholic Church. It would ordain its own priests and bishops (chosen by clergy and laity) and establish its own regulations in keeping with the national culture and customs.

The Church took roots in parts of Switzerland, Holland, and Austria, as well as Germany, and may have had as many as 250,000 members in the early 1880s. But Bismarck's ill-concealed domination of the Old Catholic Church and his exploitation of it for political ends sealed its fate. As part of the repressive Kulturkampf campaign, he fined, exiled, or imprisoned bishops and priests who failed to cooperate with the new order. German Catholics soon revolted. At the same time, the Old Catholics' internal structure began to fall apart—as doctrines were jettisoned in the interest of modernity. By 1887 Old Catholicism had ceased to be a force, but through a succession of validly (though illicitly) consecrated bishops, the Church has maintained a token existence in many countries, including the United States.

Strangely enough, Döllinger, whose rejection of Vatican I played a role in the formation of the Old Catholics, never joined the movement. Befriended by the Bavarian king after his excommunication, he continued to write and lecture for many years, mainly on the importance of Christian unity. Döllinger considered the penalty imposed on him unjust but accepted its consequences. He never afterwards said Mass or received communion. When he was eighty-seven years old in 1887, a papal nuncio urged him to accept infallibility and return to the Church. "I do not regard myself as a member of a schismatic sect," he responded. "I am alone, convinced the sentence leveled against me is unjust and improper. I persist in seeing myself as a member of the great Catholic Church and remain in a state of peace and tranquillity...." As he lay dying three years later, the last rites were performed by his lifelong friend and fellow excommunicated priest, Johann Friedrich.

A "RIGGED" COUNCIL?

The troubling question in the turmoil that followed the council was the freedom of the assembly. It was not an ecumenical council, claimed its critics, because the bishops were not free; rather, they were dominated by the pope, the Curia, and a clique of insider bishops determined to ensure that the outcome was the one they intended. In short, went the charge, Vatican I was rigged. And indeed, a review of the more peculiar occurrences at the council shows how a case could be made:

- The pope's reservation exclusively to himself of the right to propose issues to the body of bishops.
- The deliberate exclusion of minority representation on the all-important Committee on the Faith.
- The imposed rule change that allowed debate on infallibility to be cut off before all the interested parties had spoken.
- The strong pressures exerted by Pope Pius IX on council members (Cardinal Guidi, for instance) to prevent deviations from the papal position.
- The presentation and recommendation to the council in the final week of a new formula of infallibility that had not been discussed in any general session.
- The addition of a final clause in the formula that the bishops had never seen or heard of until the hour they voted on it.
- The insistent pressures (and threats) on minority members after the council in order to obtain a moral unanimity of the world's hierarchy.

Perhaps the strongest evidence that the council lacked freedom is the insistent claim by so many members that they did not feel free. It appears in speeches, in written protests, and the complaints leaked throughout the council to Döllinger. As Darboy noted in the early months, the bishops discovered on their arrival a council "already in session" under the direction of people "selected on exclusive principles" who prepared resolution "the bishops were expected to sanction."

Bishop Francis Lecourtier (the one later removed from office) put the argument in extreme terms in a letter during the council:

> Our weakness at this moment comes neither from Scripture nor the tradition of the Fathers nor the witness of the general Councils nor the evidence of history. It comes from the lack of freedom....An imposing minority, representing the faith of more than one hundred million Catholics, that is, almost half of the entire Church, is crushed beneath the yoke of a restrictive agenda which contradicts conciliar traditions. It is crushed by commissions which have not been truly elected....It is crushed by the absolute absence of discussion, response, objections and the opportunity to demand explanations....The minority is crushed above all by the full weight of the supreme authority which oppresses it with the praise and encouragement it lavishes on the priests in the form of papal briefs.[18]

This claim of lack of freedom was written about in a great wave of popular and scholarly works during the latter years of the nineteenth century, and it persists today. The Swiss theologian Hans Küng has noted, "As painful and embarrassing as it may be to admit, this council resembled a well organized and manipulated totalitarian party congress rather than a free gathering of free Christian people.[19]

August Hasler, a German theologian, argues in a two-volume work published in 1977, "There is no way to uphold the freedom of the First Vatican Council without silencing, softening or embellishing the facts....The external preconditions for a discussion were simply not there. Also missing—and this seems to me still more important—was the inner freedom to discuss and examine the doctrine. The measures taken by the pope, Infallibilists and Curia show they had no interest in [freedom]."

FREEDOM: A "RELATIVE" CONCEPT

Yet a wealth of other testimony abounds claiming the council was free, the obstacles notwithstanding, its decisions valid and binding on the faithful. Without exception, the majority bishops affirmed its freedom, and many who could be regarded as middle-of-the-roaders did so as well. Wrote Bishop Ullathorne of Birmingham:

> Every condition of a full and free debate was satisfied, the question was considered on all its sides, both by writing in the closet and by the shifting process of public discussion....In addition to the public discussion there were many private lights contributed towards the elucidation of the question; for no sooner had the doctrine been mooted than a number of pamphlets began to appear and were left at the residences of the bishops. Of these I received about 60....All that could be said in opposition was fairly said out, and had a fair opportunity of being considered.[20]

Joseph Icard, a respected council observer, wrote, "The Vatican Council incontestably had enough liberty to give value to its acts. There was freedom of speech and a moral freedom in voting."[21]

Many modern commentators agree. According to theologian George Dejaifve, "In spite of...restrictions, in spite even of the pressure from without and within the assembly—inevitable when men meet to decide upon a common action, even when they are men of God gathered together in the Holy Spirit—it is scarcely arguable that the fathers did not enjoy the freedom essential to every deliberative assembly."

Even in the classic, fully recognized ecumenical councils, like Nicea and Chalcedon, pressures were exerted from many sides, not the least of which was the emperor, says Peter Slackmeyer, and the bishops there labored under far more restrictions than existed at Vatican I.[22]

Klaus Schatz, a twentieth-century German theologian, says discussions of the relative freedom at such gatherings will not decide the issue. For him the important point is that the dogma was affirmed by a moral unanimity: "The reception of a dogma by the whole church is in itself a theologically relevant fact, even if such acceptance may not have occurred without a good deal of pressure and manipulation." For Schatz, "conciliar freedom is, historically speaking, a highly relative concept. It is contingent upon the development both of the consciousness of freedom in society as a whole and upon the Church's understanding of itself."

Many contend arguments about the council's freedom or lack thereof are moot since the vast majority of bishops were fully prepared to vote for whatever expression of infallibility was placed before them. As the historian P. Conzemius observed: "The majority...did not at all need to be pressed...their cartgories of thought led directly to a strengthening of papal prerogatives."[23]

PART THREE

The

DOCTRINE DEVELOPING

CHAPTER XI

VATICAN CENTRALIZATION AND THEOLOGICAL SHIFTS

The fundamental locus of ecclesiastical authority in the Church is not the papacy but the episcopal college. Papal authority is always...collegial.

YVES CONGAR, O.P.

Pope Pius IX, who died in 1878, never used the charism of infallibility after it was defined at the council eight years earlier. Extreme Ultramontanes were disappointed. The English publisher W. G. Ward had looked forward to finding a fresh infallible declaration on faith or morals on the front page of his newspaper almost daily. Nor were Pius's successors any more eager to speak infallibly *ex cathedra*. It was almost as if they feared the explosive potential of the new dogma. Leo XIII, who reigned as pope until 1903, and Pius X, who succeeded Leo, were much absorbed in battling what came to be known as Modernism.

In much the way that de Lammenais and his associates sixty years before had urged an accommodation of the Church to ideas like freedom of conscience and freedom of the press, Catholic intellectuals of the late nineteenth and early twentieth centuries said the Church should apply modern critical methods of analysis to its documents, including the Bible. They urged abandoning the fixed, absolutist interpretation of truth characteristic of scholasticism in favor of a more dynamic, fluid approach. Leaders of the movement included the English Jesuit George Tyrrell and the French historian Alfred Loisy. It was Loisy who extended critical analysis to the whole of Christian history and concluded somewhat sarcastically, "What Christ announced was the Kingdom of God; what came was the Catholic Church."[1]

In a series of clarifications, condemnations, and excommunications reminiscent of the *Syllabus of Errors* (especially the encyclicals *Providentissimus* in 1893 and *Pascendi* in 1907, along with the Holy Office document *Lamentabile*, also in 1907), the popes used the strongest language, labeling the Modernists as "the most pernicious of all the adversaries of the Church." To further rid the Church of this pestilence, Pius X inaugurated vigilance committees in every diocese to check on the orthodoxy of priests and bishops and to report directly to Rome on deviations. All priests and religion teachers were required to take an oath against Modernism. In 1908, on the fifth anniversary of his pontificate, Pius X had a medal struck portraying himself, sword in hand, slaying the dragon of Modernism. Under the concerted pressure, the movement did collapse.

In fact, much of what the Modernists talked about is accepted by most Catholic scholars today. For example, that dogmatic formulas are always inadequate in representing their object; that revelation was gradually unfolded in the life of the Church; and that the Bible and all sources of Christian tradition should be studied using the most scientifically critical methods available. But at the turn of the century these ideas seemed a direct assault on the well-organized, defensive fortress that had been erected at Vatican I.

Yet at no point in this crisis of thought did the pontiffs appeal directly to their powers of infallibility either in reiterating doctrine or putting down heresy. The papal reluctance would continue well into the twentieth century.

Practically every Catholic school student for most of this century learned that Mary's Immaculate Conception (1854) and her Assumption (1950) represented the only dogmas pronounced by popes *ex cathedra* in the past 150 years. What most students were only dimly aware of at best was the emergence of another parallel application of infallibility during the same period. It was the infallibility of the "ordinary universal magisterium" of the Church— a concept that has its own special history.

THE EVOLUTION OF "MAGISTERIUM"

From apostolic times, Christians maintained that the Church, the living body of the faithful as a whole, is infallible—that is, it will remain faithful to the message of Christ through the assistance of the Holy Spirit. Just how this protection would manifest itself in concrete situations remained for centuries a matter of speculation. By the year 1000, there was general agreement that ecumenical councils could speak infallibly under certain conditions, and finally, in 1870, infallibility was extended officially to the solemn pronouncements of popes. But declarations by either a council or a pope were extraordinary manifestations of infallibility issued in response to particular problems.

Was infallibility also to be attached to specific doctrines taught always and everywhere by the Church in the ordinary course of its life—even though these doctrines had never been the subject of an explicit definition? Teachings as fundamental as the existence of God and the three Persons in the Blessed Trinity had not been defined by a council. Some theologians held that all such matters fell under the umbrella of infallibility. But the question remained a speculative consideration, since it was by no means clear how one could discover what all of these universal doctrines were, nor did it seem especially important to devise a list of them. Then, as a little noticed addendum at the First Vatican Council, the concept acquired a special importance.

The term "magisterium" has deep roots. It is derived from the

Latin word for "teacher" (*magister*), and it originally meant the authority of a legitimate teacher of truth. In the primitive Church, magisterium was applied to God as the supreme teacher or to Christ as his visible incarnation. In the second and third centuries, the term was also applied to whoever in the community passed on the mysteries of the faith. To be sure, bishops had the task of leading the community, but the job of teaching was seen as not exclusively theirs. Magisterium belonged to deacons, catechists, even ordinary lay teachers, since the Church was seen as an organic thing: The charisms poured out freely by the Spirit were not and could not be limited by job description.

After the time of Constantine, as the Church took on a more formal, juridical structure, authority (whether in leading, sanctifying, or teaching) came to be vested more firmly in the bishops precisely because they were duly consecrated bishops. But in the Middle Ages the Church still recognized the "magisterium" of the doctors and theologians in the universities. Ever so gradually, though, the shift continued toward an identification of magisterium exclusively with those holding episcopal office.

Notes theologian Michael Place: "Whereas the earlier period had understood both the official solicitude of the hierarchical office and the solicitude of the theological community as being in service...to the mysteries of faith...the later period saw a growing identification of that reality with the hierarchical office. Rather than serving the truth, the official Church became the organ of the truth which was its possession."[2] By the early 1900s, the shift was complete. The Jesuit theologian John Baptist Franzelin, a major curial architect of Vatican I, spoke of the Church as a body-soul composite, with the human element, the body of the faithful, guided by the soul, the magisterium forming the single voice of the divine element.

This change could easily lead to an exaggerated state of affairs in which the status of the messenger became more important than the message. And it did in numerous instances. Advised the theologian Louis Billot in 1922: "We ought not to look to that which is believed, but rather to that which guides our belief by proposing the truth to be believed."[3] It was a simple jump from magisterium as the authority of the hierarchy to magisterium as the hierarchy itself. And from this one might easily associate Church and magisterium so closely that the terms could be used interchangeably: e.g, the magisterium becomes the Church. This evolution made it possible to determine infallible doctrine by asking what the bishops (in union with the pope) taught always and everywhere—surely not an easy task itself but less daunting than discerning what the "Church" in the larger sense believed.

ANOTHER MODE OF INFALLIBILITY

The first use of the term "ordinary universal magisterium" occurred in a letter (*Tuas Libenter*) written by Pius IX in 1863, seven years before Vatican I. He was responding to a resolution passed at a congress of theologians in Munich. The gathering had agreed in principle to a proposal by Döllinger that Catholics are bound in conscience to submit only to doctrines solemnly defined; in all other teaching they are free to dissent if they have solid reason. Declared Pius: "The subjection which must be given in an act of divine faith…must not be limited to those things which have been defined [by councils or popes] but must also be extended to those things which are handed on by the ordinary magisterium of the Church scattered throughout the world."[4]

The German theologian Joseph Kleutgen fastened on this new term and developed it prior to and after Vatican I. For him, "ordinary universal magisterium" allowed a whole range of teaching to be included in the category of infallibility. Explains theologian Richard Gaillardetz, "Kleutgen assumed that virtually all of the facts contained in scripture belonged to revelation. Since most of these facts had never been solemnly defined he maintained that they must have been taught by the ordinary magisterium. Biblical 'facts' like the sacrifice of Abraham, Jonah's being swallowed by a whale and the miracles of Jesus and the apostles all were taught infallibly by the church's ordinary magisterium."[5] Kleutgen also cited examples from tradition taught universally such as the existence of hellfire, prayer for the dead and the Church's sacraments. All, he said, merited the title of infallible doctrine.

At the First Vatican Council, Kleutgen worked closely with the Committee on the Faith in developing the much debated schema on the Church. This was the document the bishops wrestled with from January to April 1870, prior to their consideration of the primacy and infallibility of the pope. Under its title *Filius Dei*, it had passed in April by a 667-0 vote. Few council fathers, it seems, understood the meaning of a short paragraph in the middle of the document: "All those things are to be believed by divine and Catholic faith which are contained in the word of God either written or handed down and are proposed by the Church for belief as divinely revealed, either by a solemn judgment or by its ordinary and universal magisterium."[6]

Some bishops asked if "ordinary universal magisterium" referred to the pope's infallibility as distinct from that of a council. No, explained Bishop Konrad Martin of Germany: "All of you...know that before the council, of Nicea all the Catholic bishops already believed in the divinity of our Lord Jesus Christ. Before the council, not even this dogma was plainly defined or declared. Accordingly, in the time before the council of Nicea this dogma was taught by the ordinary magisterium."[7] Eighty years later, this was the argument presented by Pope Pius XII in justifying his definition of the Assumption: "From the universal consent of the ordinary universal magisterium of the church a certain and firm argument is drawn by which the bodily assumption of the blessed virgin Mary into heaven is verified...and therefore to be believed by all the children of the church."[8]

Thus it happened that Vatican I in effect defined two kinds of infallibility—that of the pope and that of the ordinary universal magisterium. Strangely enough, most histories of Vatican I are so absorbed with the controversy over papal infallibility that they scarcely notice the latter form. Yet this ordinary magisterium was destined to present the Church with far more complications and problems of interpretation.

PAPAL AUTHORITY DOMINANT

One might expect the flowering of this new mode of infallibility to bring the world's bishops into prominence. It was, after all, their teaching, scattered as they were over the whole earth, that carried the guarantee of infallibility. Yet universal ordinary magisterium seemed to buttress papal authority more than that of the episcopacy. This is due in large measure to the manualists, the authors of the basic texts on theology used in seminaries. In the afterglow of Vatican I, they tended to relate all authority to the pope and support a centralization of all things under his jurisdiction. The trend would continue (with some notable exceptions) right up to Vatican II. And it would even be reflected in some of the Vatican II documents.

Gaillardetz, who reviewed the works of major textbook authors between the councils, finds a common and tight thread running through their treatment of ecclesiology. Domenic Palmieri, whose textbook was titled appropriately *A Tract on the Roman Pontiff with a Prologue on the Church*, insisted that when the bishops around the world taught infallibly, they did so only because of their communion with the pope; he alone was the immediate subject of infallibility. Christian Pesch, whose books were used in seminaries through the 1950s, wondered if it would ever be possible to learn whether every bishop in every diocese taught a certain doctrine and how inquirers could identify a universal doctrine since it might be taught in slightly altered forms in various places because of cultural differences. The unspoken solution to these dilemmas would be to leave it up to the pope, whose individual infallibility would cut through all the doubts and red tape. The Spanish theologian Joachim Salaverri, who taught at the Gregorian University in Rome for many years prior to Vatican II, put his major emphasis not only on the Church as hierarchical but as monarchical; Peter and his successors, he said, have authority that is "universal, ordinary, immediate, truly episcopal, supreme and full, and subject to no higher judgment."[9]

The trend among manualists seemed to confirm the dark forebodings of Vatican I's Inopportunists. The minority at the council had begged for a closer connection between the pope's infallibility and the bishops, the theologians and the larger Church. It is primarily the faith of the whole Church, they had argued, that is shielded by the charism of infallibility. Only one of the manualists reviewed by Gaillardetz proposed an overt link between the exercise of magisterium and the local church. Theologian Francis Sullivan, writing just before Vatican II, asserted: "The whole Christian church, from the second century on, acknowledged solely those bishops who were true pastors of their flocks as authoritative doctors of the faith and successors to the apostles in the authentic magisterium." Therefore, concluded Sullivan, "residential bishops alone, in communion with the bishop of Rome, possess by divine law the authoritative magisterium in the church. Their collegial consensus on matters of faith and morals is infallible when they teach gathered in council or when dispersed throughout the world."[10]

For the most part, however, the authors of the theology texts that formed the minds of hundreds of thousands of clergy over four generations, remained committed to a model of Church as an entirely top-down structure overseen by a supreme authority who had within himself (and "not from the consent of the Church") all the prerogatives necessary to govern, teach, and sanctify the faithful.

It is not surprising then that the word "infallibility" came to signify for most Catholics only one thing: papal infallibility. Such an erroneous conception might have prevailed universally up to the present day if it were not for other voices and currents developing between the councils. These currents would serve as major counterbalances at Vatican II.

NEWMAN: THE SENSE OF THE FAITHFUL

The churchman who perhaps most inspired a progressive theology of the twentieth century died a decade before the twentieth century began. Yet such was the impact of John Henry Newman that Pope Paul VI would call Vatican II "Newman's council." Though Newman did not attend Vatican I, he inadvertently stirred up some controversy at that meeting when the letter he wrote about his distaste for the tactics of the Infallibilists was leaked to the press. Newman, as he later made clear, believed in papal infallibility, but it was a carefully nuanced belief, far removed from the dominant papal centralism in vogue during and after the council.

He was a strong defender of freedom of conscience—so strong that his rhetorical flourishes often seemed offensive to those accustomed to a fundamentalist interpretation of religious obedience. It was precisely in relation to the dogma of infallibility that Newman made the memorable statement, "If I am obliged to bring religion into after-dinner toasts (which indeed does not seem quite the thing) I shall drink to the Pope, if you please—still to conscience first, and to the Pope afterwards."[11]

For Newman, the assent of faith could never be reduced to a matter of passive obedience. The Holy Spirit, he insisted, was active in every member of the Church, and the Spirit moved the faithful toward assent by various "instruments of discovery" including abstract logic, experience, emotion, and other subtle influences—least of all by obedient conformity. The body of the Church, he said, has an "illative sense," that is an instinct for cutting through to the truth; and this sense must always be respected. It might be said that Newman's view was in diametric opposition to the declaration of Pius X: "The Church is essentially an unequal society...comprising two categories of persons, the pastors and the flock." Since bishops and pastors alone possess authority, "the one duty of the multitudes is to allow themselves to be led and, like a docile flock, to follow the pastors."[12]

Newman's conversion from Anglicanism to Roman Catholicism

was due in great measure to his study of the early Fathers and Doctors of the Church. These ancients presented the institution as a living body, an organism with infallibility seated first and foremost within the whole. Therefore, as he saw it, doctrine (whether by pope, council, or ordinary magisterium) could determined only through a cooperative effort of hierarchy, theologians, and laity all functioning as witnesses of the faith *per modum unius* (in a unified manner). Says Newman:

> I think I am right in saying that the tradition of the Apostles committed to the whole Church…manifests itself variously at various times—sometimes by the mouth of the episcopacy, sometimes by the doctors, sometimes by the people, sometimes by liturgies, rites, ceremonies and customs, by events, disputes, movements and all those other phenomena which are comprised by the name of history.[13]

This in no way undercuts the authority of the magisterium, he adds, because the magisterium does not have sole responsibility for preserving the Church in the truth. The "sense of the faithful" must always be heard, prayed about, and weighed carefully. In his essay "On Consulting the Faithful in Matters of Doctrine," Newman explains that the whole body is not asked to provide the wording for a proposed definition; rather:

> [T]heir belief is sought for as a testimony of that apostolical tradition on which alone any doctrine whatsoever can be defined. In like manner we may "consult" the liturgies or the rites of the Church; not that they speak, not that they can take any part whatever in the definition, for they are documents or customs; but they are witnesses to the antiquity or universality of the doctrines which they contain and about which they are "consulted."

Newman saw no reason for opposition between the magisterium and the sense of the faithful, since he viewed them as two parts of the organically unified body. He identifies three key "moments" in the interaction between the magisterium and the faithful as they witness to doctrine.

First, *articulation*: The community puts into linguistic form some aspect of its inner faith.

Second, *pedagogy*: Those in the Church charged with public office discern what and how this aspect of the faith is to be taught. They "can look within the community (its Scriptures, its traditions, its theological developments, the laity's *sensus fidelium*) for the meaning of a doctrine, since church teaching is not the prophetic inspiration of new truths. Teachers, be they a council, a pope, a diocesan bishop...pray for the guidance of the Spirit in order to discern the *mind of* the church faithfully."

Third, *reception*: At this point especially, says Newman, the sense of the faithful comes into play, as the community either recognizes or does not recognize its own faith in the doctrine presented. There is therefore in Newman's view a kind of dialectical, back-and-forth interaction of hierarchy and faithful—with theologians playing a crucial role in facilitating that third key moment, reception. They provide the "arena" where meaning and interpretation are weighed and decided.

Newman did not write specifically about the ordinary universal magisterium, but his vision of teaching as a cooperative affair was considered and developed by numerous theologians of the first half of the twentieth century—those who would have great influence at Vatican II. People like Karl Rahner, Jean Danielou, Henri de Lubac, Bernard Lonergan, and John Courtney Murray seized on various insights of Newman to balance the sterility of earlier manual writers. Jesuit theologian Avery Dulles notes that the term "collegiality"—though never used by Newman—is at the heart of Newman's thinking on Church.[14]

CONGAR AND COLLEGIALITY

A second force strongly influencing Vatican II developments was the French Dominican Yves Congar. His major works, like *Lay People in the Church* and *Mystery of the Kingdom*, written in the 1950s and 1960s, came almost a hundred years after Newman's seminal writings. The hierarchy, said Congar, exists primarily for the service of the community, not to dominate it. "We must get back to the true vision of the gospel," he wrote. "Posts of authority in the Church do indeed exist; a real jurisdictional power does exist....But this power exists only within the structure of the fundamental religious relationship of the gospel, as an organizational element....So there is never simply a relationship of subordination and superiority, as in secular society, but always a loving obedience to Christ, shaping the life of each with all and for all."[15]

The pope himself, he noted, does not stand alone possessing a kind of independent jurisdiction: "The pope is not above the community but in it....He is a baptized person, who is eventually constituted in a position of authority....Thus without denying its obligations, obedience assumes an aspect of cooperation, of co-responsibility and therefore, to some degree, of dialogue."[16]

A major contention of Congar's (and one that got him in trouble with authorities) is "that the fundamental locus of ecclesiastical authority in the Church is not the papacy but the episcopal college. Papal authority is always a collegial authority."[17] He claimed that even when the pope proclaims *ex cathedra* he does so first as a bishop—the bishop of Rome—then as the head of the episcopal college that he "personalizes" in solemn definitions.

Collegiality would be a meaningless word, he explains, if the pope, independent of the bishops, had all the resources available to the episcopal body; the head is not the body and cannot substitute for it. Congar does not see episcopal teaching as a mere echo of papal teaching.

With Congar, says Gaillardetz, "the flow of authority does not start with the top of the pyramid (the pope) and move downward, neither does it start at the base of the pyramid and move upward. Rather, the power resides, first in the church itself, laity and clergy, then, most visibly, in the college as a whole. The bishops may not be viewed as mere delegates of the pope, but neither may the pope be understood as solely a spokesperson for the bishops."[18]

Congar fully accepted the infallibility of the ordinary universal magisterium. He felt, however, that "since Pius IX there has been an over-estimation of this very office, by an absurd abuse of the category of what is 'infallible.' Today we are brought back to a more evangelical authenticity: the witness of the Word of God must dominate over any pretension to define."[19] He cautioned against a creeping infallibility that tends to put a stamp of absolute truth on anything said by a pope or authorized by the Curia or a Vatican congregation—"as if between the infallible truth and error, there did not exist an immense domain of partial truth, or probable certitude, of research and approximation, or even of the very precious truth not protected from the risks of human certitude."

It should be noted that this organic approach to Church combined with a refusal to multiply absolute certainties was not easily or quickly welcomed in every segment of the Church—nor is it universally received today. Newman in his time was forced to resign as editor of the *Rambler* magazine soon after his article on consulting the faithful appeared. He was regularly accused of minimizing papal authority and claiming that truth is a relative thing. Congar, a century later, spent much of his life under a cloud of suspicion and censure. Vatican officials delayed publication of his works and, in one case, absolutely forbade the publication of a book. He once told a reporter in France, "I am not a man of the tragic, but it is painful to be the victim of stupidity." Yet time gradually tempered the furor regarding these two.[20] Both were elevated to the rank of cardinal shortly before their deaths.

Those like John Courtney Murray, Henri de Lubac, Karl Rahner, and Bernard Lonergan who have followed in their path, all had long histories of struggle with Roman authoritarianism.

CHAPTER XII

VATICAN II
AND COLLEGIALITY

*The substance of the ancient doctrine...is one thing; the way
in which it is expressed is another.*

POPE JOHN XXIII

The 2,540 bishops who assembled in Rome in September 1962
for the opening of the Second Vatican Council were a very
different group from the 719 who met 92 years earlier for Vatican I.
They came from a world so different, it would scarcely have been
recognizable to the prelates of 1870—a world of electricity and
telephones, radio and television, automobiles and airplanes. Most
of these council fathers had lived through two world wars; they
had witnessed the birth of the atomic age, the Cold War, and the
Holocaust. Those from the Western world were fully accustomed
to constitutional governments that granted freedom of speech, freedom of worship, and freedom of the press as a matter of course.
Many had been influenced by the theology of Newman, Rahner,
and Congar.

But while the world and the Church dispersed in the world had
moved ahead, the Roman Curia had not. Their Ultramontane approach, bolstered in no small way by the definition of infallibility

at Vatican I, had produced a great centralization of authority in the Roman Rota and the various sacred congregations that determined Church policy and practice. The inflexible spirit of 1870 prevailed; here, at least, Henry Manning and Ignatius von Senestréy would have felt right at home. Notes Xavier Rynne in his *Vatican Council II*:

> Men of juridical persuasion seemed to have made the posses-sion of certain religious truths the final end of their religion. There was a saying in Rome that any slip in the moral, social or political fields would eventually be forgiven, but even a minor doctrinal deviation was fatal as far as an ecclesiastical career was concerned....One of the strangest paradoxes in his-tory was that those dyed-in-the-wool Roman theologians whose theology was oriented toward combating the older Protestant shibboleth of "justification by faith alone," had all but suc-cumbed to the temptation of proclaiming a univocal religious orthodoxy as the foremost requirement by which a Catholic participated in the Church. It was as though "justification only by the scholastic definition of religious truth" were the final test.[1]

It was widely reported that Pius XII in his later years tried to rein in the Curia and failed. So he had addressed modern issues in a series of his own writings, even urging Scripture scholars to use the latest scientific discoveries to bring about a better understanding of revelation. On his death, the insiders, operating on the adage that "popes come and go but the curia remains forever," were prepared to impose the scholastic approach to philosophy and theology in seminaries worldwide and about to condemn certain progressive scholars at Roman colleges.

They were surely not prepared for the vision and determination of John XXIII, the so-called interim pope. He was eighty years old when he convened the council, yet he insisted the outcome would not be the product of a few insiders. He wanted a wide level of participation from bishops all over the world, and a vital role was reserved for the *periti*, the nonepiscopal experts. When urged to make a heavy, authoritative statement early in the council, John said, "I am not here to *tell* the Church what the Spirit says, but to observe attentively and see *in* the Church what the Spirit is saying."[2]

There was an unmistakable irony in his opening sermon. He spoke from the papal throne in St. Peter's with Cardinal Alfredo Ottaviani, secretary of the Congregation of the Holy Office, at his right hand; Cardinal Ernesto Ruffini of Palermo and Cardinal Michael Browne of Ireland in the front tier of prelates; and Archbishop Dino Staffa of the Congregation for Seminaries in the seats reserved for the highest Vatican officials. These were men in the tradition of Pius IX, fearful of change and determined to squelch innovation. They listened in mute astonishment to this aged pontiff.

He said he was tired of listening to "prophets of doom" among his advisers. "Though burning with zeal," he said, these men "are not endowed with very much sense of discretion or measure." They were, he explained, under the illusion that "at the time of the former councils everything was a triumph for the Christian idea and way of life and for true religious liberty. We feel we must disagree with these prophets of doom, who are always forecasting disaster as though the end of the world were at hand....The world expects a step forward toward a doctrinal penetration," but it should be "according to the methods of research and literary forms of modern thought....The substance of the ancient doctrine of the deposit of faith is one thing; the way in which it is expressed is another." And he added, "Nowadays, the Bride of Christ prefers to make use of the medicine of mercy rather than that of severity. She considers that she meets the needs of the present day by demonstrating the validity of her teaching rather than by condemnation."[3]

What all this meant would be played out in the course of the next three years. John himself died less than eight months after delivering that sermon, but as Cardinal Leon-Joseph Suenens of Belgium said at the memorial celebration, his influence would prevail: "John XXIII is present in our midst in a mysterious and profound way."[4]

COLLEGIALITY SUPPORTED

Vatican II, like its predecessor, had a dominant majority and a stubborn minority. Only in this case, the theological outlooks were reversed. It was the majority, personified by Suenens, who supported the *Aggiornamento*, the opening up of the windows envisioned by Pope John, and the minority, best exemplified by the seventy-two-year-old, nearly blind Ottaviani, who fought for the status quo—and in more than a few instances managed to dilute majority victories.

Vatican II created sweeping changes in approach to liturgy, ecumenism, religious liberty, and the place of the laity. Perhaps most important of all was its call for a dialogue with the modern world. "For the first time in modern history, the Church accepts the progressive cultural and social movements...which it previously regarded with much skepticism if not outright condemnation. It notes without regret the passing of old forms of thought and feeling and social relations, and while not indulging in naive optimism, it sees the possibilities for human liberation that all of this entails."[5]

The document that caused the fiercest debate was the schema on the Church—the early version of what would finally be transformed into the council constitution *Lumen Gentium*. Suenens and other majority leaders hoped to balance the one-sided papalism on which the Curia thrived by stressing the "collegial" nature of the episcopacy. The failure of Vatican I to situate papal infallibility in a well-defined relationship with the bishops (as representatives of the larger Church community) was what had so disturbed Bishop Dupanloup and other members of that council's minority. And it seemed to many that the one-sidedness had only been exacerbated during the intervening years.

That one important phrase tacked onto the definition of infallibility at the last moment—"and not from the consent of the Church"—rankled the most. It could be interpreted, of course, in a benign light, but it appeared to many to give despotic power to the pope, to place him above and, should the situation arise, even in opposition to the rest of the Church.

For Curia leaders, that phrase was critical: The Church for practical purposes was one universal diocese headed by one supreme bishop. Local bishops were vicars or managers of their assigned territories, deriving all their authority from the pope, serving at his pleasure and having no significant relationship with one another other than through friendship or occasional, informal cooperation. The newer theology, coming from Congar, Rahner, and others, saw all the bishops, including the pope, as forming one college and having, as a college, joint responsibility for the universal Church. Without denying the unique position of the pope within the college, this second view came substantially closer to connecting papal infallibility with that fundamental infallibility rooted in the whole body of the faithful.

Cardinal Ottaviani, as chairman of the council's theological commission, oversaw the creation of the proposed schema on the Church, and it was Chapter 3, the section on hierarchy, that provoked instantaneous debate when it came up for discussion during the council's first session in December 1962. The schema, complained numerous speakers, was little more than a rehash of the old triumphalistic, Ultramontane approach, full of juridical terms and preoccupied with the Church's rights. The guardianship of the deposit of the faith is not the responsibility of the magisterium alone, as the document seems to imply, said Cardinal Joseph Ritter of St. Louis; all ranks in the Church share in it. Bishop Emile de Smedt of Belgium found the document's tone of clericalism offensive. The Church is not a pyramid of people, priests, bishops, and pope, he said, but the people of God, all endowed with rights and responsibilities for the whole organism. Another bishop said the Church appears "in this trite document" as a static entity, a kind of impersonal corporation with world headquarters in Rome.[6]

Some council fathers did rise up in defense of Ottaviani's handiwork. Italian Bishop Joseph Sarli, a curial associate, lamented that the Church was becoming too complacent, lacking in resolve to strike out against the errors of the day. And Polish bishop Louis Bernacki even regretted that papal prerogatives were not receiving more prominence in the schema. He suggested that the Creed should be altered to state, "I believe in the Holy, Catholic and Petrine Church...." The council president eventually cut him off for exceeding his time limit.

Two key speeches determined the outcome of the discussion. Cardinal Suenens said Vatican I had clearly been the council of papal primacy, so Vatican II should be the council of the larger Church, both as "the people of God and the light of the nations." He was loudly applauded. Cardinal John Baptist Montini of Milan, generally regarded as Pope John's spokesman, said it was the duty of this body to "define the collegiality of the episcopate" and raise the image of each bishop as the image of Christ. He strongly urged that the schema be returned to the theological commission for a complete revision based on the comments of the fathers and the more than three hundred suggested amendments turned in. To this the council quickly agreed.

THE "WEIGHTIEST" ISSUE

When Vatican II resumed in the fall of 1963, Pope John was dead, and Cardinal Giovanni Battista Montini had been transformed into Pope Paul VI. The redrafted schema on the Church was so remarkably different that many doubted it was the product of the original commission. Rumor had it that Karl Rahner and Jean Danielou had a hand in reconstructing it, and that it reached its new form only after a bitter struggle within the commission itself. When discussion resumed before the full council in September, both Ottaviani, the chairman, and Cardinal Michael Browne, the vice chairman, remained unusually subdued.

The subject of collegiality was debated for nine full days—the longest discussion of any issue during the council's second session. Observed Rynne: "The debate on collegiality was in fact the primary raison d'être for the second session and constituted the

core of the new vision of herself which the Church must acquire."[7]
In his opening address, Pope Paul called collegiality the "weighti-
est and most delicate issue" before the council and made clear his
personal sentiments. Approval of the doctrine, he said, "will certainly be what distinguishes this solemn and historic synod in the
memory of future ages."[8]

A first consideration was the seemingly abstruse question of
whether a bishop receives at his consecration only the power of
ordaining priests or whether he also receives jurisdiction—that is,
the authority to teach, govern and sanctify. It had long been commonly held in Rome that jurisdiction comes not from consecration but only from a canonical appointment by the pope himself.
The revised schema contradicted this, claiming a bishop obtains
the fullness of authority not from the pope but from his consecration and admission into the episcopal college. The purpose of this
shift was to elevate the bishop beyond the level of papal appointee. It soon became clear that the Curia would not mount any major
opposition on this matter, though its leadership disliked its implications.

On the grittier issue of collegiality, no quick consensus was possible. The argument was not whether bishops on occasion might
act collegially, in a unified manner, on an issue of importance.
Obviously, every ecumenical council involved collegial activity by
the whole episcopate. The real argument was about whether collegiality was of divine origin—that, is established by Christ—or
whether it was only an ecclesiastical practice that could be supported or abrogated as the pope saw fit. The newly proposed text
in the chapter on the hierarchy (section 22), asserted explicitly
that collegiality came from Christ:

> Just as, by the Lord's will, St. Peter and the other apostles con-
> stituted one apostolic college, so in a similar way the Roman
> Pontiff as the successor of Peter and the bishops as successors
> of the apostles are joined together. The collegial nature and
> meaning of the episcopal order found expression in the very
> ancient practice by which bishops appointed the world over

were linked with one another and with the bishop of Rome by
bonds of unity, charity and peace.[9]

The minority viewed this as a dangerous infringement on papal
primacy. Said Cardinal Ruffini: "I am not convinced that Christ
constituted the apostles as a college or that the episcopal college
succeeded the apostolic college, for, with the exception of the Council in Jerusalem [in the first century], the apostles did not act in a
collegial manner."[10]

Declared Cardinal Siri: "It is easy to prove that the apostles made
up one body and received a collective mission. But it is quite another thing to prove that the bishops of the Church constitute a
college....Wrongly understood, it could imply that the bishops
might sometimes force the hand of the pope, but this would contradict the teaching of Vatican I."

Brazilian archbishop de Poenca-Sigaud claimed: "Collegiality has
no basis either in the Bible, in tradition, or in the history of the
Church....It would give rise to a lack of discipline....This would
mean that the government of the Church was not monarchical
but collegiate." Bishops, he said, are not responsible for the whole
Church but only for a portion of it, which they had in their charge
by the Roman pontiff. "Care should be taken to avoid setting up
anything resembling a world parliament of bishops governing the
Church conjointly with the Roman pontiff."

One reason for the opposition (in addition to the Curia's general resistance to change) was that no one really knew what collegiality meant or how it would operate in practice. But the majority
remained convinced a balance to papal independence was impera-
tive. The speech that had the most telling effect was delivered by
the bearded, eighty-seven-year-old Patriarch Maximos IV Saigh, the
Melkite patriarch of Antioch. Since Vatican I, he said, papal primacy had been exaggerated through abusive interpretations and
was now more than ever an obstacle to reunion with the Orthodox churches of the East. If this body really hoped to set a tone for
eventual reunion of the people of God, declared Maximos, "it

should clarify and complete the doctrine of the primacy by acknowledging the rights of the episcopate."

Cardinal Franz König of Vienna and Cardinal Albert Meyer of Chicago echoed those words, insisting that collegiality was in no way a new teaching, that it now had the support of the theological commission and was fully backed by Pope Paul himself. Still, minority bishops persisted that "strange innovations," possibly even a schism, might be spawned by encouraging bishops to think and operate in an authoritative way beyond their own borders.

THREE MODES OF INFALLIBILITY

The chapter on hierarchy also contained a crucial, densely worded section (25) on the infallibility of bishops, which was in effect an attempt to clarify the meaning of the "ordinary universal magisterium":

> Although the individual bishops do not enjoy the prerogative of infallibility, they can nevertheless proclaim Christ's doctrine infallibly. This is so, even when they are dispersed around the world, provided that while maintaining the bond of unity among themselves and with Peter's successor, and while teaching authentically on a matter of faith or morals, they concur in a single viewpoint as the one which must be held conclusively.[11]

The wording used here, concerning those matters about which the bishops may proclaim infallibly, is very similar to that used regarding papal infallibility at Vatican I. They are matters "which must be held" (*tenenda* in Latin), a rather vague term that could include both doctrines contained in the deposit of faith (doctrines that must be believed) and other items that are only "related" to faith.

This was followed, however, by a sentence that seemed to restrict the scope of infallibility to faith matters strictly speaking: "This infallibility with which the Divine Redeemer willed his

Church to be endowed in defining a doctrine of faith and morals extends as far as extends the deposit of divine revelation." That seemed to finally end debate on the scope of infallibility; infallibility applies to Scripture and tradition, not to so-called "related" matters. (Yet more than thirty years after Vatican II, a wider interpretation of infallibility would be proposed again in the dispute over the ordination of women.)

The next sentence states that this narrower interpretation also affects the pope: "This is the infallibility the Roman pontiff... enjoys...when...he proclaims by a definitive act some doctrine of faith or morals." That is, the pope's charism of infallibility, like that of the Church itself, extends only to the deposit of faith.

A third paragraph stated the sort of infallibility that was appropriate to ecumenical councils: "The infallibility promised to the Church resides also in the body of bishops when that body exercises supreme teaching authority with the successor of Peter."

Thus, in less than one thousand words, Vatican II bishops had a précis of the three modes of infallible teaching the Church might exercise. Little argument or discussion ensued over these sections. One bishop, J. Discuffi of Turkey, suggested that after the phrase, "and not from the consent of the Church," there be added the qualifying words, "namely, by a special divine assistance." He also suggested the word "consent" be changed to the word "assent."[12] But he got little support for these changes. It appeared the wording on papal infallibility was too sensitive, too volatile to tinker with directly; the majority preferred to concentrate on a straightforward pronouncement concerning their own authority, thereby softening and balancing the notion of a unilateral, independent, or isolated papal infallibility.

The vote on individual articles in Chapter 3 was held during the council's third session in September 1964. Although it seemed certain that collegiality would pass by a wide margin, the minority would not surrender without a fight. At the start of this session, Pope Paul received a letter signed by fourteen bishops, including Cardinal Ruffini, urging him to remove the entire schema on the

Church from the council agenda because it was rife with "heretical doctrine." These prelates, who referred to themselves as "the remnant of Israel," were praying for divine intervention to halt the heresy of collegiality, should the pope turn a deaf ear. And he did— for the moment. "The Holy Spirit has intervened," he told the group. He inspired Pope John to summon the council and he has given us the courage to carry on the directives of his divine will."[13]

At the council sessions, Archbishop Pietro Parente, the assessor of the Holy Office, provided an unexpected boost for collegiality. As a curial member, he had opposed the concept, claimed the arguments favoring it were indecisive, and argued that a proclamation of the doctrine would be "inopportune." Now however, he urged everyone to approve the text. Fears were groundless, he said, and even though "the peace has not yet been achieved," no good would be accomplished by fighting on. Accordingly, the articles in the chapter were passed by substantial majorities—with most garnering only about 100 negative votes out of some 2,100 cast. The greatest resistance, as expected, centered on collegiality itself, with 328 bishops voting against the idea. So intransigent (and seemingly confused) were some minority members that they ended up voting against everything in the third chapter, including one article that states Holy Orders is a sacrament and another that says the pope has "supreme authority." Commented one bishop, "So determined are the opposition, they are willing to risk heresy to prove their point."[14] Thus, collegiality appeared firmly established as an important first fruit of Vatican II.

THE EXPLANATORY NOTE

But the majority underestimated the Curia's resourcefulness and overestimated Pope Paul's unambiguous commitment to a clear approbation of the collegial principle. Ten days after the vote, the theological commission was informed that "because the pope was obliged to make his own and promulgate the Constitution on the Church, he wanted an explanatory note added to it dealing with the meaning and import" of the certain parts of the text. The commission should create wording that "would relieve the doubts of the minority and thus bring about a unanimous acceptance of the schema." (The schema "as a whole" had not yet been voted on.)[15]

As dutifully prepared by the commission, the note said first: the term "college" was not to be understood in a strictly juridical sense as a body of equals who delegated their powers to a president; it should be understood in a "unique, Christian sense." Second, though the bishops do receive jurisdictional powers at consecration (as the council had just approved), the exercise of these powers must be according to "norms approved by the supreme authority." Third, the episcopal college does have full authority over the Church, but that doesn't prevent the pope from acting on his own in a noncollegial manner. And fourth, the episcopal college acts collegially only "occasionally or at intervals," and only with "the consent of its head."[16]

Proponents of collegiality were at first abashed. This complicated, obscurely worded note seemed on the surface to compromise and confuse all they had achieved. However, after considerable soul-searching and discussion, majority leaders decided the explanatory note did not eviscerate the basic concept of collegiality, and they did not object. Privately, they marveled at the exquisite resourcefulness of the entrenched Curia members, who were able to snatch a modicum of victory out of the jaws of apparent defeat. On November 17, 1964, the full Constitution on the Church, *Lumen Gentium*, was approved by a moral unanimity of council fathers, 2,100–46.

The concept of collegiality, as qualified by the papal note, has been discussed by theologians ever since, with varying interpretations on its practical applications and limits. Its most intriguing outcome may be its application to all levels of the institutional Church. Observes theologian Monika Hellwig:

> If the bishops are expected to reflect, discern and act together, being jointly responsible...in the redemptive transformation

of the world, this suggests something about the whole struc-
turing of the life of the Church. It prompts questions about
what it means to be the community of the faithful within each
diocese, within each parish. It suggests that communal dis-
cernment in which all participate actively...is an integral part
of being called into the Church.[17]

Whatever the applications, commentators tend to view the approval of collegiality as a major outcome of the council. By situat-
ing the pope within the episcopal body, by relating his infallibility
with the infallibility of the bishops, Vatican II solved, to some degree, the problems lingering from Vatican I.

Yet, for all its decrees and declarations and constitutions, Vatican
II did not make any solemn definitions. In keeping with Pope John's
appeal to the "medicine of mercy," there are no anathemas here,
no demands for submission under pain of sin. Theologians were
left to speculate on the relative theological weight of the various
sections. Though Vatican II's pronouncements are therefore not
infallible in themselves, much of what the council proclaimed had
already been defined in previous ecumenical councils or might be
considered a matter of faith through the universal ordinary
magisterium of the bishops.

HUMANAE VITAE AND ORDINARY MAGISTERIUM

In the practical order, interpreting the universal ordinary magisterium has proved to be an extraordinarily difficult task. A vexing
problem developed within a year of the close of the council in late
1965. Before his death in 1963, Pope John had authorized the formation of a special pontifical commission to advise him on the
morality of birth control. Because of the commission's existence,
the council was advised not to consider issues of birth prevention.
The commission was continued in existence by Pope Paul and eventually met for five sessions, its membership growing from six at
the first meeting to seventy-two at its last marathon gathering in
the spring of 1966.

Members of the commission included theologians, demographers, psychologists, medical doctors, sociologists, and even three married couples, all of whom were intimately conversant with various aspects of population, marital relations, the human psyche, and Catholic morality. In the early stages, the commission members felt no change was possible in the Church's traditional opposition to contraceptive acts as intrinsically evil. Pope Pius XI's 1930 encyclical *Casti Connubii* seemed a final, possibly infallible, word on the matter. Later, though, on the basis of their research and discussion (with the testimony of the married couples holding great weight), the majority of the commission (reportedly by a vote of 52–4 at one point) concurred that the absolute ban could and should be revoked. In their report to Pope Paul, they said the arguments of *Casti Connubii* were "vague and imprecise." They noted the significant changes that had occurred since 1930 in understanding the multiple purposes of sexual union and the development of doctrine on the meaning of Christian marriage. Besides, said the commission, the issue of contraception was a matter of the natural law and not of revelation; therefore it was not subject to settlement by an infallible decree.

Under the leadership of the American Jesuit theologian John Ford, the four dissenting commission members filed a minority report, which stated, in effect, that the ban on artificial contraception was irreversible because the Church had always and everywhere upheld it. If now the doctrine could be changed, they said, the Church's teaching authority would be undermined, *Casti Connubii* would be discredited, and the faithful would be led down the slippery slope of moral relativism.

Pope Paul pondered these matters for two years and eventually agreed with the minority theologians. In his 1968 encyclical *Humanae Vitae*, he reiterated that artificial contraception was forbidden. His position, he said, was based not so much on "intrinsic arguments" but on the authority of the Church as the "depository and interpreter of the moral law." In announcing the decision, however, the papal spokesman, Francesco Lambruschini, insisted

Humanae Vitae was not an infallible document, though it required "loyal and full assent both interior and exterior" as an authentic pronouncement of the papal magisterium.[18]

Humanae Vitae stirred an enormous debate about Church authority—a debate that continues thirty-four years later. Many theologians, most notably Charles Curran, said Catholics could dissent from noninfallible teaching in good conscience, especially when an official teaching is "not received" by a substantial part of the Church. In 1986 Curran was removed from his post at the Catholic University of America when the Congregation for the Doctrine of the Faith ruled that "one who dissents from the magisterium as you do is not suitable to teach Catholic theology."[19]

But the question remained: If the ban on contraception was not taught infallibly in *Humanae Vitae*, wasn't it already taught infallibly by the universal ordinary magisterium? Ten years after the encyclical, John Ford and his associate Germain Grisez made a major effort to answer that question affirmatively in an article in *Theological Studies* magazine. Basing their arguments on the precise wording of the third chapter of *Lumen Gentium*, they declared that historical studies testify that the condemnation of contraception "was universally proposed by Catholic bishops up to 1962."[20] That the consensus had weakened in recent years does not lessen the argument, they said, because "what is once infallibly proposed must always afterward be accepted with absolute assurance of its truth. Their presentation hearkened back to Pietro Olivi, the thirteenth-century so-called "inventor" of papal infallibility; it was he who hoped to use the doctrine to tie the hands of future change-minded pontiffs. Echoing Olivi, Ford-Grisez said, "Once the truth about what Christ commanded has been proclaimed infallibly, every opinion incompatible with it must always afterward be excluded."[21] Finally, they explained, it does not matter whether the ban is found in revelation, since it is "connected" with revelation; it is a truth needed to guard the deposit of faith. In other words, the ban, according to Ford-Grisez, is a "secondary object" that can be infallibly taught in order to protect a primary object—in this case, the integrity of Christian marriage.

Some theologians found the argument compelling. Most did not. Says Francis Sullivan: "It is true of course that if something was indeed taught infallibly, subsequent dissent cannot negate it. But to fulfill the conditions required for the infallible teaching of the ordinary universal magisterium, the consensus must not only be universal; it must also be constant."[22] Yet even Ford and Grisez admitted the consensus has been anything but constant in the past thirty-four years.

Richard Gaillardetz notes the extreme difficulty in determining whether a particular teaching has been universally taught over the ages or only taught by a few bishops, ignored by some, and accepted under duress by still others.

In any case, says Sullivan, Catholics may surely follow the 1983 *Code of Canon Law* which states, "No doctrine is understood to be infallibly defined unless this fact is clearly established."

If in the matter of contraception the ordinary magisterium can be established only doubtfully and amid great theologial complexity, neither can it be easily established, declare theologians, in scores of other, similar issues where Church teaching is arguably ordinary and universal. This is not to say such teaching may be ignored or disrespected—only that its infallible character cannot be assumed on casual inspection. The response to Ford-Grisez is indicative of a fairly common trend among theologians in the wake of Vatican II to proceed with extreme caution in assigning a grade of infallibility to Church teaching on the basis of the ordinary universal magisterium.

CHAPTER XIII

THE REVISIONISTS

*If infallibility is a genuine element in the mystery of the church,
then...it may be understood in a plurality of ways.*

JOHN T. FORD, C.S.C.

D uring the Second Vatican Council and for many years after,
Hans Küng was probably the most popular theologian in the
Catholic Church. He was thirty-three when he published *The Council, Reform and Reunion* one year before Vatican II got under way.
The book became a bestseller with its vision of an open, fearless
Catholicism, admitting past mistakes and opening its arms to the
world in much the way John XXIII was doing in his own person at
that time. The tremendous public expectation that swirled around
the council proceedings was due in part to the hopes raised by
Küng, a Swiss theologian at the University of Tübingen. In subsequent years, he lectured all over the world about the council and
its long range implications, while producing a series of weighty
works of progressive theology (*The Structures of the Church*, 1964,
On Being a Christian, 1966, *The Church*, 1967).

None of his earlier works had quite the impact of *Infallibility?
An Inquiry*, published in 1970. In this relatively slim volume, Küng
shocked much of the Catholic world with a full-blown attack on

173

the doctrine of infallibility from many sides. Because of who he was, the book provoked broad reaction from every segment of the Christian world and beyond. Karl Rahner was so incensed that he at first accused Küng of becoming a "liberal Protestant." Dozens of books and hundreds of articles appeared over the next five years, some congratulating Küng for his candor, others condemning him for treason. It was evident that the young man had touched a raw nerve.

To be sure, Vatican II had softened the hardest edge of papal infallibility by its appeal to collegiality. But for many Catholics as well as Küng, this wasn't enough. They saw too many problems and inconsistencies in the basic idea. An infallible pope and an infallible magisterium somehow did not seem consistent with the humble, honest Church modeled at Vatican II. More than anything since Count Joseph de Maistre's eighteenth-century book *The Pope*, Küng's work stimulated reappraisals of this complex and confusing concept.

Infallibility? An Inquiry was no masterpiece of organization. More than a few critics noticed how the tone differed from the careful, scholarly style of Küng's earlier works. He moves in many directions at once and even appears at times to be contradicting himself. Yet the overall impact is potent.

His starting point is the encyclical *Humanae Vitae*, in which Pope Paul VI condemned artificial contraception. Strangely enough, Küng agrees wholeheartedly with the argument of the so-called minority report submitted by four members of the Pontifical Birth Control Commission in 1966. John Ford and his associates had contended no pope could ever rescind (or even soften) the birth-control ban because it had been enforced universally by the Church. "The documentation produced by the conservative minority, who controlled the archives of the Holy Office...is in fact overwhelming," says Küng. "It consists of solemn statements of popes, of bishops' conferences on every continent, of many outstanding cardinals and bishops as also of the universal teaching of theologians: the aim being to prove that, according to the universal consensus of the ecclesiastical teaching office at least in the present century...it is a question of a universal teaching...binding under pain of grave sin.... In other words, the curial group did not use a particular encyclical or papal address as an argument....They appealed to the ordinary consensus in teaching of pope and bishops, that is to what is known as the *ordinary*, everyday teaching office."[1]

Küng drives home his point repeatedly: It makes no difference that the pope did not consider *Humanae Vitae* infallible; it makes no difference whether the earlier marriage encyclical, *Casti Connubii*, is infallible; it makes no difference that no council has solemnly defined the matter and no pope has proclaimed *ex cathedra* that artificial birth control is evil. It has already been infallibly declared evil by the ordinary universal magisterium—and that is all it takes. That is why, in Küng's view, Pope Paul had no choice but to repeat the ban in his encyclical. And that is why, he explains, Cardinal Pericle Felici of the Curia could state so authoritatively in *L'Osservatore Romano*: "Since they are not confronted with an *ex cathedra* definition, some conclude that the teaching is not infallible and thus that there is a possibility of change....It must be kept in mind that a truth can be sure and certain and therefore binding even with the charism of an ex cathedra definition, as in fact is the case with...*Humanae Vitae*."[2]

The best arguments of the majority members of the birth control commission were not persuasive, says Küng, because they did not take into consideration the infallible character of ordinary universal teaching.

INDEFECTIBLE OR INFALLIBLE?

For Ford, that closed the door on the subject. For Küng, it opened up a whole corridor of doors, allowing him to turn Ford's argument on its head. This clearly infallible ban on contraception, he says— a ban so unacceptable in the modern world on moral and humanitarian grounds, so generally repudiated by Catholic laity, so ignored by clergy—establishes that infallibility itself is a fatally flawed concept that must be discarded by the Church. He goes on in detail to point out the perennial weaknesses in the doctrine:

- The supportive citations from Scripture may have persuasive merit but do not prove beyond doubt the necessity for infallibility as defined at the two Vatican councils.
- Lapses by popes (and councils) are too numerous throughout history to ignore or explain away; the attempt to make everything cohere has only kept Church apologists busy trying to put out fires that won't be extinguished.
- The concept of papal infallibility itself is rooted in part on forged documents and did not appear explicitly until it was developed by an eccentric Franciscan friar in the thirteenth century.
- The qualifications imposed on papal infallibility by the councils notwithstanding, it must be recognized that even now "no one can prevent the pope from proceeding arbitrarily and autocratically in questions of doctrine—fallible or infallible. Of course, he is tied...to revelation and the faith of the Church. But the pope makes his own decision and with the means that seem to him appropriate on what this revelation is meant to say and what is the true faith of the Church." This holds for all matters of faith and morals and everything that Roman opinion includes under this heading...The teaching of Vatican I really amounts to this: if he wants, the pope can do everything even without the Church."[3]

Given the situation, Küng proposes a way out. The Church must face facts forthrightly and stop excusing itself through embarrassing subterfuges. "The Achilles heel of the Roman theory of infallibility...is ultimately a lack of faith...," he says. "People have become so accustomed to identifying the 'Church' (or better, the 'hierarchy') with the Holy Spirit that, if certain errors, aberrations, deviations and mistakes of the Church have to be admitted, they think they have to burden the Holy Spirit with those errors."[4]

A more accurate and fitting term to describe the Spirit's perennial protection of the Church, he argues, is "indefectibility": "The church will persist in the truth IN SPITE OF all ever possible errors!....What is meant here is that, no matter how ominous the

Church's deviation from truth in a particular instance may be, no matter how the Church—like Israel before her—may be constantly undecided and doubting, and sometimes even erring and falling away, 'he will be with you for ever, that Spirit of truth.' The Church will not succumb to the power of lies."[5]

Küng contends that indefectibility is more than an idealistic verbal theory and insists it does not negate the Church's authoritative teaching office, that it does not exclude certainty regarding the propositions of faith, and that it is perfectly in accord with Scripture and tradition. Also, he notes, a switch from infallibility to indefectibility would hasten the return of Protestant and Orthodox Christians into the one Church—a goal he wrote about so movingly in his first book, *The Council, Reform and Reunion.*

As many were quick to point out, Küng's argumentation is subject to serious criticism. He is, of course, especially vulnerable on his assertion that the ban on contraception is an infallible teaching by reason of the ordinary universal magisterium. As noted in the previous chapter, there is no consensus among theologians or historians that the ban has been universal and constant in the Church, nor is there agreement that the issue—contraception—is directly related to divine Revelation (and therefore eligible for an infallible judgment).

Rahner was among those who upbraided Küng for seeming to demand absolute proofs from Scripture and traditions as a condition for accepting the doctrine. There is, he pointed out, a wide and necessary berth left for the exercise of faith in Church teaching.

In his complaint about the seeming omnipotence of the pope, critics said, Küng appears to be adopting the sort of unharnessed interpretation of infallibility much preferred by Manning and other Ultramontane rather than the somewhat moderate, conditioned sort as explained by Bishop Gasser even at Vatican I.

According to many commentators in the Küng-inspired debate, popular misunderstanding of infallibility's limited nature and purpose is the doctrine's biggest drawback, and they accused Küng of fostering and exploiting misunderstanding. But others commended him for bringing the difficult doctrine out into the light of day even if he did it in a confrontational manner. Authorities in Rome proved less understanding. Citing Küng's treatment of infallibility and his "contempt for the magisterium of the Church," the Congregation for the Faith ruled in 1979, nine years after the release of the book, that "he can no longer be considered a Catholic theologian nor function as such in a teaching role."[6] Küng was removed from his faculty post at Tübingen but remained a priest in good standing and was not accused of heresy. He continued on as director of ecumenical research at Tübingen until his recent retirement.

A Flourishing of New Ideas

Among those whose ideas received greater illumination due to Hans Küng was U.S.-born Bishop Francis Simons, a missionary in India. Two years before Küng's book appeared, Simons, in his own book, *Infallibility and the Evidence,* offered a philosophical critique that can be reduced to a kind of syllogism: One can assent to something as revealed by God only if that person has moral certitude that God revealed it; but one achieves such certitude only thorough noninfallible, human judgments; therefore humans can attain at best human certitude in knowledge, religious or otherwise. His argument was similar to that posed by Anglican theologian Austin Farrar: If revelation is historical, how can it be infallibly declared, "for facts are not determined by authority" but verified through fallible historiographical methods? Accordingly, infallibility "looks like a hybrid notion arising out of confusion" between two functions—"making law and interpreting evidence."[7]

Like Küng, Simons claims the New Testament does not prove the Church's infallibility, let alone the pope's. Divine assistance is promised to the apostles and the Church, he acknowledges, but that is not the same as infallibility.

Temple University historian Leonard Swidler agrees with Küng that infallibility has caused Catholics to twist and bend history to suit their purposes. "To ignore or play with historical data, as has been done time and again in an attempt to maintain some sort of rigid notion of infallibility, of always being right, is totally unworthy of a sincere human being and Christian."[8]

Why not, asks Swidler, apply the same principles of interpretation to doctrines that are already in vogue in sacred Scripture? "It was not so long ago," he says, when "literal inerrancy of the Bible was maintained with...solemnity and vigor....Now Scripture scholars habitually [make] distinctions in scriptural texts between the time-bound language, concepts, myths and values of the periods which biblical writers used, and the essential religious and... specifically Christian messages contained in those vehicles....Such a distinction between the passing and permanent elements in the Bible is of course also applied regularly in the crucial area of social and moral values [in the Bible]. If it is legitimate to make such distinctions in the inspired word of Scripture, is it not also legitimate to make similar distinctions in the non-inspired words of ecclesiastical documents, conciliar and papal, since they presumably are of less weight than the Bible?"

Swidler leans strongly toward Küng's suggestion. "It might be better to speak of the indefectibility of the Church," he says, "and leave infallibility to be purged in the communal dark night of the soul." In any event, in Swidler's view, the development of the doctrine of infallibility is "most probably another example of a part of Catholic tradition whose significance is perhaps very largely negative in implication, that is its lesson is...largely and tragically, that of what ought not to be done in the future."

A novel approach (in this century) is that of historian Francis Oakley, whose 1969 book *Council Over Pope* received little notice until Küng stirred the waters. Oakley is an unrepentant conciliarist who believes the old doctrine can be rehabilitated for the modern age. He uses the fifteenth-century Council of Constance as his centerpiece. That was the ecumenical council that solved the dilemma of the three competing popes by deposing two, accepting the resignation of the third, and electing a new pope, Martin V. In the council document *Haec Sancta* the council fathers declared that anyone of any rank, condition, or office, "even the papal one," is obligated to obey the decrees of a lawful ecumenical assembly. In other words, a council has priority over a pope.

That decree, argues Oakley, was not (as generally assumed) a one-time, stop-gap provision: "It fulfilled all the conditions necessary to make it a dogmatic decree and one which...binds in faith."[9] Indeed, notes Oakley, the legitimacy of Martin V and all subsequent popes depends on the legitimacy of Constance as an authoritative body. What was defined, he says, was not some kind of radical conciliarism that would turn over the regular administration of the Church to the council, but rather a recognition of the ecumenical council as a "control authority" during emergency situations.

It is true of course that the decision of Constance on this matter was contradicted and annulled by a pope thirty years later, and most scholars have regarded *Haec Sancta* as an example of positive constitutional law and therefore fully subject to nullification by a later legislator. But in Oakley's view, the tenacious persistence of conciliarism long after Constance, especially in its Gallican form, means the full Church never forgot or rejected the idea of benign, conciliar control over unrestricted papal power. Since Constance and the two Vatican councils remain in direct conflict on the subject of supreme authority, Oakley hopes for a new general council "capable of dealing with the present crisis in a decisive and uninhibited fashion, a council...much more broadly and directly representative of the Church as a whole (laity as well as clergy) and much more fully in control of its agenda...than any of the great modern councils."

Realistically, he doesn't see much chance of this happening, but hopes the very predicament of competing ecclesiologies may one day force the Church to cease attaching tags of infallibility to particular council or papal decrees and admit "the historicity, the relativity, the reformability of all doctrinal pronouncements."

Küng's initiative produced an understandably positive response from Orthodox Christians, who have long viewed both papal primacy and infallibility as grave obstacles. If these obstacles could be removed, says Oreste Kéramé, secretary to the Greek-Catholic patriarch of Antioch, a great healing would occur, "for the Catholic Church is, without the Orthodox Church, only half a Church."[10] When the East separated from the West in 1094, he notes, real collegiality ceased by that very fact. Henceforth, the East did not recognize the validity of any of the subsequent ecumenical councils, since they were not really ecumenical—with episcopal representation from the whole world—but only "Western" councils. Kéramé draws encouragement from Vatican II's embrace of collegiality, but insists it must be an inclusive "collegiality of the fullest sort" if it is to bear fruit.

Reunion, he insists, will require removing the trappings of the old ways, among which is the doctrine of infallibility along with such terms as "vicar of Christ" and "supreme pontiff."

"Primacy," however, is not one of the notions that must be purged. That the pope represents "a certain real primacy...is a conclusion that could be reached on scriptural grounds and on...traditional ground....That this primacy belongs de facto to no other than the bishop of Rome is something no one can deny on historical grounds."

Brian Tierney, the historian who uncovered the thirteenth-century origins of infallibility, seized the occasion of Küng's book to argue that the doctrine is far more a historical oddity than a belief that belonged to the ancient and constant faith of the Church over the ages: "The doctrine did not emerge inevitably because it had always been presupposed. It was invented almost fortuitously because an unusual concatenation of historical circumstance arose which made such a doctrine useful to a particular group of Franciscan controversialists."[11] An inordinate amount of double-talk is required to preserve the doctrine, he says. "It is the defenders of the doctrine of papal infallibility who labor most diligently to render the doctrine meaningless. It is the defenders of the doctrine who tell us that the plain words 'irreformable in itself' really mean 'all papal definitions are open to reinterpretation.' With friends like this, one might think that the doctrine...hardly needs enemies."

NEW ASPECTS OF THE DOCTRINE

Not every scholar has been as anxious as these to throw out the baby with the bath. While admitting the validity of many objections, they insist infallibility can be understood in a positive way, especially if there is an effort to take difficulties seriously and not put them down with simplistic citations from official Church documents. Neither excessively historical analysis nor dense, abstract rational argumentation seems likely to produce much clarity. Responding to Küng, theologian Gregory Baum observed, "The reinterpretation of doctrine is not a logical, psychological or metaphysical process. It is a vital process. It includes the Church's own religious experience. It takes place as Christians understand themselves and their mission in a new way. At such times the Church will enter a crisis in regard to her truth. Only as Christians continue to listen to God's Word, take their own religious experience seriously, and engage in conversation with the whole community, will the Church gain a new self-understanding and acquire a secure perspective on the gospel."[12] Not to be overlooked by the believing Christian, says Baum, is "the creative role the Spirit enabling the Church "to discern the focal point of the gospel in new historical situations. I see no reason why this special gift should not be called 'infallibility.'"

Virtually every theologian who accepts infallibility as a viable concept also agrees on a pressing need to reconsider or "reconceptualize" it.

Says Jesuit Ladislas Orsy, "Infallibility may be a clumsy term, but it tries to express a wondrous deed—the mysterious and permanent presence of the Word in the Church."[13]

J. P. Kenny would define it as "the Uncreated Gift of the Spirit working with the church, a gift which is operative through the created gift of the sacramental character of the episcopacy."

According to A. Chavisse, "The infallibility of the Church is nothing else than the fruit of the divine fidelity to the promise of indefectibility and the efficacious assistance that does not compromise the fallibility proper to creatures."

Says John T. Ford, a Holy Cross theologian (not the Jesuit John F. Ford of the Birth Control Commission), "If infallibility is a genuine element in the mystery of the Church, then, like any other divinely bestowed gift, it may function and be understood in a plurality of ways. Such a view is unlikely to be acceptable either to those who wish an unequivocal repudiation of infallibility or to those who wish to maintain an absolutistic concept of dogma in general and infallibility in particular. Yet a commonality between absolutization and rejection should be recognized."[14]

The reconsideration is more necessary than ever now when Catholics and other Christians are taking gradual steps toward reunion. Comments Jesuit theologian Avery Dulles, "In an era of ecumenism this dogma seems to erect unnecessary barriers between Catholics and other Christians; in an era of rapid change it seems to tie the church unnecessarily to the past. Besides, papal infallibility has hardly proved fruitful in terms of concrete results. Only on one occasion in the last hundred years has the pope clearly claimed to speak infallibly, and that was in proclaiming the most notoriously problematical of dogmas—the Assumption....Unquestionably then, the dogma of infallibility is now ripe for reexamination."[15]

A substantial exercise in reexamination occurred between 1973 and 1978 as part of an ongoing dialogue between representatives of the U.S. Bishops Committee for Ecumenism and Interreligious Affairs and the national Committee of the Lutheran World Federation. The twenty-two participants, including Avery Dulles and George Tavard on the Catholic side and Paul Empie and George Lindbeck on the Lutheran side, spent nine sessions wrestling with their understanding of infallibility and looking for possible convergences. They found some, though they were unable to come to complete consensus.[16] Among the agreements:

> In accordance with scriptural promises and through the continued presence of the risen Christ...through the Holy Spirit, the church will remain to the end of time with an *indefectibility* in which the truth of the gospel...will persevere.

> This indefectibility involves a Ministry of Word and Sacrament together with structures (such as councils and synods) charged with the teaching of Christian doctrine and with... supervision...including the *mandate* for bishops or leaders to *judge doctrine and condemn doctrine* that is *contrary to the gospel.*
>
> There may appropriately be a Ministry *in the universal church* responsible to further its unity and mission.
>
> Such a ministry would have the responsibility of overseeing the church's proclamation and, as needed, of *reformulating doctrine in fidelity to the Scriptures,* the sign of such fidelity being the *harmony between the teaching of the Ministers and its acceptance by the faithful.*

This is obviously some distance from the doctrine of Vatican I and II, but it opens vistas for further exploration. An especially interesting outcome of the dialogue was the presentation of "new aspects" of infallibility as compiled by the Catholic participants. In sum, they reveal how substantially the concept of infallibility has already been reexamined and reconceptualized by theologians in the light of the Second Vatican Council.

1. Vatican II made it clearer that the infallibility of the pastors (pope and bishops) must be related to the ..."sense of faith" possessed by the entire people of God. The popes and bishops are infallible insofar as they are assisted in giving official expression...to what is *already* the faith of the Church as a whole....

2. Vatican II saw the infallibility of the pope as closely connected with the college of bishops, even referring to him as "head of the college of bishops."

3. Vatican II pointed out that while no antecedent or subsequent juridical approval by the church is necessary for the exercise of infallibility, the assent of the church can never be wanting to an authentic definition.

4. Vatican II placed the teaching of the pope in the context of a pilgrim church. His definitions reflect the situation of a church whose task is to show forth the mystery of the Lord....In other

words, such definitions will inevitably suffer from a *certain obscurity.*

5. Vatican II recognized that the Church...is always affected by human finitude and sinfulness...failings that may leave their mark even on the most solemn acts of the highest magisterium....

6. By its ecumenical orientation, Vatican II gave rise to the question: Will infallibility be able to *serve the purpose* for which it is intended without far more consultation with Christian communities not in full union with Rome?

7. Vatican II called attention to the fact that in Catholic teaching there exists an order or *hierarchy* of truths, since they vary in their relationship to the foundation of the Christian faith....This important principle suggests the possibility that authentic faith in the basic Christian message may exist without explicit belief in *all* defined dogmas.

MODERATE INFALLIBILISM

Several of these new aspects merit special attention, since they seem at variance with the Church's traditional position that every defined dogma must be held firmly on faith by all Catholics. The rationale for this intriguing approach was explained in detail by Dulles, of the Catholic University of America, in a paper delivered during a dialogue session in 1974. The position, which he calls "Moderate Infallibilism," illustrates some of the directions in which theologians move as they continue to grapple with the doctrine.

Clearly, Vatican I (and Vatican II) ruled out "the consent of the Church" as the source or cause of the absolute irreversibility of papal teaching. The source is the Holy Spirit, who assists the pope by special charisms attached to the papal office. The council did not deny, however, that the consent of the Church may be an important indicator that a teaching is in fact infallible. Vatican II followed up by stating (somewhat obscurely) that in papal definitions the assent of the Church "can never be lacking"—that is, it must be present. Dulles raises the question: What if it is lacking? That could hardly mean the whole Church has lapsed into heresy, because the Spirit is promised to the Church permanently.

What it might mean is that the pope, in preparing an infallible definition, did not fulfill the necessary requirements for an infallible definition. As Dulles explains, the pope must embody the Church's "unanimity of belief" in his definitions, and this can only be attained by his serious and sufficient investigation of what the Church's faith really is concerning the issue before him. In other words, he must use the human means available to discover the truth.

Says Dulles:

> It would not be proper to regard the pope as a mere mouthpiece for voicing what had previously been explicitly agreed to by the whole Church. As supreme pontiff and teacher he has a special responsibility and charism for doctrine. But it seems evident that definitions, if they authentically correspond to the charism of the papal office, will find an echo in the faith of the Church and will therefore evoke assent, at least eventually. If in a given instance the assent of the Church were evidently not forthcoming, this could be interpreted as a signal that the pope had perhaps exceeded his competence and that some necessary condition for an infallible act had not been fulfilled.[17]

This question of sufficient investigation has been so widely discussed that Dulles suggests it may be a "new condition" for an infallible declaration, in addition to those specified at the Vatican councils. Neither council maintained that infallibility guarantees the truth of a definition if the necessary conditions have not been met. The point is confirmed in the 1973 document of the Congregation of the Divine Faith, *Mysterium Fidei*: Since the gift of infallibility "does not come from new revelation...it does not dispense them (the pope and bishops) from studying with appropriate means the treasure of divine revelation contained both in Sacred Scripture...and in the living tradition."

Because of this and other equally murky aspects of infallibility, Dulles suggests that Catholics be given wide latitude in their adherence to certain infallible pronouncements: "I would not go so far myself as to say that one could be faithful to Vatican I while denying that the pope has any kind of infallibility under any circumstances, but I do think that the vagueness of the council gives a very large scope for interpreting what is really involved when 'infallibility' is referred to." He notes that it is "becoming increasingly difficult" to apply the old principle that questioning or denying a dogma is "to make shipwreck of the faith." He then proposes how a position of Moderate Infallibilism might relate to the three doctrines formally defined in modern times—the Immaculate Conception, the Assumption, and papal infallibility itself.

At least five attitudes toward these three dogmas appear to be current in the Roman Catholic body.

1. Some accept these dogmas at face value as unquestionably true and as obligatory upon all under pain of excommunication.
2. Some accept the dogmas...but reinterpret them in ways that would probably have surprised those who worked for the definitions....
3. Some...do not feel confident that any particular interpretation is the right one. They therefore assent with a kind of formal or implicit faith....
4. Some say these dogmas, although certainly true in some sense, are too unclear...and too peripheral in importance to be of decisive moment for good standing in the Church. They would argue therefore that Christians who fail to accept these dogmas are not for that reason alone to be considered outside the Roman Catholic communion....
5. Some say the pope (and the Council, in the case of infallibility) exceeded their rightful powers and hence these dogmas, even if true, have no binding power....

Dulles "separates" himself from the first and fifth positions; he "can accept" the second and third "if they do not mean that the definitions are meaningless or...purely arbitrary."

Finally, he says, "the fourth position is on the whole the one that I find most satisfactory. Papal infallibility is unquestionably a problematical doctrine, even for many Catholics, and is rather remote from the core of the gospel. Vatican II, in my opinion, implicitly conceded that Christians who in good faith fail to accept these dogmas are not thereby excluded from eucharistic and ecclesial communion."

Moderate Infallibilism, though much discussed among ecclesiologists, is surely not endorsed universally. Francis Sullivan says Catholics are in no way free to reject the infallibility of a defined dogma. And the *Catechism of the Catholic Church* (paragraph 891) simply repeats the words of Vatican II—"When the Church through its supreme Magisterium proposes a doctrine 'for belief as being divinely revealed,' the definitions 'must be adhered to with the obedience of faith.'" Theologian Patrick Granfield says that "to dissent from infallibly proposed teachings knowingly, obstinately, and publicly is heresy and separates the dissenter from the Church." However, he does not believe this to be the case in private dissent, provided the person is not hostile to Church authority, has tried "sincerely and prayerfully to arrive at assent," yet still finds "very convincing reasons" for disagreement.[18]

Most theologians, even conservative ones, do not today place infallibility in a very high position within the realm of divine truth. Says Sullivan:

> The sober fact is that it is far from being among the truths at the very foundation of our faith. It would be a gross misunderstanding to think that the certitude of our Catholic faith somehow depends on the infallibility of the pope. It would be an even grosser mistake to think that we put our hope for salvation in holding correct doctrine, and that our assurance that we hold correct doctrine depends on papal infallibility.[19]

CHAPTER XIV

SEARCHING FOR
INFALLIBILITY

*No doctrine is understood to be infallibly defined unless this
fact is clearly established.*
    CANON 749: 1983 CODE OF CANON LAW

Determining what doctrines are taught infallibly by the Church
and what doctrines aren't has never been an easy task, and it
is not getting any easier. For example, it is not clear whether infallible certainty can be applied only to the deposit of faith (truths
revealed in Scripture or tradition) or whether it can also apply to
other truths "related to" or "pertaining to" the deposit of faith.
And if infallibility may be applied in this latter, broader sense, it is
far from clear what are the limits of matters that might be considered "related to" the deposit.

Vatican I left the issue unsettled. As a result, two prominent
churchmen like Manning and Newman could come to absolutely
contradictory appraisals of the scope of infallibility. Vatican II
seemed to explicitly restrict infallibility in *Lumen Gentium* to "the
deposit of divine revelation." But Vatican documents since appear
to press for a wider scope of infallibility. The Congregation for the
Doctrine of the Faith in 1990 said, "When the Magisterium pro-

poses 'in a definitive way' truths concerning faith and morals, which, even if not divinely revealed, are nevertheless strictly and intimately connected with Revelation, these must be firmly accepted and held."[1]

In the judgment of Jesuit theologian Francis A. Sullivan, who taught ecclesiology at the Gregorian University in Rome for thirty-six years, the Church today maintains as official doctrine that these nonrevealed matters—that is, matters that "must be held" (*tenenda*), though not with an act of divine faith—can be taught infallibly. A question debated among theologians is whether this also extends to norms of the natural law, norms so intimately "connected with revelation" that they can be propounded by the magisterium even though not found in revelation.

The *Catechism of the Catholic Church*, promulgated by Pope John Paul II in 1992, goes several steps further (in paragraph 88): "The Church's Magisterium exercises the authority it holds from Christ to the fullest extent when it defines dogmas, that is, when it proposes truths contained in divine Revelation or *having a necessary connection with them*, in a form obliging the Christian people to an irrevocable adherence of *faith*." (Italics added for emphasis.)

This statement has mystified theologians including Sullivan, since it seems to say that revealed truths as well as "other matters" (only connected with revelation) can be proposed as dogmas requiring an assent of faith from Catholics. Such creeping dogmatism has "support in no previous document of the magisterium," says Sullivan, who hopes a moderating clarification will be issued eventually.[2]

Still more baffling is the Congregation for the Doctrine of the Faith's statement of November 1995 concerning the infallible character of the ban on the ordination of women. This will be considered in some detail in the final chapter of this book.

Another chronic problem concerns the precise wording of dogmas and other presumably infallible teachings. If a doctrine is infallible, does that mean the exact verbal formula given in the definition is absolutely unchangeable and unquestionably the best expression possible of the religious truth it communicates? That was indeed the interpretation of many Ultramontanes after Vatican I, especially since the council itself said infallible decrees are "irreformable." Yet such a rigid stance flies in the face of the notion of the development of doctrine. An excessively literal interpretation raises the specter of Peter Olivi—i.e., the universal Church bound eternally by the constraints of an infallible pronouncement.

Though theologians from Newman to Rahner and Congar argued that infallibility and doctrinal development are not necessarily mutually exclusive, official Church documents like Pius XII's 1950 encyclical *Humani Generis* warned against departing from traditional formulas of Church teaching lest the faithful be led into dogmatic relativism. That was obviously also the burden of Pope Paul VI's encyclical *Mysterium Fidei* in 1965. The formulas used in the Council of Trent, he said, "express concepts that are not tied to a certain specific form of human culture or to a certain level of scientific progress or to one or another theological school. Instead, they set forth what the human mind grasps of reality through necessary and universal experience and what it expresses in apt and exact words....These formulas are adapted to all men of all times and all places."[3]

However, Rome is not always consistent. Only seven years later, in 1972, the Congregation for the Doctrine of the Faith's declaration *Mysterium Ecclesiae* put an entirely different emphasis on Pope Paul's statement: "It sometimes happens that some dogmatic truth is first expressed incompletely (but not falsely) and at a later date, when considered in a broader context of faith or human knowledge, it receives a fuller and more perfect expression....Even though [the Church's] dogmatic formulas are distinct from the changeable conceptions of a given epoch...it can sometimes happen that these truths may be enunciated by the sacred magisterium in terms that bear traces of such conceptions....It has sometimes happened that in the habitual usage of the Church certain of these formulas gave way to new expressions which, proposed and approved by the Sacred Magisterium, presented more clearly or more completely the same meaning."[4]

The admission here is extremely guarded and cautious, but the implication is undeniable: the meaning of a doctrine may be "irreformable," yet, notes Sullivan, "the fact that this meaning can be expressed with greater clarity or be more developed shows that irreformability is not predicated of dogmatic formulas as such."[5]

This changeable character of infallible declarations is explained by German theologian Walter Kasper as a reflection of the "eschatological condition" of the Church. He writes of the "already-but-not-yet situation of the present reality of salvation that is essentially directed toward a fulfillment that will take place only in the definitive kingdom of God." This tension of incompleteness will be with the Church throughout history; as a result, every pronouncement of the Christian message will be affected by the "not yet" factor until the end of time.[6]

Says Sullivan:

> The historical circumstances that have led up to the definition of dogmas of faith have tended to focus the attention of the magisterium on certain aspects of revelation which were then being challenged. Inevitably other aspects of the truth, to which the dogmatic statement did not attend, would be left in oblivion....One can compare a dogma to the reproduction of a particular detail in a great painting. The reproduction is useful for calling our attention to the beauty of that particular detail, but it is only when the detail is seen in its place in the whole picture that one can fully appreciate its beauty. So also the full truth of any particular dogma depends on its place in the broader picture....[7]

DOGMAS FROM THE COUNCILS

In his 1996 book *Creative Fidelity: Weighing and Interpreting Documents of the Magisterium,* Sullivan attempts the mind-boggling task of explaining the relative authority of Church teachings, especially those regarded as infallible. A first guiding principle, which he repeats throughout the book, is Canon 749 of the 1983 *Code of Canon Law:* "No doctrine is understood to be infallibly defined unless this fact is clearly ('manifeste' in Latin) established."[8]

A most important word here is *manifeste*. Says Sullivan:

> The fact that a doctrine has been infallibly defined must not only be settled, undisputed, well known, but must be manifestly such. To whom would one expect a fact to be manifest if not to Catholic theologians whose business it is to evaluate the dogmatic weight or magisterium pronouncements?....I conclude that one could hardly claim that the fact that a doctrine has been infallibly defined was manifestly settled, established, undisputed, if there were serious disagreement among Catholic theologians about this alleged fact.[9]

First he considers the dogmas set forth in the Church's ecumenical councils from the fourth through the nineteenth centuries. It is of no help to look for the word "infallible" in conciliar statements, he says, because the councils don't use that word. Nor is it of great benefit to seek out those concluding canons in council documents which state that if anyone holds a position contrary to what is taught, *anathema sit*—that is, let him be cut off, excommunicated from the Church. Anathemas are hurled about rather freely by councils, Sullivan notes, often on matters that aren't revealed and have nothing to do directly or indirectly with revelation; many are strictly disciplinary injunctions.

To determine precisely what is being taught infallibly, one has to decipher precisely what the council meant to teach—an exercise that requires some knowledge of why the council was called (usually in reaction to some heresy), an understanding of the literary genre of the documents issued, and an appreciation of the different ways words like "faith" and "heresy" were understood in various eras of Church history. Failure to take into consideration how key terms may have had a broader sense than they now have, says Sullivan, would lead "to attributing dogmatic status to a good many propositions which in fact are not dogmas at all."[10]

Sullivan goes through ecumenical council documents filtering out the infallible and noninfallible doctrines as he sees them. At the first, the Council of Nicea in 325, the bishops gathered in response to the doctrines of Arius, who denied that Christ was divine. The council's Nicene Creed contains a great many articles of faith, notes Sullivan, though the only one "it intended to define was the true divinity of the Son of God." The others (including God the Father maker of all things visible and invisible and Jesus' Incarnation, death, Resurrection, and Ascension) remained undefined dogmas at that time, he says, "because the church hadn't seen need to define them."[11]

Similarly, the First Council of Constantinople in 381 was responding to the heretic Appolinarius when it proclaimed the dogma of the full humanity of Jesus and the divinity of the Holy Spirit. Chalcedon, in 451, responding to Nestorius, proclaimed only the two natures in Christ. Some early councils, says Sullivan, like Constantinople II and the first three Lateran councils issued clarifying statements or disciplinary decrees but said nothing infallibly. The Council of Constance (discussed in Chapter 3) certainly appeared to have defined the supremacy of councils over popes, but Sullivan, along with historian Brian Tierney, says its decree was merely a legislative adaptation to the unique situation of three claimants to the papacy.

Matters get considerably more complicated in later councils. Trent, for example, issued dozens of strongly worded canons affirming Church authority against the Protestant reformers. A sample: "If anyone denies that each and all of Christ's faithful of both sexes are bound, when they reach the age of reason, to receive communion once a year, at least during the paschal season… *anathema sit.*"[12]

Canons like this, says Sullivan, do not contain divinely revealed truth and therefore have no infallible character or dogmatic value. In others the reader must carefully distinguish between what is revealed doctrine and what isn't. Trent declared, "If anyone says that in the holy sacrament of the Eucharist the substance of bread and wine remains together with the body and blood of our Lord

Jesus Christ and denies that wonderful and unique change of the whole substance of bread into his body and of the whole substance of the wine into his blood while only the species of bread and wine remain, a change which the Catholic Church very fittingly calls transubstantiation, *anathema sit.*"[13]

Comments Sullivan:

> What is defined as a dogma of faith is the "wonderful and unique change of the whole substance of bread," etc. On the other hand, that the church "very fittingly" calls this change of substance by the name "transubstantiation" is hardly something God has revealed. From the fact that this clause is included within a canon that ends with "anathema sit" it does not follow that one would be a heretic...if one questioned the "fittingness" of the term "transubstantiation, provided one did not question the doctrine that Trent meant to express by the use of that term.[14]

An example of the difficulty nontheologians have in decoding council documents can be found in Trent's canon on dissolving the marriage bond: "If anyone says that the church is in error for having taught and for still teaching that...the marriage bond cannot be dissolved because of adultery on the part of one of the spouses and that neither of the two, not even the innocent one...can contract marriage during the lifetime of the other...anathema sit."[15]

This has often been seen as an unquestionably infallible conciliar definition on the indissolubility of the marriage bond and, by implication, a condemnation of the Greek Orthodox practice of allowing divorce. But Sullivan cites the painstaking examination of the canon in its historical context by theologian Piet Fransen:

> It is clear from Fransen's study...that since Trent did not intend to condemn the practice of the Greek church as heretical, it did not define as a dogma of faith the doctrine that marriage cannot be dissolved on the grounds of adultery of one of the spouses. What is strictly condemned was the position of Luther

that the church has no authority to make laws about marriage.
If Fransen's interpretation is correct, it follows that...Trent did
not define the indissolubility of marriage as a dogma of faith.[16]

VATICAN II'S "RECEPTION"

The decrees of Vatican II pose a different kind of problem because
this "pastoral" council produced no formal definitions and no
anathemas. Extreme traditionalists have held that it therefore has
not dogmatic authority (and they pray its decrees will be rescinded
in time). Yet Vatican II represents the position of the world's episcopacy united with the pope, and some of its declarations could
therefore be considered as an expression of the ordinary universal
magisterium. The council plainly connected its teaching on the
collegiality of the bishops with "the Lord's will" in setting up "the
apostolic college." Still, few have gone so far as to attribute infallibility to any Vatican II pronouncement. Cardinal Joseph Ratzinger,
prefect of the Congregation for the Doctrine of the Faith, gives
Vatican II a special preeminence but stops short of claiming infallibility: "The conciliar text by far surpasses the ordinary declarations of papal magisterium, including the encyclicals, regarding
the nature of the theological obligation which it entails. It is a
document produced by the most intense work over many years,
and it expresses the sense of its faith at which the whole Church
assembled in council has arrived....The conclusion is that it has an
importance of the first rank."[17]

Sullivan calls attention to the fact that Vatican II in several vital
matters took positions quite different from what previous popes
repeatedly taught in encyclicals: "There can be no doubt that the
teaching of the council on such issues as religious liberty, the
ecclesial status of other Christian churches, and the significance of
non-Christian religions prevails over what had been the official
position of the Catholic Church put forth by the ordinary papal
magisterium prior to Vatican II."[18]

Not every interpreter of Vatican II has come to a common conclusion about what the council intended to teach. Herman Pott-meyer, a German theologian who surveyed twenty years of Church analysis of the council, found two interpretative positions in conflict—one looking exclusively to the new beginnings promoted by the majority of bishops, the other looking exclusively to statements that reflect preconciliar theology. Pottmeyer says, "The reception of Vatican II is not yet complete. All attempts to break off the process of reception—whether through overly restrictive legislation or through a 'progressive' interpretation—are incompatible with a professed fidelity to the council."[19]

The concept of "reception" is most important in evaluating infallibility. H. J. Sieben, whose history of ecumenical councils is today considered especially authoritative, declares that the clearest sign that a conciliar decision was definitive is seen in the reception of that decision by the whole Church. Seiben, notes Sullivan, insists that such reception is not the source of the definitive authority of the decision, but is its most effective witness to it."[20]

In other words, when the whole Church in the fourth century accepted the doctrine of Christ's divinity as proposed at Nicea, that acceptance did not cause the doctrine to become infallible; it only confirmed the infallible character of the council's declaration. By the same token, when the Church of the fourteenth century did not receive the teaching of the Council of Vienne that practice of usury (taking interest on a loan) is sinful, it confirmed that the teaching was not a dogma of faith—even though it appeared to be at the time of the council.

PAPAL DEFINITIONS A RARITY

Equally fraught with difficulty is the task of identifying dogmas defined by popes outside of council situations—that is, *ex cathedra* definitions within the parameters established at Vatican I. The problem here, as with ecumenical councils, is determining the intent of the pope as well as the precise subject about which he was speaking. Was he proclaiming formally as head of the Church, or only as the provider of an opinion? Did the issue involve matters of faith (or closely related to faith), or something else entirely?

The two Marian dogmas, the Immaculate Conception and the Assumption, are relatively (but not absolutely) easy to analyze and identify. By their own admissions, both Pius IX and Pius XII meant to speak formally as heads of the Church concerning these matters, and they regarded them as part of the Church's tradition well situated within the deposit of faith. The subsequent, virtually unanimous acceptance of these doctrines by the Roman Catholic faithful would seem to confirm their infallible character for practical purposes. (However, it should be noted that some Catholic theologians still question whether these beliefs existed in the early Church, and they therefore doubt their infallible, dogmatic character.)

Since Vatican I, Ultramontane interpreters have tended to attribute infallibility to scores of papal rulings, both on matters of faith and matters "connected with" faith. Among the latter are the canonization of saints, the condemnation of certain doctrines, and the settlement of disputes on matters of morality. Some insist on attributing infallibility to Pius XI's encyclical, *Casti Connubii*, on birth control, and the ruling by Leo XIII that the ordination of priests by the Anglican church is invalid. Sullivan is most unwilling to maximize infallibility in this fashion. On the other hand, he is equally unwilling to join minimalists who limit papal infallibility to the two relatively recent pronouncements concerning Mary.

Early in this century, two authors, Louis Billot and Edmond Dublanchy, claimed to see infallible teaching in twelve papal decrees, ranging from the fifth through the nineteenth centuries. Some of these are scarcely remembered, such as the condemnation of the Quietists. Among the better-known selections were the "Tome" of Pope Leo I in the fifth century, the condemnation of Luther's doctrines by Leo X in the sixteenth century, and the *Quanta Cura* of Pius IX, which accompanied the *Syllabus of Errors*. Since then, theologians have been whittling away at this list. Members of the Lutheran-Catholic dialogue exempted the condemnation of Luther's teachings from infallibility on the grounds that it was too "global" in nature and did not specify which of his positions were heretical. Sullivan believes the condemnations of other heresies also lack specificity and are therefore should not be regarded as infallible.

The final sentence of Boniface VIII's memorable bull, *Unam Sanctam*, in the fourteenth century poses an interesting problem. It declared that "every human creature" must be "subject to the Roman pontiff" in order to achieve salvation. There is no doubt Boniface was invoking his supreme authority on what he regarded as a matter of faith and intending to oblige everyone for all time. However, says Sullivan, there are loopholes. It is by no means clear what doctrine Boniface was enunciating. If he meant membership in the Catholic Church is a requirement for all those who perceive it to be necessary for salvation, then that is still a doctrine of the Church. If he meant literal submission to the pope of Rome is an absolute requirement, then the doctrine could hardly be infallible. As theologian George Tavard has noted, the teaching was not received in the literal sense by the faithful of Boniface's day and has not been maintained as Catholic doctrine since.

As with the decrees of councils, says Sullivan, the pope can define as dogma "only a truth that is revealed and that must therefore be contained at least implicitly in the faith of the Church. The eventual failure of any papal doctrine to be received by the Church as an article of faith would show that that doctrine was not contained in the deposit of faith, and hence was not capable of being defined as dogma."[20]

On the basis of his own study, Klaus Schatz recognizes only seven instances in Church history when a pope spoke infallibly: the "Tome" of Leo I in 449; a letter of Pope Agatho in 680 concerning two wills in Christ; a bull of Benedict XII on the beatific vision in 1336, two condemnations of Jansenist teachings by Innocent X in 1653, and Pius VI in 1794, and the two Marian dogmas.

Sullivan says: "The fact is that, with few exceptions, our Catholic faith is based not on dogmas defined by popes, but on those that have been defined by councils, and on those that have never been formally defined, but are part of the faith which we profess when we participate in the liturgy."[21]

THE ORDINARY UNIVERSAL MYSTERY

The hardest job of all is identifying with a degree of certainty infallible doctrines in the ordinary universal magisterium of the Church—basic teachings representing the belief of the faithful and maintained constantly throughout the world. There are, to be sure, numberless undefined dogmas in the Christian reservoir, many of them items, as Sullivan says, in the various creeds and traditional professions of faith. He gives two examples: Mary's virginal conception and her perpetual virginity. He recognizes (along with Scripture scholar Raymond Brown) that some theologians do question the weight of these beliefs, but he finds the strength of their presence in Church tradition at least as compelling as the strength of beliefs such as the Immaculate Conception.

Beyond these relatively straightforward cases, the ordinary universal magisterium becomes a highway strewn with boulders and misleading road signs. Sullivan finds comforting guidance in Pius IX's original statement about ordinary universal magisterium. To qualify, said Pius, there must be a "constant" consensus of Catholic theologians that a doctrine is a matter of faith. Therefore, Sullivan argues "if it becomes evident that there is no longer a consensus on some point of doctrine about which in former times there was a consensus, it would seem necessary to conclude that this is not the kind of constant consensus that points to infallible teaching."[22]

A prime case concerns the age-old belief that the whole human race is descended from a single couple, Adam and Eve, as portrayed in the Book of Genesis. At the time of Vatican I, there was virtually no opposition in the Church to this position, which had been taught in catechisms and theology manuals for centuries. The council schema called for the definition of this belief as a dogma, and it assuredly would have been so defined if the council had not been interrupted by war. Some eighty years later, the belief had faded;

the theory of polygenism (the descent of the human race from many original ancestors) had taken a surprisingly firm hold in the theological world. Pope Pius XII in *Humani Generis* tried to oppose the trend by arguing that "it is not at all apparent" how polygenism could be reconciled with the biblical claim that original sin springs from a single source and is transmitted by the propagation of the race.

Nevertheless, by 1970 theologians had reached an almost universal consensus that polygenism could indeed be reconciled with the doctrine of original sin. Wrote Karl Rahner: "We may surely say that the development of Catholic theology 'since Humani Generis' has made such advances (advances that have been tolerated by the church's *magisterium*) that the opinion that polygenism is not irreconcilable with the doctrine of original sin is no longer exposed to the danger of being censured by the authorities of the church."[23]

Sullivan's argument that infallible teaching by the ordinary universal magisterium must be "constant" is identical to the one leveled against John Ford and Germain Grisez. The two claimed that the official position on contraception taught in the encyclical *Humanae Vitae* fulfilled the requirements for an infallible teaching of the ordinary universal magisterium. Not so, says Sullivan, because the official position ceased to be "constant" in the 1960s and continues even to the present day as a hotly debated topic among theologians.

On the basis of ordinary universal magisterium, infallibility has been attributed by zealous theologians to hundreds of papal bulls and encyclicals, the declarations of Vatican congregations, and various decrees like the *Syllabus of Errors*. At one time, the Church commonly taught that all pagans and Jews were destined for hell, that it was perfectly moral to own slaves and profit from their labor, and that Catholic governments had a duty to suppress Protestantism. Inevitably, these claims ran up against questions and doubts concerning these teachings' universality (that is, were they taught by all the bishops with the pope?) and their constancy (were they taught through every era?). Hence, the tendency today is to assert that—unless the contrary can be clearly manifested—all such teachings are part of the Church's ordinary (but not universal) magisterium. As such, says canon law, they merit "respect" (*obsequium* in Latin).

"*Obsequium*," says Sullivan, "denotes an *attitude* toward the teaching authority which the Congregation for the Doctrine of the Faith has described as 'the willingness to submit loyally to the teaching of the magisterium on matters per se not irreformable.' This 'willingness to submit' is said to be 'the rule,' but the congregation recognizes that 'it can happen that a theologian may, according to the case, raise questions regarding the timeliness, the form or even the contents of magisterial interventions."[24]

JOHN PAUL AND *EVANGELIUM VITAE*

This does not preclude situations from arising in which a previously undefined dogma becomes clearly defined through the ordinary universal magisterium. Sullivan cites as a potential example the March 1995 encyclical of Pope John Paul II, *Evangelium Vitae*. In it the pope uses an exceptionally strong formula concerning abortion:

> Therefore by the authority which Christ conferred upon Peter and his successors, in communion with the bishops...who... albeit dispersed throughout the world, have shown unanimous agreement concerning this doctrine—I declare that direct abortion, that is, abortion willed as an end or as a means, always constitutes a grave moral disorder, since it is the deliberate killing of an innocent human being. This doctrine is based upon the natural law and upon the written word of God, is transmitted by the church's tradition and taught by the ordinary universal magisterium.[25]

There can be little doubt what John Paul means. His appeal is not just to the natural law, Scripture, and tradition in a general sense; it is also to the bishops. In another section of the encyclical, he states that he consulted with all the cardinals on this matter in April 1991 and then polled all the bishops of the world by letter. Therefore, he apparently felt justified in calling the condemnation of abortion a teaching of the ordinary universal magisterium. (Elsewhere in *Evangelium Vitae* he included murder and euthanasia under the condemnation.)

Why did he not go one small step farther and call this an infallible teaching? According to Cardinal Ratzinger, serious consideration was given to so identifying it, but experts researching the question "found that in the past Church pronouncements on dogma had never spoken of their own infallibility." He also regarded it as "a little absurd" to solemnize teachings so clearly evident in Scripture and tradition, which was the main point of the encyclical.[26]

Because the Church has never before spoken infallibly on a matter of the natural law, says Sullivan, one might argue that it has not done so now or even that it cannot do so. Yet, he is persuaded that the teaching in this case is closely and vitally connected with Revelation: "It seems to me that the teaching of the encyclical on the immorality of murder, abortion and euthanasia meets the requirement [of an infallible teaching]."

Still, he leaves a bit of room for speculation: "It is too soon to know whether there will be the consensus that would show that it is 'clearly established' that the immorality of murder, abortion and euthanasia has been infallibly taught. What this would mean is that the church had taken an irreversible stand on these issues."[27]

CHAPTER XV

A MOUNTING TENSION

*This teaching requires definitive assent since…it has been set
forth infallibly by the ordinary and universal magisterium.*
CONGREGATION FOR THE DOCTRINE OF THE FAITH

The seemingly irreversible stand taken by the Congregation for
the Doctrine of the Faith in late 1995 concerning the ordination of women left theologians and other interested persons, including those well acquainted with the technicalities of the subject,
thoroughly puzzled. It appeared to follow the pattern of creeping
infallibility expressed by the congregation in 1990 and in the *Catechism of the Catholic Church*. The tone of finality and certitude in
the statement did nothing to dispel the ambiguity and confusion.
It was titled in Latin *Responsum ad Dubium* (Response to a Doubt),
as if a question had been presented to the congregation by an
anonymous seeker for clarification.

The *Dubium*: "Whether the teaching that the Church has no
authority whatsoever to confer priestly ordination on women,
which is presented in the apostolic letter *Ordinatio Sacerdotalis*
[which stated the Church has "no authority" to ordain women]…is
to be understood as pertaining to the deposit of faith."

The *Responsum*: "This teaching requires definitive assent, since, founded on the written word of God and from the beginning constantly preserved and applied in the tradition of the Church, it has been set forth infallibly by the ordinary and universal magisterium....Thus in the present circumstances the Roman pontiff, exercising his proper office of confirming the brethren...has handed on this same teaching by a formal declaration explicitly stating what must be held always, everywhere and by all as pertaining to the deposit of faith.

"The sovereign pontiff John Paul II at the audience granted to the undersigned cardinal prefect, approved this reply...and ordered it to be published."

The document was signed by Cardinal Ratzinger, prefect of the Congregation for the Doctrine of the Faith (CDF), and dated October 28, 1995.

What was being claimed here was obvious: The ban on women priests represented, in the judgment of the congregation, an infallible doctrine of the ordinary universal magisterium. It was clear that the response itself was not being proposed as an *ex cathedra* definition of John Paul II, even though he approved the statement and ordered it promulgated. Theologians agree universally that papal infallibility cannot be delegated by the pope to the CDF or any other body or individual. Nor was it being claimed that *Ordinatio Sacerdotalis* was an *ex cathedra* teaching; that document was to be understood as an assertion by the pope that the ban's infallibility stemmed from the ordinary universal teaching of the Church.

A "NEW CHAPTER" OF INFALLIBILITY?

When *Ordinatio Sacerdotalis* was released, most commentators regarded its teaching as an exercise of the pope's ordinary magisterium—an authoritative, noninfallible teaching deserving the external and internal respect of the faithful. On the contrary, declared the *Responsum*, *Ordinatio Sacerdotalis* really intended to present the ban as a constant, infallible doctrine that "must be held" (*tenenda*) by all Catholics because it "pertains" to the deposit of the faith. This is where the confusion starts. The word "pertains" (*pertinens* in Latin) admits of several meanings.

Was the congregation stating (with the pope in full agreement) that the ban is "within" the deposit of the faith—a truth fully established in Scripture or tradition? Or was it saying the ban is only "related" to the deposit of faith—a truth that, though not revealed, is considered necessary to protect revelation? And if the ban is "within" the deposit of faith, why didn't the congregation call it a truth that must be believed (*credenda*) instead of one that "must be held?"

The distinctions have more than esoteric significance. The question of these nonrevealed, "related" truths has been a source of confusion since Vatican I, which left the matter vague. As noted in Chapter 12, Vatican II in the document *Lumen Gentium* appeared to settle the confusion by stating that infallibility is coextensive with the deposit of faith; therefore, other matters that are "only related" to the deposit are not taught infallibly. The CDF response muddied the waters by placing the mantle of infallibility over both categories—both *tenenda* and *credenda* doctrines.

Said theologian John T. Ford:

> The congregation's response effectively initiates a new chapter in the history of infallibility. On the one hand, theologians favoring a "principle of minimizing" will have difficulty generalizing about what apparently is a unique instance of infallibility being officially extended to tenenda. Simultaneously, theologians who maintain that tenenda come within the scope of infallibility will have difficulty drawing the line between... new categories of tenenda.[1]

Ford suspected the CDF did not state explicitly that the ban on women is "within" the deposit of faith (and therefore a matter "that must be believed") because the congregation really has doubts that this can be established theologically. "If it [the congregation] could have pushed the ban into a matter of belief, 'credenda,' it would have," said Ford. "It went right up to the frontier between 'tenenda' and 'credenda' but refused to cross it." Consequently, he said, the response represents a "high level disciplinary decree" of the present administration in Rome, not a dogmatic statement; as such, it could be rescinded by some future pope.[2] Yet Ford remained perplexed and concerned about how a mark of infallibility could possibly be applied to a nonrevealed, disciplinary directive. In the absence of objective criteria to determine what truths can reasonably be considered "related" to revelation, it seems infallibility could be applied in unlimited situations. This extension was precisely the dream of extreme Infallibilists at Vatican I like Archbishop Manning.

DOCTRINAL DOUBTS

Francis Sullivan avoided some of this complexity by interpreting the congregation's words "pertaining to the deposit of faith" to mean "within" the deposit of faith. In other words, he believed the congregation did cross the frontier into *credenda*, even though it did not say the ban represents a doctrine that "must be believed." But this only brought him up squarely against the biggest problem of all in the response. Said Sullivan:

> I take the CDF's statement to mean that it is clearly established fact that the world-wide Catholic episcopate is in agreement with Pope John Paul II in teaching that the exclusion of women from ordination to the priesthood is a divinely revealed doctrine that must be held definitively by all the faithful. I think it is a fair question to ask how they know that this is a clearly established fact.[3]

There are several recognized ways to determine if a doctrine is clearly established as infallible by the ordinary universal magisterium. As Pope John Paul II observed in the encyclical *Evangelium Veritatis*, it can be verified by consultation with the world's bishops. Second, it can be manifested, as Pius IX declared, in the consensus of Catholic theologians. Finally, it can be confirmed, as Canon 750 of the 1983 *Code of Canon Law* states, by the "common adherence of Christ's faithful."

Said Sullivan:

> Official documents then have proposed three ways of establishing that a doctrine is taught by the ordinary and universal magisterium....The CDF has not invoked any of these criteria in support of its assertion that the doctrine excluding women from the priesthood has been set forth infallibly by the ordinary and universal magisterium....
>
> The question that remains in my mind is whether it is a clearly established fact that the bishops of the Catholic Church are as convinced...as Pope John Paul II evidently is, and that, in exercising their proper role as judges and teachers of the faith, they have been unanimous in teaching that the exclusion of women...is a divinely revealed truth. Unless this is manifestly the case, I do not see how it can be certain that this doctrine has been taught infallibly by the ordinary and universal magisterium.[4]

Indeed, the history of the Church is replete with doctrines that seemed at one time to be the unanimous teaching of the bishops (with the pope), the theologians, and the faithful. Yet later developments convinced the Church to reformulate or, in some cases, to jettison the doctrines—for example, the common belief that non-Catholics could not attain salvation. In all matters of interpretation, explained Sullivan, one may rely safely on Canon 749's declaration that no doctrine should be regarded as infallibly defined unless that fact is manifestly established. Nor would he abandon that principle even in the face of the explicit assertion by the congregation that the ban on women priests is infallibly taught by the Church.

CATHOLICS SHOULD BE WARNED

Like Ford, Avery Dulles regarded the doctrine as not necessarily "within" the deposit of faith but as one of those truths "related to" the deposit. "In saying that the doctrine 'pertains' to the deposit of faith," Dulles told a meeting of the National Conference of Catholic Bishops in June 1996, the CDF "does not necessarily mean that it is divinely revealed. And in saying that the faithful must 'hold' rather than 'believe' the doctrine, they may wish to leave some latitude for the opinion that the doctrine is a deduction or inference from the word of God and is not itself a revealed truth." In any case, added Dulles, it is not the kind of truth that belongs to the basic profession of Christian faith....If it is a revealed truth, it would stand relatively low in the hierarchy of truths." Those who doubt or deny the doctrine should not be regarded as heretics, he says, "but if they show obstinacy, such dissenters are subject to just canonical penalties."[5]

Nevertheless, Dulles then argues vigorously that, in his view, Scripture, tradition, and the Church's episcopacy all concur on the legitimacy of the prohibition; therefore, we have here an infallible teaching of the ordinary universal magisterium: "In confirming the consensus of the episcopate, the pope is not acting outside the college [of bishops]. He is exercising the leadership that properly belongs to his office." The teaching, Dulles said, comes from a "powerful convergent argument, backed by the insistent declarations of the highest doctrinal authorities in the church," and as such is beyond question or criticism.

Dulles absolutely rejected the suggestion that the movement favoring women's ordination may be (as Elizabeth Johnson suggested) a "God-intended development of doctrine." Rather, he claimed it stems from "the general ethos of secular society, which treats the exclusion of women from public positions as unjust discrimination....In this radicalized climate a new coalition has been formed under the slogan 'We are the church.' It includes the Women's Ordination Conference, Call to Action, CORPUS...and some gay and lesbian groups. The member groups of this coalition share the conviction that the church can reconstruct or reinvent itself to conform to the needs of the times." Catholics should be warned, he believes, about coalitions "that would subvert the authority of scripture and the nature of the church as a divinely established hierarchical society." He urged the bishops to make "an unambiguous statement" to end speculation that they themselves are divided on this issue.

Ironically, several bishops at the meeting took immediate issue with Dulles's observations—a hint that the moral unanimity Dulles assumes to be present may be less than unanimous. One bishop, Kenneth Untener of Saginaw, Michigan, argued that since the subject of women's ordination is being seriously discussed for the first time in history in the context of the equality of men and women, the Church has "a different window" to look through and a "different question" to answer.

"THE DIVINE WILL IS NOT ARBITRARY"

The Catholic Theological Society of America also maintained that this issue requires further investigation. In June 1996 the organization appointed a task force to draw up a document on the matter for discussion and debate at future meetings. A draft text for that document declares that the society "is convinced that the grounds on which the Church has based its tradition regarding the ordination of women have not received the reexamination which the full resources of the Catholic theological community can and should give."

It notes that the scriptural arguments consistently used in the past (such as Saint Paul's demand in 1 Corinthians that women "keep silent" in church and in 1 Timothy that women should not teach or hold any authority over men) are no longer invoked at any level in the Church, yet such arguments have played a major part in justifying the ban throughout history. The more recent scriptural citations in Vatican documents, which concern Jesus' choice of men only as his immediate followers, are also less than persuasive today, says the draft: "Since Jesus left the Church to make so many decisions on its own regarding the organization of its ministry, scholars judge it very doubtful that he intended to lay down such a particular prescription regarding the sex of future candidates for ordination or indeed that he explicitly set up the practice of ordination itself."[6]

While tradition deserves respect, the draft says, it should not exclude a priori the possibility of change. Cited is the 1970 declaration from the Congregation for Divine Worship prohibiting women "from serving the priest at the altar, even in women's chapels, houses, convents, schools and institutes." The draft declares, "The numerous decrees of popes and councils, which through the centuries had repeatedly inculcated this norm, show that this exclusion was based on the belief that there was something gravely improper about any kind of ministry of a woman in the sanctuary at the celebration of the eucharist. There was not only a traditional practice but a traditional belief that justified it. The abrogation of this norm means that the Church no longer holds the belief on which its practice had been based This in turn must mean that the Church has reexamined the grounds for this traditional belief and found them wanting."

As Cardinal Ratzinger has noted, says the draft, "Not everything that exists in the Church must for that reason be also a legitimate tradition. In other words, not every tradition that arises in the Church is a true celebration and keeping present of the mystery of Christ. There is a distorting as well as a legitimate tradition....Consequently, tradition must not be considered only affirmatively, but also critically."

Before the Immaculate Conception was defined by Pope Pius IX in 1854, it is noted, several important conditions were present: Theologians expressed no objections to the doctrine, the faithful favored it, and the worldwide episcopate responded positively when polled by the pope. Yet today, "none of these conditions is clearly and certainly fulfilled with regard to the teaching that the Church must exclude women from ordination to the priesthood out of fidelity to the revealed will of Christ," says the draft paper.

The argument that the ordination of women is prohibited by the will of Christ and must be accepted on pure faith is not a satisfactory one, says the draft: "The Catholic tradition of moral thought and practice has been profoundly shaped by the belief that the divine will is not arbitrary and thus moral norms overall 'make sense.' Hence, it is never sufficient to say simply, 'This is the law'; God's will asks not only for obedience but also for some degree of understanding."

Equally unconvincing, according to the paper, is the claim that natural differences between men and women legitimize the differentiation of their roles in the Church: "A theological anthropology built upon this understanding of gender complementarity... faces serious problems. It has not been shown satisfactorily to belong to the revealed word of God, either by direct word or by the diverse example of biblical men and women. Practically speaking, beyond anatomical and physiological differences, it is notoriously difficult to identify gender-specific traits or capabilities that translate into different social roles."

THE RATZINGER CLARIFICATION

In the midst of all this speculation, the CDF in early 1997 attempted a resolution. Yet the attempt left observers more baffled than before. The occasion was the formal excommunication of the aged Sri Lankan theologian Tissa Balasuriya. A Marianist priest, he had long sought to give the Church a distinctively Asian identity. But the congregation claimed he had gone too far in his book *The Eucharist and Human Liberation;* he was ordered to sign a specially composed declaration of faith that stated, among other things, "I firmly accept and hold that the Church has no authority whatsoever to confer priestly ordination on women." When Balasuriya declined to sign, a sentence of excommunication was pronounced against him as one who denied the faith. Commentators immediately speculated that the inclusion of the ban on women priests in the profession was a clear indication the CDF held that teaching to be a matter of faith.

However, in a press conference in early January, Cardinal Ratzinger said, "It is not true that Balasuriya was excommunicated for not wishing to recognise that the Church has no authority to admit women to the priesthood." There are, he said, "many things which are unacceptable" in Balasuriya's book, including his treatment of the doctrine of Original Sin. Ratzinger then turned his attention to the 1995 *Responsum ad Dubium*. That document, he explained, was not only approved by the pope, but "the Holy Father had actually wanted this text"—apparently referring to the document's invocation of infallibility. What the *Responsum* really intended to teach, said Ratzinger, is that the ban on women's ordination belongs to "the second level" of religious truths—that is, truths which "though not formally revealed," are nevertheless "connected in such a way with revelation that one destroys the fabric of revelation itself by denying the content of the second level." But since they are not matters contained in the deposit of faith, Ratzinger said, rejecting them "would not be heresy in the strict sense of the word." The CDF position thus amounted to this: The teaching that women may not be ordained, though not necessarily founded in Scripture or tradition, must still be regarded as infallibly certain in order to protect "the fabric" of revealed truth.

John Ford called the explanation "a most remarkable statement." First, it backed off entirely from the traditional argument that the teaching on women's ordination has a firm basis in Scripture or tradition or both. Second, it assumed as a clear and undisputed fact that infallibility can be extended to the vague and broad category of "secondary truths." Said Ford, "I have serious doubts about extending infallibility in this area, and given the uncertainty, "I do not see how this extension can be called Catholic doctrine."[7] Vatican I left the matter open, he noted, Vatican II was ambiguous, and the general trend among theologians since Vatican II had been to view infallibility as applicable exclusively to truths revealed in

Scripture or tradition. Yet under John Paul II, there is a decided trend to stamp a wider range of Church teaching with an absolute and definitive character.

At the very least, the Ratzinger clarification is likely to heat up the old argument between maximizers of infallibility (in the tradition of Henry Edward Manning) and the minimizers (in the footsteps of John Henry Newman).

CONSULTING THE CHURCH

Like the huge tectonic plates beneath the earth's surface, which cause great earthquakes when they crash into one another, so these two highly sensitive forces—pressure for women's admission to the priesthood and the presumed infallibility of the ordinary universal magisterium—are colliding, creating a historic upheaval in the world of Catholicism. Church landscape will not be the same again.

Easy solutions are unavailable, and the level of polarization is extraordinarily high. It is most unlikely proponents of a gender-inclusive priesthood will grow weary and reconcile themselves to the status quo. A considerable number of people have left the Church over this issue, and others may follow, but the substantial number who are bound and determined to remain will be neither content nor quiet. The prohibition of ordination, unlike most Church teaching, is one of those high profile, extremely visible doctrines; it is on display every Sunday in every Catholic church in the world— on display at the very center of the action considered most sacred and most essential to the Church's existence, the Eucharist. Perhaps it is, as Dulles suggests, far down in the hierarchy of beliefs, but it is not so regarded by those who view the continued prohibition as an act of injustice eroding the Church at its core.

It is also unlikely that opponents of women's ordination will yield. How can they, after investing so much of the Church's moral capital in the ban? Here, it seems, as in few other matters in modern times, authority has drawn a line in the sand.

Some will say all this confusion can be easily ended if the present pope or a future pontiff were simply to assert on his own authority in an *ex cathedra* definition that, by the will of Christ, women are not eligible for priestly ordination. Surely, many Catholics believe, this would remove all doubt, halt all speculation, and label stubborn dissenters as outside the body of the Church. Yet it's not that simple now, and despite what many Catholics believe, it never was. In the only two examples of *ex cathedra* definitions in modern times, Mary's Immaculate Conception in 1864 and her Assumption in 1950, the popes consulted the worldwide episcopate before making these proclamations, and they reportedly encountered virtually unanimous agreement among the bishops. The subsequent acceptance by the universal Church seemed to confirm the truth of the papal definitions.

It is now perfectly clear that such consultations are not a mere courtesy but an absolute requirement. Vatican II's insistence on the collegiality of the bishops with the pope and the council's assumption that the pope will "listen to the word of God" before functioning as the supreme teacher create specific obligations.

Said Francis Sullivan:

> If then, before he can define anything as divinely revealed, the pope must "listen to the word of God"...and if this word of God has been "entrusted to the church"...and is handed on "in her teaching, life and worship"...it follows that before the pope can define a dogma he must listen to the Church, and that he can define as dogma only what he finds in the faith of the Church. The pope has no source of revelation that is independent of the faith-life of the Church.[8]

Commenting on the dilemma, *Commonweal* magazine asked editorially how the bishops of the world can confirm the pope's teaching "if in fact they have not been consulted? And how can they be consulted if they have not been permitted to discuss the matter? And how can they discuss the matter if they cannot freely inquire into the sense of the faithful?"[9]

Would it be theoretically possible that a pope could make the sort of consultations he thinks appropriate, define a doctrine infallibly—and still be wrong? Could theologians and other Catholics dispute a teaching of this kind without falling into immediate heresy?

This is precisely where the idea of reception by the Church becomes relevant. It should be recalled first that the Church's reception of a teaching does not give that teaching its authority. That old Gallican tenet was rejected at Vatican I. But Vatican II stated the Church's acceptance of infallible teaching "can never be lacking"—it must be present. If it is lacking, that could mean one of two things. Possibly, those who reject the doctrine represent a minority that has indeed broken away from the body of the Church. Or it could mean, especially if the rejection is massive and of long duration, that one or more of the conditions necessary for an infallible dogma was not fulfilled in the pope's definition. Those conditions—especially that the doctrine is founded on Scripture or tradition—were spelled out at Vatican I and have never been disputed (except by those who deny the possibility of infallible teaching in the first place). Nor can a pope declare with his charism of infallibility that all the conditions for an infallible teaching have been met. Only the subsequent acceptance of the doctrine by the Church makes it clear the conditions had been met; the nonacceptance by a substantial number would necessarily raise questions about the presence of the conditions.

According to theologian Patrick Granfield:

> Reception is a multilayered reality. It is not a purely juridical concept, a technical device, nor a sociological norm. Nor is it the exclusive task of the magisterium. When the church teaches a doctrine or mandates a discipline, the process of reception is not ended. Reception of papal and episcopal teaching involves the entire people of God; the hierarchy and the faithful are together the bearers of reception....Christian truth is not an abstraction but exists only in the living faith of people. Church officials play a critical role in the process of reception by their formal teaching and also by their continued preaching and explaining of that teaching. But it is the faithful themselves who appropriate the teaching of the Church.[10]

One is tempted to ponder the significance of the intriguing nonreception of the church's authoritative ban on women's ordination by many Catholics in the present day. Equally intriguing is speculation about what might occur if the ban were raised to the level of an *ex cathedra* papal definition. Yet even conservative theologians agree that nonreception, regardless of the level of a teaching, merits serious consideration by the magisterium.

Despite his conviction that the ban on women's ordination is a dogma, Avery Dulles acknowledges that a lack of assent within the Church "could be interpreted as a sign that the pope had perhaps exceeded his competence and that some necessary condition for an infallible act had not been fulfilled."

And Cardinal Ratzinger, prefect of the CDF, goes further: "Where there is neither consensus on the part of the universal Church nor clear testimony in the sources, no binding decision is possible. If such a decision were formally made, it would lack the necessary conditions and the question of the decision's legitimacy would have to be examined."[11]

A Groaning of the Spirit

Would it be possible for a future ecumenical council to settle a serious dispute—the ban on women's ordination or some other controversial Church doctrine of the time? To be sure, a council has not only the moral presence of the pope but the assembled presence of the world's bishops behind its decrees. Yet the teaching of Vatican II has ironically raised questions about who should be invited to the next ecumenical council and how its decisions should be made.

Sullivan poses the questions in stark form: "If we no longer exclusively identify the Church of Christ with the Roman Catholic Church, but recognize the presence and saving activity of Christ's Church in other Christian churches and ecclesial communities, can we still attribute infallibility to the belief of the Catholic faithful, if their belief in a particular doctrine is not shared by the majority of other Christians? Should 'universal agreement of the whole body of the faithful' now require agreement among the faithful of all major Christian communities? Would only a truly ecumenical agreement now satisfy the requirements for infallibility of belief?"[12]

Sullivan believes a valid ecumenical council could still be convoked without such broad participation. Yet in the light of the ecumenical initiatives taken at Vatican II and continued since, it is difficult to see how the belief of the Christian faithful can be determined without at least some input from Orthodox Christian and Protestant churches—bodies Vatican II specifically acknowledges as "providing access to the community of salvation."[13]

In addition, Vatican II's recognition of the sense of the faithful as an important determiner of belief suggests that a future council would appropriately require some direct input from Catholic laity before proclaiming "the faith of the whole Church" to the world. Such radical changes would be heartily welcomed by some, and they would be fiercely opposed by others, including many in Church authority. Nevertheless, the fact that changes are being discussed indicates the ambiguous situation of infallible teaching as the Church enters a new millennium.

Some find speculation and controversy alarming realities that must be settled as quickly and firmly as possible. Others are more inclined to regard these conditions as the groaning of a living body in the process of change and growth. The history of infallibility— like the history of the Church itself—is replete with such groanings. Saint Paul reminds the Church that it is the Holy Spirit that groans within the body, and in its deepest meanings that is what the doctrine of infallibility is all about: the abiding presence—and groaning—of the Spirit within the body.

The Second Vatican Council speaks about it in these words:

> It happens rather frequently, and legitimately so, that with equal sincerity some of the faithful will disagree with others on a given matter...Solutions proposed by one side or another may be confused by many people with the gospel message.... They should always try to enlighten one another through honest discussion, preserving mutual charity and caring above all

for the common good....The Church also realizes that she has great need of the ripening which comes with the experience of the centuries. Led by the Holy Spirit, Mother Church unceasingly exhorts her children to purify and renew themselves so that the sign of Christ can shine more brightly on the face of the Church.[14]

NOTES

INTRODUCTION

1. Quotations from Vatican I proceedings in this section are cited in Cuthbert Butler, The Vatican Council, Vol. II (London: Longmans, Green & Co., 1930), 295.
2. Cited in ibid., 163.
3. *The New York Times*, July 17, 1970.
4. "The Church Faces the Modern World," The General Council (Washington, D.C.: Catholic University of America Press, 1962), 135.
5. Cited in Patrick Granfield, *The Limits of the Papacy* (New York: Crossroad, 1987), 42.
6. A variety of the pope's eccentricities are cited in August Hasler, *How the Pope Became Infallible* (New York: Doubleday, 1981), 114–121.
7. *National Catholic Reporter*, September 2, 1994.
8. Ibid., July 26, 1996.
9. *The Table*, December 2, 1995.
10. *Commonweal*, January 26, 1996.
11. *National Catholic Reporter*, December 8, 1995.
12. Ibid., December 29, 1995. Unless otherwise noted, the quotations in the rest of this section are from the same issue.
13. Ibid., December 8, 1995.
14. Ibid., December 15, 1995.
15. Ibid., December 8, 1995.

CHAPTER I

1. Karl Rahner, *Foundations of the Christian Faith* (New York: Crossroad, 1978), 379.
2. Francis Sullivan, *Magisterium: Teaching Authority in the Catholic Church* (New York: Paulist Press, 1983), 42.
3. Cited in ibid., 50.
4. Richard McBrien, *Catholicism* (San Francisco: Harper, 1994), 744–745.

5. Sullivan, *Magisterium*, 85.
6. Ibid.
7. Quotations in this paragraph are cited in Nicolas Cheetham, *Keepers of the Keys: A History of the Popes From Peter to John Paul II* (New York: Chas. Scribner's & Sons, 1986), 47.
8. Cited in Sullivan, *Magisterium*, 70.
9. Francis Sullivan, *Creative Fidelity: Weighing and Interpreting Documents of the Magisterium* (New York: Paulist Press, 1996), 62–63.
10. Sullivan, *Magisterium*, 87.
11. Thomas Bokenkotter, *A Concise History of the Catholic Church* (New York: Doubleday, 1977), 111.

CHAPTER 2

1. Thomas Bokenkotter, *A Concise History of the Catholic Church* (New York: Doubleday, 1977), 121.
2. Francis Sullivan, *Magisterium: Teaching Authority of the Catholic Church* (New York: Paulist Press, 1983), 89.
3. Cited in ibid., 72–73.
4. Cited in Brian Tierney, *The Origins of Papal Infallibility: 1150–1350* (Leiden: E. J. Brill, 1972), 83.
5. Brian Tierney, "Origins of Papal Infallibility," *Journal of Ecumenical Studies*, Vol. VIII, 1971, 847–852.
6. Citations in this section are from Tierney, *The Origins of Papal Infallibility: 1150–1350*, 99–117.
7. Cited in Tierney, *Journal of Ecumenical Studies*, 860.
8. Ibid.
9. Ibid., 862.
10. Cited in Tierney, *The Origins of Papal Infallibility: 1150–1350*, 239.

CHAPTER 3

1. Cited in Richard McBrien, *Catholicism* (San Francisco: Harper, 1994), 628.
2. Ibid., 629.
3. Ibid., 631.
4. Cited in Leonard Swidler, "The Ecumenical Problem Today: Papal Infallibility," *Journal of Ecumenical Studies*, Vol. VIII, 759.
5. Thomas Bokenkotter, *A Concise History of the Catholic Church* (New York: Doubleday, 1977), 198.
6. Yves Congar, *The Church of St. Augustine and the Modern Era* (Paris: St. Sulpice, 1970), 244–245.
7. Bokenkotter, *A Concise History of the Catholic Church*, 199.
8. Cited in ibid., 204.
9. Ibid., 210.

CHAPTER 4

1. Cited in Cuthbert Butler, *The Vatican Council*, Vol. I (London: Longmans, Green & Co., 1930), 37.
2. Thomas Bokenkotter, *A Concise History of the Catholic Church* (New York: Doubleday, 1977), 251.
3. Cited in Butler, *The Vatican Council*, Vol. I, 27.
4. Ibid., 27–30.

5. August Hasler, *How the Pope Became Infallible* (New York: Doubleday, 1981), 39.

CHAPTER 5

1. Joseph de Maistre, *The Pope* (New York: Fertig, 1975), xvi.
2. Ibid., xxi.
3. Ibid., 19–110.
4. Brian Tierney, "Origins of Papal Infallibility," *Journal of Ecumenical Studies*, Vol. VIII, 1971, 843.
5. Cited in Cuthbert Butler, *The Vatican Council*, Vol. I (London: Longmans, Green & Co., 1930), 64.
6. Ibid., 77.
7. Ibid., 74.
8. Citations in this section are from Thomas Bokenkotter, *A Concise History of the Catholic Church* (New York: Doubleday, 1977), 276–278.
9. John Tracy Ellis, "The Church Faces the Modern World," *The General Council* (Washington, D.C.: Catholic University of America Press, 1962), 115.
10. Ibid., 122.

CHAPTER 6

1. J. B. Bury, *History of the Papacy in the 19th Century* (New York: Schocken, 1964), 84.
2. August Hasler, *How the Pope Became Infallible* (New York: Doubleday, 1981), 111.
3. Cited in Richard McBrien, *Catholicism* (San Francisco: Harper, 1994), 1092–1102.
4. Cited in Bury, *History of the Papacy in the 19th Century*, 50.
5. Ibid., 8.
6. Quotations in this section are cited in ibid., 1–45.
7. Cited in Cuthbert Butler, *The Vatican Council*, Vol. I (London: Longmans, Green & Co., 1930), 71.
8. Cited in Thomas Bokenkotter, *A Concise History of the Catholic Church* (New York: Doubleday, 1977), 295.
9. Cited in Butler, *The Vatican Council*, Vol. I, 56.
10. Ibid., 85.
11. Ibid., 87.
12. Cited in Bokenkotter, *A Concise History of the Catholic Church*, 302.
13. Cited in Bury, *History of the Papacy in the 19th Century*, 62.
14. Cited in Hasler, *How the Pope Became Infallible*, 180.
15. Cited in Bokenkotter, *A Concise History of the Catholic Church*, 292.
16. Cited in Bury, *History of the Papacy in the 19th Century*, 66.
17. Cited in Butler, *The Vatican Council*, Vol. I, 97.
18. Cited in Bury, *History of the Papacy in the 19th Century*, 69.
19. Cited in Hasler, *How the Pope Became Infallible*, 65.

CHAPTER 7

1. Cited in Cuthbert Butler, *The Vatican Council*, Vol. I (London: Longmans, Green & Co., 1930), 298.

2. Cited in J. B. Bury, *History of the Papacy in the 19th Century* (New York: Schocken, 1964), 78.
3. Cited in Butler, *The Vatican Council*, Vol. I,124.
4. Ibid., 127.
5. *The New Catholic Encyclopedia*, Vol. 9 (New York: McGraw, Hill, 1967), 169.
6. Cited in August Hasler, *How the Pope Became Infallible* (New York: Doubleday, 1981), 178.
7. Butler, *The Vatican Council*, Vol. I, 150.
8. Cited in Bury, *History of the Papacy in the 19th Century*, 83.
9. Ibid., 84.
10. Ibid., 88.
11. Quotations from council members in this section are from Butler, *The Vatican Council*, 190–233.
12. Cited in ibid., 213.
13. Cited in Bury, *History of the Papacy in the 19th Century*, 105.
14. Ibid., 110–120.
15. Ibid,. 110–111.
16. Ibid., 114.
17. Ibid., 116.
18. Cited in Butler, *The Vatican Council*, Vol. I, 271–272.
19. Cited in Butler, *The Vatican Council*, Vol. II, 41–42.
20. Cited in Bury, *History of the Papacy in the 19th Century*, 120.

CHAPTER 8

1. Cited in Cuthbert Butler, *The Vatican Council*, Vol. II (London: Longmans, Green & Co., 1930), 49–50.
2. Hefele's quotes in this section are cited in ibid., 47.
3. Cited in Butler, *The Vatican Council*, Vol. II, 200–201.
4. Ibid., 48.
5. Ibid., 52–53.
6. Ibid., 55.
7. Cited in James Hennesey, *The First Council of the Vatican: The American Experience* (New York: Herder and Herder, 1963), 244–245.
8. Cited in Butler, *The Vatican Council*, Vol. II, 72.
9. Ibid., 130.
10. Cited in J. B. Bury, *History of the Papacy in the 19th Century* (New York: Schocken, 1964), 131.
11. The following citations in this section are from Butler, *The Vatican Council*, Vol. II, 75–85.
12. Cited in ibid., 133. I have altered the translation of the words "to be held by the universal Church" to "must be held by the universal Church" as more faithful to the Latin text *tenenda*.
13. Ibid., 125.

CHAPTER 9

1. Citations in this section are from Cuthbert Butler, *The Vatican Council*, Vol. II (London: Longmans, Green & Co., 1930), 94–98.
2. Cited in ibid., 98. Practically every author has a slightly different version of what the pope allegedly said.
3. Cited in August Hasler, *How the Pope Became Infallible* (New York: Doubleday, 1983), 92.

4. Cited in Butler, *The Vatican Council*, Vol. II, 92–103.

5. Gasser's citations in this section and the next are from ibid., 136–140.

6. Butler, *The Vatican Council*, Vol. II, 147.

7. Cited in Hasler, *How the Pope Became Infallible*, 187.

8. Cited in Butler, *The Vatican Council*, Vol. II, 157.

9. Citations in this section are from ibid., 158–161.

10. Ibid., 295.

11. Ibid., 163.

12. Ibid., 164–165.

CHAPTER 10

1. Cited in Margaret O'Gara, *Triumph in Defeat: Infallibility, Vatican I and the French Minority Bishops* (Washington, D.C.: Catholic University of America Press, 1988), 183–185.

2. Cited in Cuthbert Butler, *The Vatican Council*, Vol. II (London: Longmans, Green & Co., 1930), 141.

3. Cited in O'Gara, *Triumph in Defeat*, 182.

4. Ibid., 192.

5. Cited in Butler, *The Vatican Council*, Vol. II, 171.

6. Ibid., 182.

7. Butler, *The Vatican Council*, Vol. II, 168.

8. Cited in Francis Sullivan, *Creative Fidelity: Weighing and Interpreting Documents of the Magisterium* (New York: Paulist Press, 1996), 176–177.

9. Citations in this section are from O'Gara, *Triumph in Defeat*, 211–215.

10. Cited in Butler, *The Vatican Council*, Vol. II, 232.

11. Cited in August Hasler, *How the Pope Became Infallible* (New York: Doubleday, 1983), 215.

12. Ibid., 224.

13. Ibid.

14. Cited in Butler, *The Vatican Council*, Vol. II, 174.

15. A full account of the Kenrick story can be found in James Hennesey, *The First Council of the Vatican: The American Experience* (New York: Herder and Herder, 1963), 318–324.

16. Cited in Hasler, *How the Pope Became Infallible*, 203.

17. A full account of the Old Catholic schism can be found in Butler, *The Vatican Council*, Vol. II, 178–185.

18. Cited in Hasler, *How the Pope Became Infallible*, 13.

19. Cited in ibid., 142–145.

20. Cited in Butler, *The Vatican Council*, Vol. II, 192.

21. Cited in O'Gara, *Victory in Defeat*, 248.

22. Ibid.

23. Cited in Hasler, *How the Pope Became Infallible*, 304.

CHAPTER 11

1. Cited in Thomas Bokenkotter, *A Concise History of the Catholic Church* (New York: Doubleday, 1977), 328–333.

2. Cited in Richard Gaillardetz, *Witnesses to the Faith: Community, Infallibility, and the Ordinary Magisterium of Bishops* (New York: Paulist Press, 1992), 14.

3. Ibid., 17.

4. Cited in ibid., 25.

5. Ibid., 27.
6. Cited in ibid., 31.
7. Cited in ibid., 30.
8. Cited in ibid., 32.
9. Cited in Richard McBrien, *Catholicism* (San Francisco: Harper, 1994), 658.
10. Cited in Gaillardetz, *Witnesses to the Faith*, 54.
11. John Henry Newman, *A Letter Addressed to His Grace, the Duke of Norfolk* (London: Pickering, 1875), 66.
12. Cited in Robert McClory, *Turning Point: The Inside Story of the Papal Birth Control Commission* (New York: Crossroad, 1995), 28.
13. The remaining quotations of Newman in this section are cited in Gaillardetz, *Witnesses to the Faith*, 66–68.
14. Avery Dulles, "Notes on Infallibility," *Theological Studies*, Vol. 51, 1990, 448.
15. Yves Congar, *The Hierarchy as Service in Power and Poverty in the Church* (London: Chapman, 1964), 98.
16. Yves Congar, *Blessed Is the Peace of My Church* (Denville, N.J.: Dimension, 1973), 78.
17. Cited in Gaillardetz, *Witnesses to the Faith*, 108.
18. Gaillardetz, *Witnesses to the Faith*, 108.
19. Cited in ibid., 104–106.
20. *National Catholic Reporter*, June 23, 1994.

CHAPTER 12

1. Xavier Rynne, *Vatican Council II* (New York: Farrar, Strauss & Giroux, 1968), 20.
2. Cited in Monika Hellwig, *What Are the Theologians Saying Now?* (Westminster, Md.: Christian Classics, 1992), 20.
3. Rynne, *Vatican Council II*, 46–47.
4. Ibid., 139.
5. Thomas Bokenkotter, *A Concise History of the Catholic Church* (New York: Doubleday, 1977), 389.
6. The quotations from council members in this section are cited in Rynne, *Vatican Council II*, 112–117.
7. Rynne, *Vatican Council II*, 176.
8. Cited in ibid., 288.
9. Ibid., 175.
10. Quotations in this section are cited in Rynne, *Vatican Council II*, 177–181.
11. Walter Abbott, *The Documents of Vatican II*, "Dogmatic Constitution on the Church" (New York: Guild Press, 1968) 47–50. I changed the words "to be held" in section 25 to "must be held" as closer to the meaning of the Latin word *tenenda*.
12. Cited in Rynne, *Vatican Council II*, 182.
13. Ibid., 313.
14. Ibid., 316.
15. Ibid., 410.
16. Ibid., 411.
17. Hellwig, *What Are the Theologians Saying Now?* 52.
18. Cited in Robert McClory, *Turning Point: The Inside Story of the Papal Birth Control Commission* (New York: Crossroad, 1995), 138.
19. Ibid., 152.

20. Francis Sullivan, *Creative Fidelity: Weighing and Interpreting the Documents of the Magisterium* (New York: Paulist Press, 1996), 105.
21. Cited in Richard Gaillardetz, *Witnesses to the Faith: Community, Infallibility, and the Ordinary Magisterium of Bishops* (New York: Paulist Press, 1992), 131.
22. Cited in Sullivan, *Creative Fidelity: Weighing and Interpreting the Documents of the Magisterium*, 106.

CHAPTER 13

1. Hans Küng, *Infallible? An Inquiry* (New York: Doubleday, 1983), 61–62.
2. Cited in ibid., 67.
3. Ibid., 111.
4. Ibid., 182.
5. Ibid., 181–187.
6. Ibid., 11.
7. Austin Farrar, "Infallibility in the Catholic Church," *Catholic Biblical Quarterly*, Vol. XXIX, 1967, 512–523.
8. Leonard Swidler, "The Ecumenical Problem Today: Papal Infallibility," *Journal of Ecumenical Studies*, Vol. VIII, 1971, 759–765.
9. Francis Oakley, "The New Conciliarism," *Journal of Ecumenical Studies*, Vol. VIII, 1971, 825–833.
10. Oreste Kéramé, "The Basis for Reunion of Christians," *Journal of Ecumenical Studies*, Vol. VIII, 1971, 794–813.
11. Brian Tierney, "The Origin of Papal Infallibility," *Journal of Ecumenical Studies*, Vol. VIII, 1971, 863–864.
12. Gregory Baum, *The Infallibility Debate* (New York: Paulist Press, 1971), 37.
13. Orsy and the following two quotes are cited in John T. Ford, "Infallibility—From Vatican I to the Present," *Journal of Ecumenical Studies*, Vol. VIII, 1971, 786–787.
14. Ibid., 790.
15. Cited in ibid., 789.
16. Quotations in this section are from Paul Empie, *Lutherans and Catholics in Dialogue* (Philadelphia: Fortress Press, 1981), 128–135.
17. Cited in Paul Empie et al, editors, *Teaching Authority and Infallibility in the Church* (Minneapolis: Augsburg, 1978), 81–100.
18. Patrick Granfield, *The Limits of the Papacy* (New York: Crossroad, 1987), 155–159.
19. Francis Sullivan, *Magisterium: Teaching Authority and Infallibility in the Catholic Church* (New York: Paulist Press, 1983), 117.

CHAPTER 14

1. Francis Sullivan, *Creative Fidelity: Weighing and Interpreting Documents of the Magisterium* (New York: Paulist Press, 1996), 15.
2. Ibid., 17.
3. Ibid., 117.
4. Ibid., 34.
5. Ibid., 35.
6. Cited in ibid., 38.
7. Ibid., 39–40.
8. Cited in ibid., 106.
9. Sullivan's quotations in this section are from ibid., 55–133.

10. Ibid., 51.
11. Ibid., 57.
12. Ibid., 51.
13. Cited in ibid., 123.
14. Ibid., 51–52.
15. Cited in ibid., 132.
16. Ibid., 133.
17. Cited in ibid., 167.
18. Ibid., 168.
19. Cited in ibid., 174.
20. Ibid., 88.
21. Ibid., 86.
22. Ibid., 104.
23. Cited in ibid., 104.
24. Ibid., 23.
25. Cited in ibid., 155.
26. Cited in ibid., 157.
27. Ibid. 160.

CHAPTER 15

1. John T. Ford, "Responses to Rome," *Commonweal*, January 26, 1996.
2. Ford, phone interview, October 9, 1996.
3. Francis Sullivan, *Creative Fidelity: Weighing and Interpreting the Documents of the Magisterium* (New York: Paulist Press, 1996), 182.
4. Ibid., 184.
5. *National Catholic Reporter*, July 27, 1996.
6. Quotations in this section are cited in *Origins*, June 27, 1996, 90–94.
7. Ford, phone interview, March 25, 1977.
8. Francis Sullivan, *Magisterium: Teaching Authority in the Catholic Church* (New York: Paulist Press, 1983), 104.
9. *Commonweal*, December 1, 1995.
10. Patrick Granfield, *The Limits of the Papacy* (New York: Crossroad, 1987), 148.
11. Cited in ibid., 150.
12. Sullivan, *Magisterium*, 19.
13. Walter Abbott, *The Documents of Vatican II*, "Decree on Ecumenism" (New York: Guild Press, 1968), 346.
14. Ibid., 244-245.

INDEX

229

ABOUT THE AUTHOR

Robert McClory is currently an associate professor at North-western University's Medill School of Journalism, where he has been teaching since 1987. He has also taught several courses at the graduate level, including "Religion and the News Media." In addition, McClory is a staff writer for *National Catholic Reporter* and *Chicago Reader* and a contributor to numerous publications, including *U.S. Catholic, Chicago* magazine, and *Illinois Issues.*

A former Roman Catholic priest in the Chicago archdiocese, he holds an M.A. in theology from St. Mary of the Lake Seminary in Mundelein, Illinois, and a master's degree in journalism from Medill. Prior to his current position, he was a lecturer in theology at Loyola University and in journalism at Columbia College, both in Chicago.

The author of four previous books, including *Racism in America* and *Turning Point: The Inside Story of the Papal Birth Control Commission,* McClory is also the recipient of awards from the National Newspaper Publishers Association, Women in Communications, the Chicago Headline Club, and the Catholic Press Association. He resides with his wife in Evanston, Illinois.